Equilibrium Unemployment Theory

D0168937

Equilibrium Unemployment Theory

second edition

Christopher A. Pissarides

The MIT Press
Cambridge, Massachusetts
London, England

This book was set in Times Roman by Best-set Typesetter Ltd., Hong Kong.

Printed and bound in the United States of America.

Library of Congress Cataloging-in-Publication Data

Pissarides, Christopher A.
    Equilibrium unemployment theory / Christopher A. Pissarides. — 2nd ed.
        p.   cm.
    Includes bibliographical references and index.
    ISBN 0-262-16187-7 (alk. paper)
    1. Unemployment—Mathematical models.   2. Equilibrium (Economics)
I. Title.
HD5707.5.P55   2000
331.133'7'01—dc21   99-41746
                                                                        CIP

to Antony and Miranda

Contents

Preface

The approach to labor market equilibrium and unemployment followed in the first edition of this book has found many applications since the book's publication. This was helped by the emergence of new data on job and worker flows at the micro level and the success of the approach in their analysis and explanation. Also the approach proved successful in the modeling of the labor market in equilibrium business cycle models and in the analysis of policy associated with the welfare state. The second edition incorporates the most important of the new developments and discusses a variety of new results. The structure of the book remains, however, unaltered, and the logical development of the theory explained in the preface to the first edition is still the one followed.

The most important new theoretical development is the analysis of endogenous job destruction. In the first edition the rate of job destruction was constant. This feature of the model was criticized by reviewers and contradicted by micro data that became available at about the time of the book's publication. In the second edition a new chapter is devoted to the analysis of job destruction, following the approach taken in my joint work with Dale Mortensen. Although many results are still more conveniently derived in a model with constant job destruction, the model with endogenous job destruction becomes the central model in the second edition. It turns out, however, that despite the endogeneity of job destruction, not much needs to be changed in the modeling and discussion of results of the first edition. The model becomes richer and empirically implementable, but the results of the model in the first edition are not contradicted. Although this may appear surprising, in fact it is not. The model of the first edition was built on the job creation choices of the firm and the job search behavior of the worker. The introduction of job destruction choices along the lines of my joint work with Mortensen does not alter the nature of job creation and job search decisions.

The second important revision is the analysis of search on the job and job-to-job quitting. The neglect of job-to-job quitting is a criticism often made of search and matching models of unemployment. In a new chapter I show that on-the-job search and job-to-job quitting can be analyzed following the same modeling principles as those in the analysis of endogenous job destruction. Moreover the results of the model of unemployment without on-the-job search remain largely unaltered by this extension, so the discussion in other parts of the book ignores it. Many of the features of job-to-job quitting, such as those associated with the accumulation of human capital on the job, learning about nonpecuniary characteristics, and the quality of the match are, however, not modeled.

Apart from the two new chapters, there has been a lot of rewriting and simplifying of the analysis in the first edition. Many peripheral results in parts II and III have been omitted, and new policy issues are addressed. The treatment of capital has also been simplified. Under the assumptions of the model about capital markets, not much generality is gained by carrying capital through the notation, as was done in the first edition. In the second edition, the necessary assumptions are stated, and it is demonstrated that they imply that capital can be ignored without loss of generality. Our assumptions are that capital is reversible, and there is a perfect second-hand market for capital goods. These assumptions are natural extensions of the neoclassical assumptions about capital, but they assume away important "holdup" problems that might arise in the environment of the model. Recently there has been important work in the holdup problem and in the complementarities associated with the capital and training decisions of firms and workers, which are not modeled in this book. Some references to the literature are given in notes at the end of relevant chapters.

The chapter on adjustment dynamics in the first edition has been omitted, though the most important results about the uniqueness of the adjustment path have been incorporated into other chapters, where relevant. The sections on growth and the endogeneity of the interest rate have also been re-written, in the light of recent work in growth theory and "creative destruction."

Finally the notes on the literature at the end of each chapter have been substantially extended to include recent work. Several of the recent papers cited are unpublished and some may never be published. Although I have tried to give references to a lot of the recent literature, the literature has grown enormously since the first edition, and a comprehensive bibliography would require many more pages than the several devoted to it here.

In revising the book I have benefited from many people who have commented on the first edition and who used the book in their teaching and research. My greatest debt is to my coauthor Dale Mortensen. Chapter 2 is based on our joint work, as is much of the discussion of policy in chapter 9. His influence is also present in revisions made to other chapters. His review article in the *Journal of Monetary Economics* helped me focus my ideas and led to our joint projects. Others with whom I have had discussions about this approach to labor markets and whose influence is present, include Daron Acemoglu, Philippe Aghion, Charlie Bean, Olivier Blanchard, Simon Burgess, Steve Davis, Peter Howitt, Richard Jackman, Richard Layard, Espen Moen, Steve Nickell, Andrew Oswald, Robert Shimer and numerous graduate students at LSE and elsewhere, including Jozef Konings, Pietro Garibaldi, Barbara Petrongolo, Claudio Michelacci and Etienne Wasmer. Able research assistance was provided by Paloma Lopez-Garcia. This project was supported by the Centre for Economic Performance (the successor to the Centre for Labour Economics, which supported the first edition), a designated research center of the Economic and Social Research Council at the London School of Economics.

Preface to the First Edition

This book is about a particular approach to the theory of unemployment. The equilibrium unemployment stock in this approach is derived from the transitions in and out of unemployment, which can be influenced both by aggregate events and by individual decisions. The book concentrates on the modeling of the transition out of unemployment and on the implications of this approach to unemployment for macroeconomic equilibrium and for the efficiency of the labor market. Entry into unemployment is assumed to be exogenous; it results from stochastic structural change and from new entry into the labor force.

The transition out of unemployment is modeled as a trading process, with unemployed workers and firms with job vacancies wanting to trade labor services. Unlike Walrasian theory, trade in this approach to unemployment is an economic activity that requires the input of time and other resources. The book aims to give a thorough and rigorous explanation of how an equilibrium model with these features works. It avoids some potentially important applications of the model, in order to concentrate on its central theme of the interaction between unemployment transitions and macroeconomic equilibrium. It also avoids a comparison of the model with other theories of unemployment and a detailed discussion of its compatibility with the empirical evidence. Many aspects of the model are too abstract to be empirically implementable as they are presented here. The main objective of the book is to develop a usable model that can be extended to deal with many problems in the theory of labor markets and in the empirical analysis of unemployment. Its purpose is not to explain particular episodes or particular time-series properties that might be found in the history of unemployment.

The implications of exogenous structural change and costly exchange reach beyond the trivial ones of the existence of some "frictional" unemployment in otherwise conventional models. Since Walrasian and traditional Keynesian theory ignore trade, not much can be learned from them about its implications for macroeconomic equilibrium, even if the rest of the model is conventional. Keynes's famous statement that the unemployment of workers between jobs can be ignored in the study of more important kinds of unemployment is unverified conjecture. Descriptively it is false: With the exception of a few "discouraged" workers, unemployed workers are always between jobs, or between some other state and a job. The approach taken in this book leads to the view that the decomposition of unemployment into frictional, cyclical, voluntary, involuntary, and so on is unhelpful in the theoretical and empirical analysis of unemployment. In this book unemployment consists of workers who lose their jobs because it is not to their advantage (and to their employer's advantage) to continue employed, and who find another job after a length of time that depends on aggregate events, on institutional constraints and on what they, firms, and other workers do. The book discusses whether the unemployment obtained from these processes is unique, stable, optimal, and responsive to aggregate parameters and policy, and not whether it is frictional, voluntary, and so on.

The theory of unemployment in this book is an "equilibrium" theory. By this we mean that firms and workers maximize their payoffs under rational expectations, given the stochastic process that breaks up jobs and the one that leads to the formation of new jobs. By equilibrium we also mean that wages are determined so as to exploit all the private gains from trade available to those who set them. The latter requirement is critical in the efficiency analysis of equilibrium. In general, we show that the assumptions that give rise to unemployment in our model imply that the interests of the employed and the unemployed diverge. Therefore, if wages are determined at the level of the firm, where only employed workers are present, equilibrium will not, in general, be efficient. Not all gains from trade available to unemployed workers and to firms with job vacancies are exploited, so the inputs into trade by the unemployed and by the firms with vacant jobs are not socially efficient.

In addition to being an equilibrium theory, the theory of unemployment in this book is a "macroeconomic" one. It is in terms of two representative agents, firms and workers, who move between two states, employment and unemployment, and aims to derive an equilibrium unemployment rate for the economy as a whole. Our assumptions ensure that the equilibrium unemployment rate is unique. These assumptions are natural extensions of the ones underlying the neoclassical model of growth, and part I is devoted to the development of a balanced-growth model with unemployment and job vacancies. Special attention is paid to the "stylized facts" of long-run growth; the model is shown to explain the existence of a constant unemployment rate and constant vacancy rate, in a growing economy that is also characterized by the other conventional stylized facts of balanced growth. As in other areas of macroeconomics, the emphasis on the neoclassical model of balanced growth is not driven by the belief that the model is empirically the most suitable one for the analysis of unemployment. Rather, it is driven by the belief that if a model of unemployment conforms to the long-run equilibrium requirements of balanced growth, it is the most suitable starting point for the extensions that will eventually explain unemployment in real economies. The "starting-point" model of part I is shown to imply that in steady-state equilibrium there is a downward-sloping and convex-to-the-origin curve in vacancy-unemployment space—the Beveridge curve. When the steady state is disturbed, the stable adjustment path traces an anticlockwise loop around the curve. The Beveridge curve and the loops around it are stylized facts of modern economies. The model also implies the existence of a long-run Phillips curve in inflation-unemployment space, with a negative slope if there is an inflation-tax effect that affects the equilibrium real interest rate. The real rate of interest is one of the determinants of the natural rate of unemployment.

In part II the labor-market model of part I is extended in two important directions. Both give a bigger role to the supply of labor than in part I and introduce plausible shift variables in the Beveridge curve. Empirical evidence from several countries shows that the Beveridge curve does shift, in ways that cannot easily be explained by the simple model of part I. The two extensions are, first, endogenous search intensity and second, job-specific variations in productivities that lead to the possibility of job rejection. The traditional labor-supply questions of the choice of hours of work and the participation decision are also analyzed in part II. With regard to the latter, the conventional discouraged- and added-worker effects are given new rigorous interpretations.

Search intensity is introduced into the model in a way that parallels the "efficiency unit" approach to productivity differences in production theory. Job-specific productivity differences are given the similar interpretation of differences in the efficiency units of labor that can be utilized in a particular job match. The analysis of each follows the equilibrium principles established in the macroeconomic model of part I, and each is shown to lead to usable models with strong empirical content. The analysis of the participation and hours decision is also done for a labor market in equilibrium.

The efficiency of the equilibrium of the labor market described in parts I and II is examined in part III. The existence of "search externalities" gives rise to the possibility of inefficiencies. The critical questions here are whether wages can, and whether they do, internalize the externalities. The answer we give to the first question is yes, and to the second no. The wage that internalizes the search externalities is feasible, but the decentralized approach to wage determination followed in this book does not lead to the efficient wage outcome. Unemployed workers suffer in this game, so their returns from participation are less than what they would be if wages were socially efficient. As a result too few workers come into the market, they do not search for a job with high enough intensity, and they are too ready to accept job offers and give up search.

The equilibrium unemployment rate derived in the models of parts I and II depends on several policy parameters, such as unemployment compensation, wage taxes, and employment subsidies. The positive question of the dependence of equilibrium unemployment and vacancies on policy, and the normative question of how policy can be used to move the economy toward the social equilibrium, are studied in part III. One important result is that there are nondistortionary combinations of policy instruments, even when there is unemployment insurance. Another is that there is a policy package that internalizes the search externalities.

The book develops its argument in a logical sequence, but busy readers will be able to follow most chapters without having to read all chapters that precede them. The foundation chapters of the book are chapters 1 and the first two sections of chapter 2. Readers interested in the interaction between the labor market and the macroeconomy will find an analysis of steady states in the rest of chapter 2 and an analysis of fluctuations in chapter 3. Chapters 4, 5, and 6 can be read individually after reading chapter 1 and the first two sections of chapter 2. Chapters 7 and 8 consist of virtually self-contained sections that follow on from the analysis of chapters 1, 2, 4, 5, or 6. Readers interested in the efficiency or policy analysis of the issues raised in each of these chapters can move directly to the relevant sections of chapter 7 or 8. In order to achieve continuity, there is reference to the results of previous chapters in virtually all chapters of the book, though other chapters are not essential to understanding a chapter's argument.

Many of the ideas in the book have appeared in journal articles that I published between 1979 and 1987. However, the book was completely written (and rewritten) in a uniform style and notation, and all of the results were completely re-derived within a consistent framework. In many cases the emphasis has changed, and new results have emerged from the more general framework of the book. Needless to add, the book has also been influenced by the work of many other authors, who published papers on these topics over the same period. The notes on the literature that follow each chapter explain the relation between the chapter's results and those in the published literature. References in the text have been kept to a minimum to avoid breaks in the argument. For the same reason, footnotes have been eliminated completely: If the point is important enough, it is in the text; if not, it is not in the book.

I have received useful comments on the work reported in this book from too many people to mention. My greatest debt is to my colleagues at the Centre for Labour Economics at the London School Economics, especially to Richard Layard and Richard Jackman, with whom I co-authored one of the first empirical papers on this subject, which convinced me of the usefulness of this approach to unemployment. I am also indebted to the Economic and Social Research Council and the Department of Employment for their financial support (through their financing of the Centre's programme on unemployment), to Bob Gross for compiling the bibliography, and to Ellen Byrne and Pam Grace for expert typing, patience, and devotion to the project.

I FOUNDATIONS

1 The Labor Market

The purpose of this chapter is to describe a simple version of the labor-market model that captures the salient features of the theory of unemployment developed in this book. The model does not yet claim to be realistic or empirically implementable. At this stage many of the variables that are likely to be important in an empirical analysis of unemployment are left out. Its purpose is to point out the nature of unemployment in the steady state and to show how wages and unemployment are jointly determined in an otherwise standard equilibrium model.

The model of this chapter is suitable for macroeconomic analysis, and it is with this objective in mind that it is being developed. Chapter 2 extends it in an important direction, by introducing endogenous job destruction. Chapter 3 embeds it into the standard neoclassical model of growth and considers the properties of the balanced growth path. The model is shown to add a rich theory of the natural rate of unemployment to the full-employment models that form the basis of much of modern macroeconomics.

1.1 Trade in the Labor Market

The central idea of the model is that trade in the labor market is a decentralized economic activity. It is uncoordinated, time-consuming, and costly for both firms and workers. Firms and workers have to spend resources before job creation and production can take place, and existing jobs command rents in equilibrium, a property that does not characterize Walrasian labor markets.

We use a simple modeling device to capture the implications of trade for market equilibrium, which has its parallel in the neoclassical assumption of the existence of an aggregate production function. We assume that there is a well-behaved *matching function* that gives the number of jobs formed at any moment in time as a function of the number of workers looking for jobs, the number of firms looking for workers, and possibly some other variables (which are introduced in later chapters).

Trade in the labor market is a nontrivial economic activity because of the existence of heterogeneities, frictions, and information imperfections. If all workers were identical to each other and if all jobs were also identical to each other, and if there was perfect information about their location, trade would be trivial. But without homogeneity on either side of the market and with costly acquisition of information, firms and workers find it necessary to spend resources to find productive job matches. The heterogeneities may be in the skills possessed by workers, on the one hand, and those required by firms, on the other. They may be in the information possessed about the job. Or, they may be in the location of jobs and workers and in the timing of job creation in different locations. In this environment there is uncertainty about the arrival of good jobs to job-seekers and good workers to hiring firms, and firms and workers have to decide whether to accept what is available, wait for a better alternative, or influence the arrival process itself by spending resources on the acquisition of information, retraining employees, or changing location.

The matching function gives the outcome of the investment of resources by firms and workers in the trading process as a function of the inputs. It is a modeling device that captures the implications of the costly trading process without the need to make the heterogeneities and other features that give rise to it explicit. In this sense it occupies the same place in the macroeconomist's tool kit as other aggregate functions, such as the production function and the demand for money function. The production function summarizes a relationship that depends on a physical technology that is not made explicit in macroeconomic modeling. The demand for money function summarizes a transaction technology and a portfolio choice that is also rarely made explicit. Similarly the matching function summarizes a trading technology between heterogeneous agents that is also not made explicit.

Like the other aggregate functions in the macroeconomist's tool kit, the usefulness of the matching function depends on its empirical viability and on how successful it is in capturing the salient features of exchange in the labor market. Of course, if an empirically successful microfoundation for the matching function were known, that would make it more convincing, but it is not uncommon to find aggregate functions in the macroeconomist's tool kit without explicit microfoundations. Empirical success and modeling effectiveness are usually sufficient. One of the aims of this book is to show that the matching function is a useful modeling device and that many new and plausible results can be derived from it.

Matching functions have been estimated for a number of countries with good and largely uniform results. Some of these studies are discussed in the Notes on the Literature at the end of this chapter. Matching functions have also been derived from explicit trading processes, but there is as yet no microfoundation for it that dominates all others. In this book we will assume the existence of a general matching function of a few variables and impose some regularity restrictions on it that have been shown to be empirically valid in a large number of studies.

Trade and production are completely separate activities. In order to emphasize this, we assume that there is full specialization in either trade or production. A firm with many jobs may have some of them filled and some vacant, but only vacant jobs can engage in trade. Thus, although firms do not specialize, jobs do. Similarly, in the model of this chapter and in most of the applications in this book, a worker may be employed or unemployed, but only unemployed workers search for jobs. In view of the empirical importance of search on the job and job-to-job moves, however, we will also characterize market equilibrium with search on the job (chapter 4). We will argue that the justification for the assumption that only the unemployed search is naturally not its descriptive accuracy. It is the claim that the theory of unemployment obtained under the assumption of no on-the-job search is not significantly different from the one obtained when on-the-job search is introduced. It will be shown in chapter 4 that although some new results are derived, there are no significant modifications to the theory of unemployment in this and the next chapter, and it is not necessary for equilibrium-matching models to abandon the assumption of a simple matching function with only unemployed workers searching. The assumption of full specialization in either production or trade is a useful modeling device for both jobs and workers.

Vacant jobs and unemployed workers become matched to each other and move from trading to production activities gradually, according to the prevailing matching technology. Unemployment persists in the steady state because during the matching process and before all unmatched job-worker pairs meet, some of the existing jobs break up, providing a flow into unemployment. The separations result from firm-specific shocks, which summarize mainly changes in technology or demand, due to shifts in production or utility functions.

Firms and workers decide what to do with full knowledge of the job-matching and job-separation processes but without any attempt to coordinate their actions. There are many firms and many workers, and each operates as an atomistic competitor. The equilibrium that we describe is a full rational expectations equilibrium. The aggregate equilibrium state is one where firms and workers maximize their respective objective functions, subject to the matching and separation technologies, and where the flow of workers into unemployment is equal to the flow of workers out of unemployment. Our assumptions ensure that there is a unique unemployment rate at which these two flows are equal.

We begin with a formalization of the equilibrium condition for unemployment. Suppose there are L workers in the labor force. We let u denote the unemployment rate—the fraction of unmatched workers—and v the number of vacant jobs as a fraction of the labor force. We refer to v as the vacancy rate, and we assume that only the uL unemployed workers and the vL job vacancies engage in matching. The model is specified in continuous time. The number of job matches taking place per unit time is given by

$$mL = m(uL, vL). \tag{1.1}$$

Equation (1.1) is the matching function. It is assumed increasing in both its arguments, concave, and homogeneous of degree 1. Homogeneity, or constant returns to scale, is an important property, and our reasons for assuming it are similar to the reasons that aggregate production functions are assumed to be of constant returns: It is empirically supported and plausible, since in a growing economy constant returns ensures a constant unemployment rate along the balanced-growth path. Of course one does not need constant returns everywhere, both at the micro and macro levels, to derive a balanced growth path. There are by now, however, convincing empirical reasons for assuming constant returns in matching functions, which are discussed at the end of this chapter and later (chapter 3). The empirical literature has further found that a log-linear (Cobb-Douglas) approximation to the matching function fits the data well. We do not need to impose this additional restriction on the matching function for the results derived in this book.

The job vacancies and unemployed workers that are matched at any point in time are randomly selected from the sets vL and uL. Hence the process that changes the state of vacant jobs is Poisson with rate

$m(uL,vL)/vL$. By the homogeneity of the matching function, this rate is a function of the ratio of vacancies to unemployment only. It is convenient to introduce the v/u ratio as a separate variable, denoted by θ, and write the rate at which vacant jobs become filled as

$$q(\theta) \equiv m\left(\frac{u}{v}, 1\right). \tag{1.2}$$

During a small time interval δt, a vacant job is matched to an unemployed worker with probability $q(\theta)\delta t$, so the mean duration of a vacant job is $1/q(\theta)$. By the properties of the matching technology, $q'(\theta) \leq 0$ and the elasticity of $q(\theta)$ is a number between 0 and -1. Its absolute value is denoted by $\eta(\theta)$.

Unemployed workers move into employment according to a related Poisson process with rate $m(uL, vL)/uL$. Making use of the θ notation, this rate is equal to $\theta q(\theta)$ and has elasticity $1 - \eta(\theta) \geq 0$. The mean duration of unemployment is $1/\theta q(\theta)$. Thus unemployed workers find jobs more easily when there are more jobs relative to the available workers, and firms with vacancies find workers more easily when there are more workers relative to the available jobs. The process that describes the transition out of unemployment is related to the process that describes the filling of jobs by the fact that jobs and workers meet in pairs. By the structure of the model, θ is an appropriate measure of the *tightness* of the labor market. In much of what follows, labor market tightness, θ, is a more convenient variable to work with than the vacancy rate, v.

The dependence of the functions $q(\theta)$ and $\theta q(\theta)$ on the relative number of traders (tightness) is an example of a trading externality that will play a central role in our analysis. The trading externality arises because during trade, price is not the only allocative mechanism. During a short interval of time δt, there is a positive probability $1 - q(\theta)\delta t$ that a hiring firm will not find a worker and another positive probability $1 - \theta q(\theta)\delta t$ that an unemployed worker will not find a job, whatever the set of prices. There is stochastic rationing, which cannot be eliminated by price adjustments. But it can be made better or worse for the representative trader by adjustments in the relative number of traders in the market. If the ratio of hiring firms to searching workers increases, the probability of rationing is higher for the average firm and lower for the average worker, and conversely. We refer to these trade externalities as *search* or *congestion* externalities because they are caused by the congestion that searching firms and workers cause for each other during trade. Their existence is important for most of the properties of equilibrium unemployment that we derive. It also has important implications for the efficiency of equilibrium, which we consider in chapter 8.

The flow into unemployment results from job-specific (idiosyncratic) shocks that arrive to occupied jobs at the Poisson rate λ. The job-specific shocks may be caused by structural shifts in demand that change the relative price of the good produced by a job, or by productivity shocks that change the unit costs of production. In either case they are real shocks associated with a shift in either tastes or technology. Once a shock arrives, the firm has no choice but either to continue production at the new value or to close the job down. In the full specification of the model, we will assume that when an idiosyncratic shock arrives, the net product of the job changes to some new value that is a drawing from a general probability distribution. In the simpler model in this chapter, however, we assume that the probability distribution of idiosyncratic productivity values is a very special one. The relative price of output of an occupied job is either high enough (and constant) to make production profitable or low enough (and hence arbitrarily small) to lead to a separation. Idiosyncratic shocks move the value of output from the high level to the low one at rate λ.

Job creation takes place when a firm and a searching worker meet and agree to form a match at a negotiated wage. When the decision to create a job is made, the firm has a choice of which product value to choose, so it always chooses the high value. Goods or technologies are differentiated but irreversible. Before job creation, there is full choice of technology and product type; once job creation has taken place, the firm has no choice of either. Thus, once the firm and worker meet and a job is created, production continues until a negative idiosyncratic shock arrives, at which point the productivity of the job moves to the low value. *Job destruction* then takes place, which in the framework of this model is equal to job separations: The worker moves from employment to unemployment, and the firm can either withdraw from the market or reopen a job as a new vacancy (in equilibrium firms are indifferent between these two options).

We assume that the job-worker pairs that experience the adverse shocks are randomly selected. During a small time interval δt a worker moves from employment to unemployment with exogenous probability $\lambda \delta t$, and an occupied job separates with the same probability. Thus job separations follow a Poisson process with rate λ which is independent of the processes that describe the filling of jobs, and which in this version of the model is exogenous.

Without growth or turnover in the labor force, the mean number of workers who enter unemployment during a small time interval is $\lambda(1 - u)L\delta t$, and the mean number who leave unemployment is $mL\delta t$. We rewrite the latter as $u\theta q(\theta)L\delta t$, where $\theta q(\theta)\delta t$ is the transition probability of the unemployed. The evolution of mean unemployment is given by the difference between the two flows,

$$\dot{u} = \lambda(1-u) - \theta q(\theta)u. \tag{1.3}$$

In the steady state the mean rate of unemployment is constant, so

$$\lambda(1 - u) = \theta q(\theta)u. \tag{1.4}$$

We assume that the market is large enough, so deviations from the mean can be ignored. We can rewrite (1.4) as an equation determining unemployment in terms of the two transition rates:

$$u = \frac{\lambda}{\lambda + \theta q(\theta)}. \tag{1.5}$$

Equation (1.5) is the first key equation of the model. It implies that for given λ and θ, there is a unique equilibrium unemployment rate. λ is a parameter of the model; θ is an unknown. We show in the next section that θ is determined by an equation derived from the assumption of profit maximization and that it is unique and independent of u. Hence the solution for u is also unique. By the properties of the matching function, (1.5) can be represented in tightness-unemployment space or in vacancy-unemployment space, by a downward-sloping and convex to the origin curve. This curve is known as the *Beveridge curve*.

We stated the steady-state condition (1.4) in terms of the flows in and out of unemployment. Alternatively, it can be stated in terms of job flows, which we do here for future reference. The number of jobs created at any moment in time is $m(v, u)$. The empirical literature on job flows defines the job creation rate as the ratio of the number of jobs created to employment, namely as $m(v, u)/(1 - u)$. The job destruction rate is similarly defined as the ratio of the total number of jobs destroyed, $\lambda(1 - u)$, to employment, $1 - u$. Equating the constant job destruction rate, λ, to the job creation rate gives (1.4). Restating the steady-state condition in terms of the job flows makes it clear that the key driving force in this version of the model is job creation. It also makes it easier to compare some of the model's results with the empirical findings, which we do in later sections.

1.2   Job Creation

Job creation takes place when a firm and a worker meet and agree to an employment contract. Before this can take place, however, the firm has to open a job vacancy and search, and unemployed workers also have to search. The employment contract specifies only a wage rule that gives the wage rate at any moment in time as a function of some commonly observed variables. Hours of work are fixed (and normalized to unity), and either side can break the contract at any time.

For convenience, we assume that firms are small. Each has one job that is vacant when it first enters the market, but the job is occupied by a worker after an employment contract has been signed. When the job is occupied, the firm rents capital and produces output, which is sold in competitive markets. The capital decision is not important for our main results, so we will suppress it for the time being and introduce it later in this chapter. We assume instead that the value of a job's output is some constant $p > 0$. When the job is vacant, the firm is actively engaged in hiring at a fixed cost $pc > 0$ per unit time. During hiring, workers arrive to vacant jobs at the rate $q(\theta)$, which for now is independent of what the firm does.

The hiring cost is made proportional to productivity on the ground that it is more costly to hire more productive workers. In a long-run equilibrium it is a natural assumption to make, since the costs of the firm have to rise along with productivity to ensure the existence of a steady state. The assumption may, however, be less easy to justify over the business cycle, when it might be more natural to assume that hiring costs depend on wages, on the ground that hiring is a labor-intensive activity. But even if wages are not proportional to productivity in the short run, assuming proportionality of the hiring cost to productivity is still a good assumption to make. The derivation and explanation of the results that follow are easier with this assumption, and there are no new results of interest that can be derived by making the alternative assumption that hiring costs depend on wages.

The number of jobs is endogenous and determined by profit maximization. Any firm is free to open a job vacancy and engage in hiring. Hence profit maximization requires that the profit from one more vacancy should be zero. In the environment of the simple model of this chapter, with each firm having one job only, profit maximization is equivalent to a zero-profit condition for firm entry. In chapter 3 we show that the same condition can be derived from a standard model of a competitive firm with costs of adjustment for employment, when the firm maximizes the present-discounted value of profits. We follow the single-job approach in this chapter to motivate the wage equation, which plays a key role in the analysis. Some of our later results, however, especially those derived for endogenous job destruction depend critically on this assumption.

Let J be the present-discounted value of expected profit from an occupied job and V the present-discounted value of expected profit from a vacant job. With a perfect capital market, an infinite horizon and when no dynamic changes in parameters are expected, V satisfies the Bellman equation

$$rV = -pc + q(\theta)(J - V). \tag{1.6}$$

A job is an asset owned by the firm. In a perfect capital market the valuation of the asset is such that the capital cost, rV, is exactly equal to the rate of return on the asset: The vacant job costs pc per unit time and changes state according to a Poisson process with rate $q(\theta)$. The change of state yields net return $J - V$. Since we are in a steady state, there are no capital gains or losses from expected changes in the valuation of jobs. Both V and J are constant.

In equilibrium all profit opportunities from new jobs are exploited, driving rents from vacant jobs to zero. Therefore the equilibrium condition for the supply of vacant jobs is $V = 0$, implying that

$$J = \frac{pc}{q(\theta)}. \tag{1.7}$$

This is the second key equation of the equilibrium model. For an individual firm, $1/q(\theta)$ is the expected duration of a vacancy. Condition (1.7) states that in equilibrium, market tightness is such that the expected profit from a new job is equal to the expected cost of hiring a worker. Since in the environment of this model a firm cannot enter the market with a filled job, there are rents in equilibrium associated with filled jobs. Competition for vacant jobs drives those rents down to the expected cost of finding a worker.

The asset value of an occupied job, J, satisfies a value equation similar to the one for vacant jobs. The flow capital cost of the job is rJ. In the labor market, the job yields net return $p - w$, where p is real output and w is the cost of labor. The job also runs a risk λ of an adverse shock, which leads to the loss of J. Hence J satisfies the condition,

$$rJ = p - w - \lambda J. \tag{1.8}$$

The firm takes the interest rate and product value as given, but the wage rate is determined by a bargain between the meeting firm and worker. Making use of equation (1.8) to substitute J out of the equilibrium condition (1.7), we derive the equation,

$$p - w - \frac{(r + \lambda)pc}{q(\theta)} = 0. \tag{1.9}$$

Equation (1.9), as we will see in chapter 3, corresponds to a marginal condition for the demand for labor. p is the marginal product of labor and $(r + \lambda)pc/q(\theta)$ is the expected capitalized value of the firm's hiring cost. If the firm had no hiring cost, c would be 0 and (1.9) would reduce to the standard marginal productivity condition for employment in the steady state. Because of the properties of the arrival rate $q(\theta)$, equation (1.9) can be represented by a downward-sloping curve in θ, w space. In this model the properties of the matching technology ensure that the demand for labor is downward-sloping, even for a constant marginal product of labor. We will refer to it (and to the equation representing it) as the *job creation* condition.

The Beveridge curve and job creation condition, (1.6) and (1.9), contain four unknowns—unemployment, the number of jobs, the real wage rate, and the real rate of interest. Between them they yield solutions for the two quantities—unemployment and jobs—in terms of the two prices—real wages and rate of interest—which are still to be determined. To determine them, we have to close the model by considering the behavior of workers and the demand side of the model.

1.3 Workers

Workers normally influence the equilibrium outcome through their job search and their influence on wage determination. In the simple version of the model in this chapter, the size of the labor force and each worker's intensity of search are fixed, whereas the assumption of common productivity in all jobs makes the job-acceptance decision trivial. So the only influence that workers have on the equilibrium outcome is through wages. In this section we derive the typical worker's returns when employed and when unemployed, which we use in the next section to derive the wage equation and in later chapters in other applications.

A typical worker earns w when employed and searches for a job when unemployed. During search the worker enjoys some real return z, which we measure in the same units as real wages. z may include a number of things, distinguished by the fact that they have to be given up when the worker becomes employed. We ignore any income that the worker receives regardless of whether he is employed or unemployed, since with risk neutrality and perfect capital markets such incomes do not play a role in the determination of unemployment.

The most obvious component of z is unemployment insurance benefits. Another component of z is the income that the unemployed worker may be able to earn by doing odd and irregular jobs in a secondary sector of the economy, if such a sector exists. z includes also the imputed real return from any unpaid leisure activities, such as home production or recreation. We show later in this and subsequent chapters that the way in which we specify z is important for many of our results. To begin with, we assume that z is constant and independent of market returns.

Let U and W denote the present-discounted value of the expected income stream of, respectively, an unemployed and an employed worker, including the imputed return from nonmarket activities. The unemployed worker enjoys (expected) real return z while unemployed, and in unit time he expects to move into employment with probability $\theta q(\theta)$. Hence U satisfies

$$rU = z + \theta q(\theta)(W - U). \tag{1.10}$$

Equation (1.10) has the same interpretation as the firm's asset equations (1.6) and (1.8). The asset that is valued is the unemployed worker's human capital and the valuation placed on it by the market is U, which is made up of the yield z and the expected capital gain from change of state $q(\theta)(W - U)$. rU can be given two useful interpretations. Since it is the average expected return on the worker's human capital during search, it is the minimum compensation that an unemployed worker requires to give up search. This makes it the unemployed worker's reservation wage (see also chapter 6). rU is also the maximum amount that the unemployed worker can spend without running down his (human) capital. Hence it is also the unemployed worker's normal or permanent income, with permanent income defined broadly to include imputed non-market returns.

Employed workers earn a wage w; they lose their jobs and become unemployed at the exogenous rate λ. Hence the valuation placed on them by the market, W, satisfies

$$rW = w + \lambda(U - W). \tag{1.11}$$

The permanent income of employed workers, rW, is different from the constant wage w because of the risk of unemployment. If there were job quitting in the model, rW would be the minimum net compensation that the worker would require to give up his job. Without on-the-job search, workers stay in their jobs for as long as $W \geq U$. The necessary and sufficient condition for this to hold is $w \geq z$. Although w is still an unknown, this inequality is assumed to hold. We show later that a sufficient condition for this to hold is $p \geq z$, which is imposed.

Equations (1.10) and (1.11) can be solved for the permanent incomes of unemployed and employed workers, in terms of the returns z and w and the discount and transition rates:

$$rU = \frac{(r + \lambda)z + \theta q(\theta)w}{r + \lambda + \theta q(\theta)}, \tag{1.12}$$

$$rW = \frac{\lambda z + [r + \theta q(\theta)]w}{r + \lambda + \theta q(\theta)}. \tag{1.13}$$

Since $w \geq z$, it follows from (1.12) and (1.13) that with discounting, employed workers have higher permanent incomes than unemployed workers: Unemployment is more costly to those currently experiencing it than to those who expect to experience it some time in the future. But without discounting, unemployed workers are not worse off than employed workers in permanent-income terms. The reason is that with infinite horizons all workers eventually participate equally in employment and unemployment, and the timing of their experience does not affect their ex ante returns.

1.4   Wage Determination

In equilibrium, occupied jobs yield a total return that is strictly greater than the sum of the expected returns of a searching firm and a searching worker. If the firm and worker who are together separate, each will have to go through an expensive process of search before meeting another partner. Since all job-worker pairs are equally productive, the expected joint return of the firm and the worker after they form new matches must be the same as the joint return from their current match. Hence a realized job match yields some pure economic rent, which is equal to the sum of the expected search costs of the firm and the worker (including forgone wages and profits). Wages need to share this economic (local-monopoly) rent, in addition to compensating each side for its costs from forming the job. We assume that the monopoly rent is shared according to the Nash solution to a bargaining problem.

The wage rate for a job is fixed by the firm and the worker after they meet. Because all jobs are equally productive and all workers place the same value on leisure, the wage fixed for each job is the same everywhere. But an individual firm and worker are too small to influence the market. When they meet, they fix the wage rate by taking behavior in the rest of the market as given.

Given our assumptions on productivity and the arrival process of idiosyncratic shocks, a firm and worker who are brought together by the matching process will always form a productive job. An employment contract between the meeting firm and worker is a wage w_i for each period of time that they are together and a separation rule that is contingent on the arrival of an idiosyncratic shock. We assume both here and throughout the analysis that the wage contract is renegotiated whenever new information arrives. This amounts to assuming that the wage rate continually satisfies the Nash sharing rule for the life of the job.

For a wage rate w_i the firm's expected return from the job, J_i, satisfies,

$$rJ_i = p - w_i - \lambda J_i. \tag{1.14}$$

Recall that if the firm is unoccupied the job is worth $V = 0$. The job is worth to the worker W_i, where

$$rW_i = w_i - \lambda(W_i - U). \tag{1.15}$$

The expected return from search, U, is independent of w_i and satisfies, as before, equation (1.12), with w denoting wages in the rest of the market.

The wage derived from the (generalized) Nash bargaining solution is the w_i that maximizes the weighted product of the worker's and the firm's net return from the job match. In order to form the job match, the worker gives up U for W_i and the firm gives up V for J_i. Therefore the wage rate for this job satisfies

$$w_i = \arg\max(W_i - U)^\beta (J_i - V)^{1-\beta}, \tag{1.16}$$

where $0 \leq \beta \leq 1$. In symmetric situations β is equal to $\frac{1}{2}$. More generally, there may be plausible bargaining situations that imply a different β, for example, when firms and workers have different rates of impatience. In those more general situations, β may be interpreted as a relative measure of labor's bargaining strength, other than the one implied by the "threat points" U and V. We will treat β as a constant parameter strictly between 0 and 1 throughout the analysis and think of $\frac{1}{2}$ as the most plausible value, since we are modeling symmetric situations.

The first-order maximization condition derived from (1.16) satisfies

$$W_i - U = \beta(J_i + W_i - V - U). \tag{1.17}$$

So in the model of this chapter, β is labor's share of the total surplus that an occupied job creates.

Condition (1.17) can be converted into a wage equation in a number of ways; we show here two. First, by substituting W_i and J_i from (1.15) and (1.14) into (1.17), and by imposing the equilibrium condition $V = 0$, we derive the flow version of (1.17),

$$w_i = rU + \beta(p - rU). \tag{1.18}$$

Workers receive their reservation wage rU and a fraction β of the net surplus that they create by accepting the job: product value net of what they give up, rU. rU is not a particularly interesting variable in the equilibrium solution of the model. A simpler and more appealing version of the wage equation may be derived by noting that (1.18) implies that all jobs will offer the same wage, and by making use of (1.17) and the equilibrium condition for jobs, (1.7), to substitute $W - U$ out of (1.10). This gives the following expression for rU:

$$rU = z + \frac{\beta}{1-\beta} pc\theta, \tag{1.19}$$

which, when substituted into (1.18) yields the aggregate wage equation that holds in equilibrium,

$$w = (1 - \beta)z + \beta p(1 + c\theta). \tag{1.20}$$

Equation (1.20) is the most convenient form of the wage equation for the applications that we will study. It is intuitive for a market equilibrium if we note that $pc\theta$ is the average hiring cost for each unemployed worker (since $pc\theta = pcv/u$ and pcv is total hiring cost in the economy). Workers are rewarded for the saving of hiring costs that the representative firm enjoys when a job is formed. The way that market tightness enters the wage equation in our model is through the bargaining power that each party has. A higher θ indicates that jobs arrive to workers at higher rate than workers do to vacant jobs, relative to an equilibrium with lower θ. The worker's bargaining strength is then higher and the firm's lower, and this leads to a higher wage rate.

Equation (1.20) replaces the labor supply curve of Walrasian models. Labor supply in our model is fixed: The labor force size is constant, workers search with constant intensity, and they work a fixed number of hours when in a job. The Walrasian labor supply curve in our model is a vertical line at the fixed labor force size. But the existence of local monopoly power in this model and the sharing rule used to solve for wages imply that even with fixed labor product and labor supply, there is an upward-sloping relation in θ, w space (or alternatively, for given vacancies, a downward-sloping relation between wages and unemployment). We refer to this curve as the *wage curve* for brevity, though it can also be referred to as the wage-setting function or wage-determination curve.

We finally note one more property of the sharing rule (1.17). A job in equilibrium creates a positive surplus for both the firm and the worker, which is equal to the sum of the expected cost of search and the expected cost of hiring. The firm's net return from the job is J which, by (1.7), must be positive and equal to the expected hiring cost. From (1.14) and (1.20) it follows that the product p must be strictly greater than the worker's nonmarket return, z, and labor's share β must be strictly less than 1; otherwise, no firm will have an incentive to open a job. The worker's return from a job, $W - U$, may then be strictly positive, if $\beta > 0$, but it is also feasible to have $\beta = 0$, where the firm enjoys the entire surplus from the job. We will assume that p is sufficiently high to ensure the existence of a nontrivial equilibrium and that β is strictly less than 1.

1.5   Steady-State Equilibrium

Equilibrium is a triple (u, θ, w) that satisfies the flow equilibrium condition (1.5), the job creation condition (1.9), and the wage equation (1.20). The real interest rate is left out of this analysis and for the time being assumed to be exogenous and constant. For given interest rate, equations (1.9) and (1.20) determine the wage rate and the ratio of vacancies to unemployment; given the ratio of vacancies to unemployment, equation (1.5) determines unemployment. With knowledge of θ, the evolution of employment is obtained from the assumption of a constant labor force and the evolution of output from the assumption of a constant output per job.

Because of the structure of the model, it is convenient to refer to θ as the unknown, in place of the number of jobs or job vacancies. Recall that the number of jobs is equal to employment, $(1 - u)L$, plus job vacancies, $\theta u L$; therefore, if we know θ and u, we also know the number of jobs. As before, we refer to θ as labor-market tightness (or as the v/u ratio). The three equations determining steady-state equilibrium are reproduced here for convenience:

$$u = \frac{\lambda}{\lambda + \theta q(\theta)}, \tag{1.21}$$

$$p - w - \frac{(r + \lambda)pc}{q(\theta)} = 0, \tag{1.22}$$

$$w = (1 - \beta)z + \beta p(1 + c\theta). \tag{1.23}$$

Equilibrium is easily shown to be unique with the help of two diagrams, one that replaces the conventional demand and supply diagram for labor and a new diagram with the Beveridge curve as its centerpiece.

Figure 1.1 shows equilibrium for tightness and wages. Recall that (1.22) is the job creation curve, and in tightness-wage space it slopes down: Higher wage rate makes job creation less profitable and so leads to a lower equilibrium ratio of jobs to workers. It replaces the demand curve of Walrasian economics. Equation (1.23) is the wage curve and slopes up: At higher market tightness the relative bargaining strength of market participants shifts in favor of workers. It replaces the supply curve. Equilibrium (θ, w) is at the intersection of the two curves and it is unique.

Consider now figure 1.2, the Beveridge diagram. Figure 1.1 shows that the equilibrium θ is independent of unemployment. The equation for this θ can be explicitly derived by substituting wages from (1.23) into (1.22), to get

$$(1 - \beta)(p - z) - \frac{r + \lambda + \beta\theta q(\theta)}{q(\theta)} pc = 0. \qquad (1.24)$$

In the vacancy-unemployment space of figure 1.2, this is shown as a line through the origin, with slope θ. The steady-state condition for

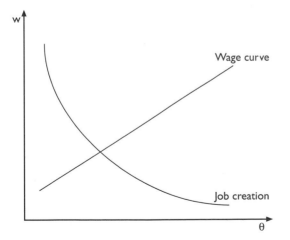

Figure 1.1
Equilibrium wages and market tightness

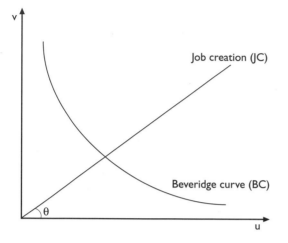

Figure 1.2
Equilibrium vacancies and unemployment

unemployment, (1.21), is the Beveridge curve, and it is convex to the origin by the properties of the matching technology. When there are more vacancies, unemployment is lower because the unemployed find jobs more easily. Diminishing returns to individual inputs in matching imply the convex shape. Equilibrium vacancies and unemployment are at the unique intersection of the job creation line and the Beveridge curve.

Some of the more interesting properties of equilibrium can be shown in the diagrams. Higher labor productivity increases p and shifts the job creation line in figure 1.1 to the right and the wage curve up. Since $\beta < 1$, the job creation curve shifts by more, so both wages and market tightness increase (see also equation 1.24). In figure 1.2 this rotates the job creation line anticlockwise, increasing vacancies and reducing unemployment.

Examination of the wage equation and (1.24) shows that the productivity effect on market tightness and unemployment takes place because of the fixed income (imputed or actual) of unemployed workers, z. The fixed z stops wages from fully absorbing productivity changes, so at higher productivity the profit from job creation is higher, leading to more job creation and lower unemployment. Although this is intuitive within the framework of the model of this chapter, it is not a desirable property of a model in long-run equilibrium. In the long run, wages should fully absorb productivity changes, at least when they are labor-augmenting, and a balanced-growth equilibrium with constant unemployment should exist.

Extensions that imply that wages fully absorb productivity changes are easy to find. The easiest, though not most general, is when z is primarily unemployment insurance income which is fixed in terms of the average wage rate. If we let $z = \rho w$, where ρ is the replacement rate (a policy parameter), then the wage equation becomes

$$w = \frac{\beta(1+c\theta)}{1-(1-\beta)\rho} p. \tag{1.25}$$

With this wage equation the job creation condition (1.22) becomes

$$1 - \frac{\beta(1+c\theta)}{1-(1-\beta)\rho} - \frac{(r+\lambda)c}{q(\theta)} = 0, \tag{1.26}$$

making the equilibrium θ independent of productivity. Equilibrium unemployment is then also independent of the average level of productivity.

Other more general assumptions about the value of nonmarket time also have such neutrality implications, though not necessarily with respect to the rate of growth of productivity. We return to this question in chapter 3, where we argue that some inflexibility in z may be a reasonable feature of short- to medium-run equilibrium but not of long-run equilibrium, and where we look at the effects of productivity growth.

A higher nonmarket return for workers, shown by a higher z (or higher ρ if the wage equation is (1.25)), shifts the wage curve in figure 1.1 up and therefore increases wages but reduces market tightness. Workers claim a higher wage when z is higher because the cost of unemployment is lower, and with higher wages firms create fewer jobs. A higher β has similar effects, for similar reasons. The job creation line in figure 1.2 rotates clockwise, reducing vacancies and increasing unemployment. Note that these effects of unemployment income are obtained by ignoring the disincentive effects that this income has on job search and job acceptance, a question that we address in chapters 5 and 6.

A higher real interest rate or arrival rate of negative idiosyncratic shocks (and so higher job destruction rate at given unemployment rate) shifts the job creation curve in figure 1.1 to the left. The reason is that in the case of the higher interest rate, the future revenues from a job are discounted more heavily, and in the case of the higher destruction rate, the life of the job is on average shorter. They both lead to lower tightness and wage rate because the costs of job creation have to be paid up front. In the Beveridge diagram both changes rotate the job creation line down, but the increase in the arrival rate of idiosyncratic shocks also shifts the Beveridge curve out. The higher interest rate increases unemployment and reduces vacancies. The higher job destruction rate increases unemployment but has uncertain effect on vacancies.

The higher λ shifts the Beveridge curve out because at given unemployment rate a higher λ implies a bigger flow into unemployment than out of it. Unemployment needs to increase to bring the flow out of unemployment into equality with the higher inflow. Another change that can shift the Beveridge curve out is an exogenous fall in the rate of job matching, namely a downward shift in the matching function for given vacancies and unemployment. We have not yet discussed reasons for such a shift in this chapter, but we show in chapters 5 and 6 that exogenous changes in job matching can be caused by changes in a small number of parameters that affect, in equilibrium, the searching behavior of firms and workers. There is, however, another cause of exogenous changes in the rate of job matching, which is related to the usefulness of the concept of the aggregate matching function, and which we discuss here.

This cause is the degree of mismatch in the economy. As we have already argued, job matching in a real economy does not take place instantaneously because of heterogeneities in the qualities of jobs and workers, differences in their location, and imperfect information about these and other relevant parameters. The matching function in our model is a convenient modeling device that summarizes the effects of these factors on the speed of job formation. Mismatch can be thought of as an empirical concept that measures the degree of heterogeneity in the labor market. If mismatch in an economy were identically zero, the matching function would not exist and jobs and workers would meet instantaneously. It is because of the existence of some mismatch that meetings take place only after a search and application process. Therefore, if there is an exogenous rise in mismatch, the rate of job matching at given labor-market tightness must fall, and so the Beveridge curve must shift to the right, away from the origin. Since a fall in the rate of job matching also reduces the arrival rate of workers to jobs at given market tightness, it also shifts the job creation curve in figure 1.1 down and to the left, reducing wages and equilibrium tightness. In figure 1.2 this is shown by a downward rotation of the equilibrium job creation line, giving rise to more unemployment but to no apparent change in vacancies.

Of course, if empirically mismatch changes are frequent, the usefulness of the concept of the matching function is reduced. But the requirement that changes in mismatch are not frequent is not different from the one of other aggregate functions, such as the aggregate production function and the money demand function. If empirically there are many shifts in the aggregate production function because of problems associated with the aggregation of capital and labor, its usefulness in macroeconomic modeling is reduced. Our use of an aggregate matching function relies as much on the absence of serious aggregation problems as do the other aggregate functions used in macroeconomics. Whether in practice the matching function is a useful device or not is an empirical question. The available empirical evidence supports it sufficiently well to justify its use in the macroeconomic modeling of unemployment (see the notes on the literature at the end of this chapter).

In the empirical literature, mismatch bears some relationship to the frequently discussed sectoral shifts hypothesis, and to the older view of structural unemployment, which was thought to be unemployment arising from fast structural change in the economy as a whole. For example, it has been argued that the oil, technology, and other supply shocks of the 1970s and 1980s increased the speed with which unemployed workers needed to adapt to the changing requirements of employers. This led to increased mismatch, which increased unemployment at given vacancies. However, neither the sectoral shifts hypothesis in the United States, nor the mismatch hypothesis in Europe, has had much success in accounting for a large fraction of fluctuations in employment, which is another indication of the stability of the aggregate matching function.

1.6   Capital

We now introduce the capital decision in the model of the preceding sections and show that under the assumption that there is a perfect second-hand market for capital goods, on the one hand, the essential features of the unemployment model remain unaltered and on the other hand the capital decision is unaffected by the existence of matching frictions. We continue assuming that the interest rate is exogenous, an assumption that we relax in chapter 3. The assumptions that follow will justify our use of the model without capital in later chapters.

Suppose that the firm can buy and sell capital at the price of output in a perfect market. No time lapses between the decision to trade in capital and the execution of the decision. Since capital is costly, the firm will buy it only when there is a worker occupying the job; that is, vacancies do not own capital.

The productivity p of the model of preceding sections is reinterpreted as a labor-augmenting productivity parameter that measures the efficiency units of labor. Letting K and N, respectively, denote aggregate capital and employment, there is an aggregate production function $F(K, pN)$, with positive but diminishing marginal products and constant returns to scale. Defining k as the ratio K/pN (i.e., the capital stock per efficiency unit of labor), we define $f(k)$ as output per efficiency unit of labor, $F(K/pN, 1)$. The per-unit production function $f(k)$ satisfies $f'(k) > 0$ and $f''(k) < 0$.

When the job is vacant, its asset value is given by V and satisfies the same value equation as before, (1.6). But when a worker arrives and a wage rate agreed, the firm hires capital k for each efficiency unit of labor. The capital stock owned (or rented, it makes no difference with a perfect second-hand market for capital goods) by the firm becomes part of the value of the job, so the asset value of an occupied job is now given by $J + pk$, the sum of the present-discounted value of profits and the value of the rented capital stock. The real capital cost of the job is $r(J + pk)$. In the labor market the job yields net return $pf(k) - \delta pk - w$, where $pf(k)$ is real output, δpk is capital depreciation, and w is the cost of labor. The job also runs a risk λ of an adverse shock, which leads to the loss of J but not of k, which can be sold in the second-hand market. Hence J is determined by the asset-valuation condition

$$r(J + pk) = pf(k) - \delta pk - w - \lambda J, \tag{1.27}$$

which generalizes (1.8).

The firm takes the interest rate and the wage rate as given and rents as much capital as is necessary to maximize the value of the job. The maximization of J with respect to k gives the familiar equilibrium condition for the firm's capital stock,

$$f'(k) = r + \delta. \tag{1.28}$$

The marginal product of capital is equal to the marginal cost of capital, the rental plus the depreciation rate.

A rearrangement of equation (1.27) shows that it is equivalent to (1.8) with the generalization that job product p is replaced by $p[f(k) - (r + \delta)k]$. Of course, with (1.28) holding, the term in the square brackets is the marginal product of an efficiency unit of labor, $f(k) - kf'(k)$. None of the other asset value equations is affected by the introduction of the capital stock. Also, because the firm can buy and sell capital in a free market, the wage bargain is not affected by the introduction of capital—the worker cannot hold up the firm that has committed itself to a capital investment because capital investments are liquid (and reversible, although technology is still irreversible). Therefore the model can be solved as before but with the generalization that product p is multiplied by $[f(k) - (r + \delta)k]$ in all expressions. We restate here the equilibrium conditions with this generalization:

$$f'(k) = r + \delta, \tag{1.29}$$

$$p[f(k) - (r + \delta)k] - w - \frac{(r + \lambda)pc}{q(\theta)} = 0, \tag{1.30}$$

$$w = (1 - \beta)z + \beta p[f(k) - (r + \delta)k + c\theta], \tag{1.31}$$

$$u = \frac{\lambda}{\lambda + \theta q(\theta)}. \tag{1.32}$$

For given interest rate, the equilibrium system in (1.29) to (1.32) is recursive. With knowledge of r, equation (1.29) gives the capital-labor ratio. With knowledge of r and k, the block (1.30) to (1.31) gives wages and market tightness, very much along the lines illustrated in figure 1.1. Finally, for given tightness, equation (1.32) determines unemployment, along the lines of figure 1.2. The parametric effects described with the aid of figures 1.1 and 1.2 are not altered by the introduction of capital.

The equilibrium aggregate capital stock in this economy is $L(1 - u)pk$ and equilibrium employment $L(1 - u)$, so aggregate output is $L(1 - u)pf(k)$. Since we assumed a constant interest rate, the supply of

capital needs to be infinitely elastic to satisfy the equilibrium conditions
(1.29) to (1.32). We will return to this issue in chapter 3, when we consider the determination of the interest rate for an endogenous supply of
capital.

1.7   Out-of-Steady-State Dynamics

The discussion of the preceding sections was entirely about steady states.
The theory of unemployment in it, however, was explicitly derived from
(1) a dynamic equation for the evolution of the unemployment stock,
which was derived from models of the job creation and job destruction
flows, and (2) forward-looking rational expectations behavior by firms
and workers in job creation and wage determination. We now examine
the implications of these assumptions for the dynamic behavior of the
economy out of steady state.

Although the analysis of out-of-steady-state dynamics suggests various
directions for the development of a stochastic model of fluctuations, we
do not pursue the development of a full model of the business cycle here.
Our focus is on the dynamic behavior of unemployment, vacancies, and
wages when there is a matching function. A full model of the cycle would
require a more general treatment of capital than the one offered in the
preceding section and would also require the introduction of consumption and savings (see the Notes on the Literature for some recent work
in this area of research). Instead, here we ignore capital and focus on the
dynamics of the triple (θ, w, u) with the help of figures 1.1 and 1.2, ignoring all markets other than the one for labor. In this context the questions
of interest are whether (1) there is a unique stable path to the steady
state of figures 1.1 and 1.2, and (2) the out-of-steady-state dynamics of
unemployment and vacancies are consistent with the cyclical stylized
fact, that when the economy is off the Beveridge curve of figure 1.2 it
traces anticlockwise loops around the curve.

In the steady-state model we derived the equilibrium value of tightness from the assumption that the expected profit from the creation of
a new job vacancy was zero. We now assume that this property holds out
of the steady state as well. To ensure that this assumption can hold, job
vacancies, and so market tightness, have to be "jump" variables; that is,
firms have to be able to open up or close vacancies instantaneously so
as to ensure that the value of a new vacancy is always zero.

Similar assumptions are made about wage determination. Wages in the steady state were derived from the assumption that the firm and worker shared the rents from a job according to (1.17). We now assume that the same sharing rule holds out of steady state, consistent with our assumption that the firm and worker can renegotiate any time new information arrives. This assumption also requires that wages are a jump variable and change without delay and as necessary during adjustment, which is needed if (1.17) is to be always satisfied.

The dynamic behavior of unemployment contrasts with that of vacancies and wages. Although firms and workers can decide in isolation and without delay whether to form or break a match once they meet, at the aggregate level match formation is governed by the matching technology. The matching technology does not allow jumps in job formation; it describes a slow, stable and backward-looking process that is governed by the difference between the job creation and job destruction flows, as shown in equation (1.3). This makes unemployment a predetermined variable at any moment in time.

It is natural to expect the out-of-steady-state dynamics of a model that combines a backward-looking stable process with forward-looking jump variables to be characterized by a saddle path. Under the assumption of rational expectations we can show that the saddle path is the unique stable path that takes the economy to its steady-state equilibrium.

In order to derive the dynamic equations for wages and market tightness, we need to specify the expected returns of firms and workers out of steady state. The net worth of jobs and workers is now an explicit function of time. The arbitrage equations determining their value are similar to the ones that hold in the steady state, except that now they recognize the fact that there may be capital gains or losses from changes in the valuation placed by the market on jobs and workers.

Let again V denote the asset value of a vacant job. With a perfect capital market and perfect foresight it satisfies the arbitrage equation

$$rV = -pc + \dot{V} + q(\theta)(J - V). \tag{1.33}$$

As in the steady state, the left-hand side of (1.33) is the capital-market cost of the asset. The right-hand side is the labor-market return: a yield $-pc$, expected capital gains from changes in the valuation of the asset $\dot{V}$, and expected capital gains from the chance of finding a worker to take the vacancy. Comparison of (1.33) with (1.6) shows that the only thing that has changed in the valuation of a vacant job is that now account has to be taken of the changes in the value of the job during adjustment.

The value of a filled job, J, satisfies a similar arbitrage condition. In the absence of capital we get

$$rJ = p - w + \dot{J} - \lambda J. \tag{1.34}$$

$\dot{J}$ is the expected capital gain from changes in job value during adjustment.

Our assumption that firms exploit all profit opportunities from new jobs, regardless of whether they are in the steady state or out of it, implies that $V = \dot{V} = 0$. Therefore J is determined by the two equations

$$J = \frac{pc}{q(\theta)}, \tag{1.35}$$

$$\dot{J} = (r + \lambda)J - (p - w). \tag{1.36}$$

The net worth of employed and unemployed workers are given by two arbitrage equations that are similar to (1.33) and (1.34). As before, U denotes the net worth of an unemployed worker and W the net worth of an employed worker. The arbitrage equations when changes in valuations take place because of out-of-steady-state dynamics are

$$rU = z + \dot{U} + \theta q(\theta)(W - U) \tag{1.37}$$

and

$$rW = w + \dot{W} + \lambda(U - W). \tag{1.38}$$

All differential equations for asset values are unstable because of arbitrage and perfect foresight.

Wages are determined by the Nash solution to the bargaining problem, which as before implies the sharing rule (1.17). Because we allow wages to be renegotiated continually, (1.17) holds also in rates of change. Going through the same substitutions as for the steady-state wage equation, we derive the same equation as before, (1.20), which now holds both in and out of the steady state. Thus, for given productivity and income during unemployment, the out-of-steady-state dynamics of wages are driven entirely by the dynamics of labor-market tightness.

We are now ready to describe the out-of-steady-state dynamics of wages and tightness (figure 1.1). By (1.35), the job value J is a monotonically increasing function of tightness. Because wages are also a monotonically increasing function of tightness without sticky dynamics, the dynamic system in (1.35) and (1.36) can have only one rational expectations solution, $\dot{J} = \dot{\theta} = 0$. (To see this more explicitly, substitute J from (1.35) and wages from (1.17) into (1.36).) Therefore the out-of-steady-state equilibrium of tightness and wages is still given by the intersection of the two curves in figure 1.1. Whatever the initial conditions in this economy, vacancies and wages instantaneously jump to the intersection of the two curves.

This contrasts with the dynamics associated with the Beveridge curve. To demonstrate this, we combine the dynamics of unemployment with those of tightness into a two-equation system with u and θ as the unknowns. The equation for the evolution of unemployment, (1.3), is stable with driving force θ. Substitution of wages and job value J from (1.17) and (1.35) into (1.36) gives an unstable equation in θ, with no other unknown in it. The critical point (equilibrium) of the two-equation system is a saddle point. The sign pattern of a first-order linear approximation to the two differential equations is

$$\begin{pmatrix} \dot{u} \\ \dot{\theta} \end{pmatrix} = \begin{pmatrix} - & - \\ 0 & + \end{pmatrix} \begin{pmatrix} u \\ \theta \end{pmatrix}. \tag{1.39}$$

With negative determinant in (1.39), the necessary and sufficient conditions for a saddle-point equilibrium are satisfied.

The saddle point arises because one of the variables, unemployment, is sticky and stable, whereas the other, vacancies, is forward-looking and unstable. Firms in this model treat vacancies as an asset; it is the price that has to be paid now in order to attract employees in the future. The expected arrival of employees is the rate of return on the asset held by the firm, and as with other assets, there is an instability inherent in the supply of vacancies. If the arrival rate of employees is expected to fall, the firm wants to have fewer vacancies when the fall takes place. It therefore endeavors to reduce its vacancies by hiring its employees before the expected fall. But to hire more employees sooner, the firm needs to open up more vacancies. Thus, an expected fall in the arrival rate of employees leads to more vacancies coming into the market and to an immediate fall in the arrival rate of employees to each vacancy.

The expected changes in the arrival rate of employees play the role of expected capital gains or losses on the firm's outstanding vacancies. The unique feature of vacancies as an asset is that to get to a situation where the firm needs fewer of them, it needs to open more of them initially. This implies that vacancies overshoot their equilibrium value when an adjustment is expected to take place. This can also be shown more formally.

The perfect foresight path in the neighborhood of equilibrium is unique: The number of stable roots in (1.39) is equal to the number of predetermined variables. The initial condition on the predetermined variable, and the requirement that the perfect foresight path should converge (a terminal condition), uniquely define an initial point in (θ, u) space, from which adjustment to equilibrium takes place. In the absence of anticipated changes in the exogenous variables, the initial point is always on the saddle path, since this is the unique convergent path.

In system (1.39) the saddle path is easily found because of the independence of the second equation from unemployment. Since θ is the unstable variable, if θ is not in equilibrium, it will diverge. So the saddle path is the θ-stationary (figure 1.3). If at any point in time unemployment is, say, equal to u_0, in the absence of anticipated future changes in the equilibrium position, the system must be at point A on the saddle path. Adjustment then takes place along the saddle path, with θ constant and unemployment falling until there is convergence to equilibrium.

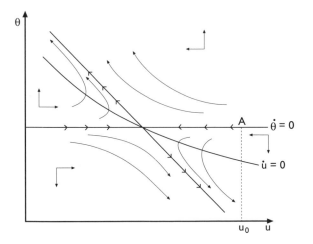

Figure 1.3
Adjustment paths in labor-market tightness and unemployment space

The translation of the dynamics of figure 1.3 to vacancy-unemployment space is straightforward (figure 1.4). Since the θ-stationary is a line through the origin in vacancy-unemployment space, the saddle path is this line. So in the absence of anticipated changes, the perfect foresight adjustment path implies that both unemployment and vacancies change in the same direction during adjustment, even though their equilibrium locus (the Beveridge curve) is downward-sloping. This is the overshooting feature of vacancies. If, say, unemployment is expected to fall from some initial value u_0 toward the intersection of the two curves in figure 1.4, the return from vacancies when unemployment is at u_0 is higher than the anticipated return during adjustment. This is because at higher unemployment, the rate at which workers arrive to vacancies is higher. So firms open up more vacancies at the beginning of adjustment than the number they expect to have in equilibrium. During adjustment the number of vacancies falls through the matching process. But generally, the ratio of vacancies to unemployment does not stay the same when vacancies and workers are matched in pairs, unless in equilibrium vacancies and unemployment happen to be equal (i.e., unless by chance, $\theta = 1$). If vacancies and unemployment are not equal to each other ($\theta \neq 1$), vacancies enter or exit during adjustment so as to maintain the ratio θ constant.

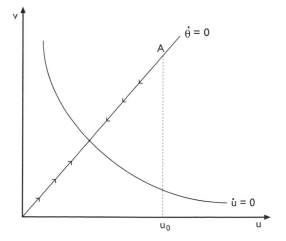

Figure 1.4
Adjustments in vacancy-unemployment space

How do wages, vacancies, and unemployment respond to changes in productivity p? A rise in p shifts the wage curve up and the job creation curve to the right, causing an immediate rise in both market tightness and wages (figure 1.1). The two variables jump to their new equilibrium; there are no adjustment dynamics. In the Beveridge curve diagram, figure 1.5, the impact effect is an anticlockwise rotation of the job creation line. If the initial equilibrium point is A, initially equilibrium jumps to B, as firms open more vacancies to take advantage of the higher productivity. This sets in motion unemployment dynamics, which move the economy down the new job creation line, toward the new steady-state equilibrium point C. In the case of a fall in p, the adjustment dynamics move the economy in the opposite direction, from C to D and then up to A.

Thus wages and tightness move in jumps in response to news about productivity changes, whereas vacancies and unemployment trace anti-clockwise loops around the Beveridge curve. Although the loops have spikes due to the overshooting of vacancies, which is not a feature of the data, the out-of-steady-state dynamics derived here are broadly consis-tent with the stylized observation that over the business cycle vacancies and unemployment trace anticlockwise loops in vacancy-unemployment space. Whether the model is consistent with other business cycle facts of

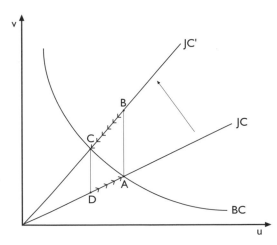

Figure 1.5
Adjustments in response to productivity changes in vacancy-unemployment space

labor markets is a difficult question that needs more explicit modeling of the business cycle and the capital market.

1.8   Notes on the Literature

The idea that a theory of unemployment can fruitfully be built on the assumption that trade in the labor market is an economic activity was first explored by a number of authors in the late 1960s, in what became known as search theory. The most influential papers in this tradition were Alchian (1969), Phelps (1968), and Mortensen (1970); they were collected with other contributions in the same spirit in the Phelps volume (Phelps et al. 1970). The impetus to this research came from Phelps's (1967) and Friedman's (1968) reappraisal of the Phillips curve and the natural rate approach to which this led.

Early search theory assumed the existence of a distribution of wage offers for identical jobs; unemployment arose in equilibrium because workers rejected low-wage jobs. This aspect of the theory was criticized both on logical grounds (Rothschild 1973) and on empirical grounds (Tobin 1972; Barron 1975). An equilibrium model that met Rothschild's criticisms, but with a trivial role for workers looking for alternative jobs, was first presented in Lucas and Prescott (1974).

Lucas and Prescott's model did not consider matching problems. Several early contributions (most notably Phelps 1968) had a matching function relating unemployment and vacancies to hirings, but this device was not generally used to bypass the need to model reservation wages as the main economic mechanism driving unemployment. Early applications of the concept of the matching function that downplay the role of reservation wages include Hall (1979), Pissarides (1979), and Bowden (1980). Diamond and Maskin (1979) used the similar concept of "search technology" in a related context.

The application of zero-profit conditions for new jobs, leading to a closed model with endogenous demand for labor, was first discussed in Pissarides (1979, 1984b).

Early search theory (e.g., Mortensen 1970) had a theory of monopolistic wage setting by firms. The Nash solution was first applied in this context with fixed numbers of traders by Diamond (1982b), though earlier papers by Mortensen (1978) and by Diamond and Maskin (1979) discussed similar sharing rules for the division of the surplus from a job match. Pissarides (1984a, 1985a, b) also applied the Nash rule to derive a wage equation. The use of the Nash solution to the bargaining problem in models of this kind is justified by Binmore, Rubinstein, and Wolinski (1986) by an application of sequential bargaining theory. For alternative assumptions about wage setting, see Burdett and Mortensen (1998), Moen (1997), and the survey of Mortensen and Pissarides (1999b).

The unemployment-vacancy curve has a long history in the British literature on structural change in the labor market. Its existence was noted by Beveridge (1944) and now bears his name. Pioneering work on the Beveridge curve was done by Dow and Dicks-Mireaux (1958), Holt and David (1966), and Hansen (1970). Hansen derived the curve from a model of distinct labor markets interacting at different levels of disequilibrium. His approach does not rely on the existence of a stable matching function but, as he points out, is consistent with it. Much of the early work on vacancy-unemployment interactions was motivated by the desire to find a suitable measure of the excess demand for labor to use in wage-inflation (Phillips curves) studies. In this context, see Dicks-Mireaux and Dow (1959), Lipsey (1960, 1974), and Phelps (1968).

The Phillips curve motivation has been absent from the recent literature (but see the recent paper by Cooley and Quadrini 1998). Instead, authors have been preoccupied with (1) understanding the dynamics of labor markets within explicit dynamic models and (2) building real macroeconomic models with frictions that can better match the business cycle facts. The matching function has played a key role in both strands of the literature.

Despite its importance there are very few attempts to derive the matching function from primitive assumptions about trade. Hall (1979), Pissarides (1979), and Blanchard and Diamond (1994) have borrowed Butters's (1976) urn-ball game to derive an exponential function. Their derivation is, however, mechanical and assumes the absence of all information about potential trading partners. Julien, Kennes, and King (1998) derive a similar function by assuming that job candidates auction their labor services to potential buyers. Ioannides (1997), Lagos (1997), and Lagos and Violante (1998) have studied micro models of agent interaction and derived some properties of the matching technology from more primitive assumptions about market exchange.

In most empirical applications, matching functions are usually assumed to be of the Cobb-Douglas form with constant returns to scale. Coles and Smith (1998) proposed an alternative form where the existing stock of unemployed workers can match only with the inflow of vacancies and the existing stock of vacancies can match only with the inflow of unemployed workers. A similar model was also estimated by Gregg and Petrongolo (1997).

There is now a large number of empirical estimates of aggregate matching functions and the implied Beveridge curves. They generally establish the existence and stability of an aggregate matching function with constant returns to scale. The empirical literature, both micro and macro, is surveyed by Divine and Kiefer (1991). For studies directly relevant to the approach taken in this chapter and using aggregate data, see Pissarides (1986) and Layard, Nickell, and Jackman (1991) for the United Kingdom; Abraham (1987), Blanchard and Diamond (1989) and Berman (1997) for the United States; Gross (1997) and Entorf (1998) for Germany; Schager (1987) for Sweden; Feve and Langot (1996) for France; and van Ours (1991) and Broersma and van Ours (1998) for the Netherlands. These studies generally accept the assumption of a log-linear function with constant returns to scale. An exception is Warren (1996), who estimates a translog matching function by making use of monthly U.S. manufacturing data and finds increasing returns to scale.

For estimates using disaggregated regional data, see Anderson and Burgess (1995), Burda and Profit (1996), Linderboom, van Ours, and Renes (1994), Gorter and van Ours (1994), Boeri and Burda (1996), Coles and Smith (1996), and Burgess and Profit (1998).

Structural estimation of the Beveridge curve and the other equilibrium conditions of the model was undertaken by Yashiv (1997b). The vacancy (job creation) curve was also estimated with Dutch data by van Ours and Ridder (1991, 1992). Evidence for a wage curve of the kind drawn in figure 1.1 was accumulated by Blanchflower and Oswald (1994).

The out-of-steady-state analysis of unemployment and vacancies was first discussed in Pissarides (1985a, 1987). In Pissarides (1985a), imputed unemployment income was assumed fixed, but the model contained more features than the models in this chapter. In Pissarides (1987) unemployment income was allowed to depend on wealth (see chapter 3).

Real business cycle extensions of the model of this chapter have been calibrated by Merz (1995), Andolfatto (1996), and Yashiv (1997a). The existence of frictions in the labor market and the noncompetitive elements that it implies provide a richer framework for the analysis of fluctuations in employment than usually found in other models. The search explanation of unemployment is consistent with the assumptions of Hansen (1985) and Rogerson (1988) of indivisible labor because the assumption that workers either search or work follows naturally from the existence of indivisibilities. In calibrations, matching models are usually compared with Hansen's calibrated model and shown to perform at least as well. Shi and Wen (1997) integrated the search equilibrium model with capital accumulation derived from an intertemporal utility maximization framework and derived various analytical results, including a hump-shaped response of output to a productivity shock. For an alternative model of the cycle where job matching drives the fluctuations in employment, see Howitt (1988).

The anticlockwise loops around the Beveridge curve were present in the data examined by the pioneering works on unemployment-vacancy dynamics, such as Dow and Dicks-Mireaux (1958) and Holt and David (1966), as in more recent data. Various explanations have been put forward, for example, by Phelps (1968), Hansen (1970), and Bowden (1980), that rely on the idea that labor demand is more flexible than employment. The phenomenon is regular enough to have the status of a stylized fact of business cycles.

The framework of the model of the next chapter is more suitable for the study of sectoral shifts, so discussion of the relevant literature is postponed.

2 Endogenous Job Destruction

The model of the preceding chapter highlighted an important property of equilibrium: In the steady state the rate of job creation is equal to the rate of job destruction. Differences in the two rates induce out-of-steady-state employment dynamics. In the simple model of chapter 1, however, the rate of job destruction was a constant λ. So, with the exception of exogenous changes in the rate of job destruction, the influence of shocks and parameter changes on the natural rate of unemployment operated through the rate of job creation.

But empirical evidence shows that both job creation and job destruction respond to exogenous shocks. In some instances, as in the case of business cycle shocks, there is evidence that the rate of job destruction is even more responsive than the rate of job creation. This chapter generalizes the simple model of chapter 1 by making job destruction an unknown of the model that depends on the optimizing actions of firms and workers. Parameter or policy influences on unemployment now work through both job creation and job destruction. The assumptions of the model are consistent with the evidence of Davis, Haltiwanger, and Schuh (1996) and others on the nature of the job destruction and job creation processes in industrial countries.

2.1 Productivity Shocks and Reservation Rules

We endogenize the job destruction decision by considering a more general distribution of idiosyncratic productivity shocks than assumed in chapter 1. At some of the idiosyncratic productivities that firms now face production is profitable, but at some others it is not. The firm chooses a *reservation productivity* and destroys jobs whose productivity falls below it. The productivity of a job falls below the reservation value either because of the arrival of an idiosyncratic shock or because of the arrival of a general shock that hits many firms. In the steady state we consider only idiosyncratic shocks, which is consistent with the evidence that the main reason for job destruction is the arrival of idiosyncratic shocks. But when we consider out-of-steady-state dynamics, we show that general productivity shocks can also cause changes in the rate of job destruction.

When job destruction takes place, the firm and worker separate. This generates an endogenous flow of workers into unemployment, which in the steady state is equal to the matching rate. We continue assuming that the only reason for job separations is job closure, an assumption relaxed in chapter 4.

In the model of the preceding chapter, newly created jobs had constant productivity p until a negative shock arrived, which led to the destruction of the job. Without loss of generality, we can assume that the negative shock reduced the productivity of the job to 0. We now generalize this assumption by writing px for the productivity of the job, where p denotes, as before, a general productivity parameter and x an idiosyncratic one. The model of the preceding chapter can be reinterpreted as one that allowed only two values for the idiosyncratic parameter, 1 and 0. In this chapter we assume that when an idiosyncratic shock arrives, the productivity of the job moves from its initial value x to some new value x', which is a drawing from a general distribution $G(x)$ with support in the range $0 \le x \le 1$. No other assumptions are needed to derive the results of this chapter, though for convenience we will also assume that the distribution is free of holes. As with the model of job creation, the capital decision does not play an important role in the determination of the rate of job destruction provided that there is a perfect market in second-hand capital, so we will first develop the model without explicit reference to capital.

As before, idiosyncratic shocks arrive to jobs at Poisson rate λ. The idiosyncratic productivity that is drawn after the arrival of the shock is independent of initial productivity and is irreversible. The firm has the choice either to continue production at the new productivity or to close the job down and separate from the worker. The idiosyncratic shock process has persistence because $\lambda < \infty$, it is memoryless because the new x' after the shock is independent of initial x, and it is irreversible because the only choice that the firm has is either to produce at the new x' or shut down. But as previously, at job creation the firm has complete choice of job productivity. Profit maximization trivially requires that all new jobs are created at maximum productivity, p.

The intuition behind our new assumptions is similar to the one that was briefly discussed in preceding sections. Jobs are differentiated by product and technology. Changes in tastes and technologies move the relative value of products up or down a scale, here from 0 to p. The firm cannot adapt its technology or influence tastes for its product once production has started, but it can choose its product and technology before the job is created.

The assumption of complete irreversibility is obviously extreme and is made for convenience. Firms might be able, in some situations, either to update their technologies or destroy one job and immediately create another one, switching production to another product that commands higher value, without dismissing the worker. These are complications that do not influence the main results that we discuss here, provided that there is at least *some* irreversibility that necessitates job destruction and separation of firm and worker when a negative shock arrives. The empirical literature, mainly for data reasons, defines as job destruction the joint event of job destruction and separation of firm and worker, as we do here.

Because now jobs are distinguished by productivity, we have to make productivity explicit in the expression for the value of a filled job. Let $J(x)$ be the value of a filled job with idiosyncratic productivity x, and let $w(x)$ be the wage associated with it. When an idiosyncratic shock arrives, the firm has the choice of either destroying the job, with return 0, or continuing at the new productivity. Since free disposal is always a choice, the optimal decision is that production should continue if $J(x) \geq 0$ but stop if $J(x) < 0$. We show below that $J(x)$ is a continuous function of x, so the job destruction rule $J(x) < 0$ satisfies the reservation property with respect to the *reservation productivity* R, defined by

$$J(R) = 0. \tag{2.1}$$

By the reservation property, firms destroy all jobs with idiosyncratic productivity $x < R$ and continue producing in all jobs with productivity $x \geq R$. This, and the property that all jobs are created at maximum productivity, makes the productivity of a filled job a stochastic Poisson process with initial value p and terminal value pR.

Equilibrium unemployment is obtained as before from the equality of the flow into unemployment with the flow out of it. The flow into unemployment in this model is equal to the fraction of jobs that get hit by a productivity shock below reservation value. In a large market this is given by the product of the fraction of firms that get hit by a shock, λ, and the probability that the shock is below reservation, $G(R)$. Therefore the flow into unemployment (job destruction) is given by $\lambda G(R)(1 - u)$. As before, the flow out of unemployment is equal to job creation, $m(v, u) = \theta q(\theta)u$. The evolution of unemployment is therefore given by

$$\dot{u} = \lambda G(R)(1-u) - \theta q(\theta)u, \tag{2.2}$$

and its steady-state value by

$$u = \frac{\lambda G(R)}{\lambda G(R) + \theta q(\theta)}. \tag{2.3}$$

Equation (2.3) is the Beveridge curve for the economy with endogenous job destruction. But because the Beveridge curve now depends on both R and θ, which are both unknowns, it is less useful as a tool of diagrammatic analysis than it was in the model with exogenous job destruction rate. Most of the variables that shift the job creation line in vacancy-unemployment space in this model also shift the Beveridge curve through their influence on the reservation productivity. We will return to this diagram when we derive the equilibrium conditions for R and θ.

2.2   Steady-State Equilibrium

To derive the conditions that characterize equilibrium, we first need to derive the asset values of jobs and workers with the more general distribution of productivity shocks. Equilibrium is fully characterized by the employment contract, which is now a wage rate $w(x)$ for each productivity x and a reservation value R, a market equilibrium condition for tightness θ that is to be derived from the job creation decision and the condition for the evolution of unemployment, (2.2).

The asset value of a job with productivity in the range $1 \geq x \geq R$ satisfies

$$rJ(x) = px - w(x) + \lambda \int_R^1 J(s)dG(s) - \lambda J(x). \tag{2.4}$$

For the worker the returns from working at a job with idiosyncratic productivity x satisfy

$$rW(x) = w(x) + \lambda \int_R^1 W(s)dG(s) + \lambda G(R)U - \lambda W(x). \tag{2.5}$$

In (2.4), whenever an idiosyncratic shock arrives, the firm has to give up the value $J(x)$ for a new value $J(s)$ if the new idiosyncratic productivity is in the range $1 \geq s \geq R$, or destroy the job for a zero return otherwise. In (2.5) the worker in a job with productivity x enjoys expected returns $W(x)$, which he has to give up when a shock arrives. If the new productivity is in the range $1 \geq s \geq R$, the worker remains employed, but if it is below that range, he becomes unemployed for an expected return U.

As before, we assume that the wage rate divides the job surplus in fixed proportions at all x, so the sharing rule that generalizes (1.17) is

$$W(x) - U = \beta[J(x) + W(x) - V - U] \tag{2.6}$$

for all $1 \geq x \geq R$. Implicit in this sharing rule is the assumption that the wage rate is renegotiated every time a productivity shock arrives. V is the firm's expected return from a vacancy. Since U and V are both independent of x, it follows immediately from (2.4), (2.5), and (2.6) that $J'(x) \geq 0$, which is a sufficient condition for the optimality of the reservation rule in (2.1).

Also as before, job creation follows the same rules as when idiosyncratic productivity took only two values. Noting that all jobs are created at maximum idiosyncratic productivity, $x = 1$, the expected profit from a new job vacancy satisfies

$$rV = -pc + q(\theta)[J(1) - V]. \tag{2.7}$$

$q(\theta)$ is the rate at which workers arrive to job vacancies. Firms open vacancies until all rents from vacant jobs are exhausted. Therefore job creation satisfies a condition similar to (1.7),

$$J(1) = \frac{pc}{q(\theta)}. \tag{2.8}$$

The four equations that uniquely solve for the four unknowns in the steady state—unemployment, the reservation productivity, wages, and market tightness—are (2.3), (2.1), (2.6), and (2.8). We solve the model by deriving first the wage equation at all productivities, use it to substitute wages out of the job creation and job destruction conditions, and then use the latter two conditions to solve for R and θ. With knowledge of R and θ, unemployment can then be obtained from the Beveridge curve. Unlike the model of chapter 1, the key two-equation block now is not the wage equation and job creation condition but the reduced form job creation and job destruction conditions.

To derive the wage equation, we proceed as in chapter 1 and use the job creation condition (2.8) and the sharing rule (2.6) to write the unemployed worker's expected returns as

$$rU = z + \theta q(\theta)[W(1) - U]$$
$$= z + \frac{\beta}{1 - \beta} pc\theta.$$

(2.9)

Multiplying the asset equation for the firm, (2.4), by β and the one for the worker, (2.5), by $1 - \beta$, then subtracting one from the other and making use of the sharing rule (2.6), the zero-profit condition $V = 0$, and equation (2.9), gives a wage equation that is the natural generalization of (1.20):

$$w(x) = (1 - \beta)z + \beta p(x + c\theta).$$

(2.10)

Wages depend on job productivity and the worker's unemployment income but not on other jobs' productivities. Market conditions influence wages only through market tightness, θ. As before, the reason for this influence is that θ influences the firm's and the worker's bargaining strength. A higher θ makes it easier for workers to find a job elsewhere, and more difficult for the firm to recruit a worker, so wages are higher at all productivities.

Following the derivation of the wage equation, we derive two new expressions, one for the job creation condition and one for the job destruction condition. The two equations will form a self-contained block that will give a unique solution for R and θ, which can then be used in (2.10) and (2.3) to solve for wages and unemployment.

We note first that by the nature of the sharing rule (2.6), the firm and worker agree about the jobs that should be destroyed. The firm wants to destroy all jobs with productivity below the R that satisfies $J(R) = 0$. By the zero-profit condition for new vacancies, $V = 0$, and so (2.6) implies that R also satisfies $W(R) = U$. But this is precisely the point where the worker will want to quit a job and join unemployment, since at all productivities $x < R$, $W(R) < U$ and the worker is better off in the unemployment pool than in the job. Thus there are no voluntary job separations for one side and involuntary for the other; all job separations are privately efficient. (They are not socially efficient because of the search externalities discussed in chapter 1, a question that we address in chapter 8.) Private efficiency implies that once we make use of the wage equation, we can derive the expression for the reservation productivity by analyzing either the firm's decision or the worker's. We concentrate on the firm's decisions.

Substitution of the wage equation into (2.4) gives

$$(r + \lambda)J(x) = (1 - \beta)(px - z) - \beta pc\theta + \lambda \int_R^1 J(s)dG(s). \tag{2.11}$$

Evaluating now (2.11) at $x = R$ and subtracting the resulting equation from (2.11) after noting that $J(R) = 0$ by the definition of the reservation productivity in (2.1), we get

$$(r + \lambda)J(x) = (1 - \beta)p(x - R). \tag{2.12}$$

Substitution now of $J(x)$ from (2.12) into the integral expression of (2.11), gives

$$(r + \lambda)J(x) = (1 - \beta)(px - z) - \beta pc\theta + \frac{\lambda(1 - \beta)p}{r + \lambda} \int_R^1 (s - R)dG(s). \tag{2.13}$$

The conditions for job creation and job destruction can be obtained by making use of (2.12) and (2.13). To derive first the condition for job creation, we make use of (2.12) for $x = 1$ and the zero-profit condition (2.8) to arrive at the key equation

$$(1 - \beta)\frac{1 - R}{r + \lambda} = \frac{c}{q(\theta)}. \tag{2.14}$$

Equation (2.14) says that the expected gain from a new job to the firm must be equal to the expected hiring cost that the firm has to pay. This is drawn in figure 2.1 as a downward-sloping curve and labeled the job creation curve. It slopes down because at higher R the expected life of a job is shorter, because in any short interval of time δt the job is destroyed with probability $\lambda G(R)\delta t$. Firms create fewer jobs as a result, leading to a fall in market tightness, θ.

The parameters that shift the job creation curve for given R are few. General productivity p does not enter this expression because both the firm's expected revenues and costs are proportional to p. Higher β leads to less job creation because it decreases expected profits by giving labor more of the surplus from new jobs. Higher r or λ also decrease job

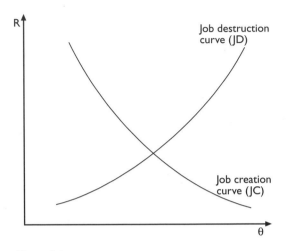

Figure 2.1
Equilibrium reservation productivity and market tightness

creation because the future returns from new jobs are discounted at higher rates. Finally, higher mismatch, in the sense of lower arrival rate of workers at given tightness, also reduces job creation because it increases the expected duration of a vacancy and, by implication, the expected hiring cost facing the firm. All these changes shift the job creation curve to the left.

The job destruction condition is derived from (2.13) by evaluating it at $x = R$ and substituting the result into the zero-profit condition for the reservation job, (2.1):

$$R - \frac{z}{p} - \frac{\beta c}{1-\beta}\theta + \frac{\lambda}{r+\lambda}\int_R^1 (s - R)dG(s) = 0. \tag{2.15}$$

Equation (2.15) is the second of the two key equations that we use to solve for R and θ. It is shown in figure 2.1 as an upward-sloping curve and labeled the job destruction curve. It slopes up because at higher θ, the worker's outside opportunities are better (and wages are higher) and so more marginal jobs are destroyed.

Before discussing the properties of the equilibrium R and θ, we note an important property implied by the job destruction condition. By equation (2.9), the reservation productivity is less than the reservation wage of unemployed workers, rU. The reason for this is that occupied jobs have a positive option value, which implies that there is some labor hoarding. This option value is shown by the integral expression in (2.15). Because of the possibility that a job productivity might change, the firm keeps some currently unprofitable jobs occupied. By doing this, it is able to start production at the new productivity immediately after arrival, without having to pay a recruitment cost and forgo production during search. As intuition would justify, if productivities change more frequently (higher λ), the option value of keeping a worker is higher. The option value is also higher if the discount rate is lower, because the returns from a productivity change accrue in the future, and if the expected gain that can be obtained from new productivities, shown by the integral expression, is higher.

Now, at given θ, the reservation productivity is higher when unemployment income is higher and also when labor's share of profits, β, is higher. As with θ, both these effects work through the worker's reservation wage. From (2.9) labor's reservation wage is higher when z, β, θ, and c are higher. The reservation productivity is also higher when the rate of arrival of idiosyncratic shocks is lower and when the interest rate is higher, in each case because the option values of the job is lower.

Finally the reservation productivity is lower when productivities in all jobs increase by the same proportion, represented by an increase p. The reason for this is that with higher general productivities, the worker's opportunity cost becomes relatively less attractive because z is independent of p. As we emphasized in chapter 1, this is a plausible effect of higher p in a short- to medium-run equilibrium but not in a long-run growth equilibrium. If we follow the suggestion made in chapter 1 and write z as a proportion of the mean wage, the effect of p on the reservation productivity disappears. (See also chapter 3 for more discussion of this point.)

To see this, suppose that z is a fixed proportion of the mean wage rate observed in the market,

$$z = pE[w(x)\,|\,x \geq R], \tag{2.16}$$

where $0 \leq \rho \leq 1$ is the replacement rate. Then from (2.10),

$$E[w(x)\,|\,x \geq R] = (1 - \beta)z + \beta p[E(x\,|\,x \geq R) + c\theta]. \tag{2.17}$$

Therefore

$$z = \frac{\rho\beta}{1-\rho(1-\beta)} p[E(x \mid x \geq R) + c\theta].$$ (2.18)

As expected, unemployment income is higher when the replacement rate, labor's wage share, expected productivities, and market tightness are higher. Crucially, unemployment income is now proportional to the general productivity parameter, p.

Substitution of z from (2.18) into (2.15) gives the new job destruction condition:

$$R - \frac{\rho\beta}{1-\rho(1-\beta)} E(x \mid x \geq R) - \frac{\beta}{1-\beta}\frac{c\theta}{1-\rho(1-\beta)} + \frac{\lambda}{r+\lambda}\int_R^1 (s-R)dG(s) = 0.$$ (2.19)

The reservation productivity is now independent of p. It depends positively on the replacement rate ρ and on all the other parameters as before. The positive slope of the job destruction curve in figure 2.1 is not affected by these substitutions. In the remainder of this chapter, we will use the simpler expression (2.15) for the reservation productivity, though we will return to something like (2.19) when we discuss growth.

Figure 2.1 shows that the equilibrium θ and R are unique and so the equilibrium wage rate for each productivity and equilibrium unemployment are also unique. The equilibrium wage rate at each productivity x is obtained by substituting the solution for θ into (2.10), and equilibrium unemployment is obtained by substituting both θ and R into (2.3). We examine the properties of equilibrium in the next section.

2.3 Unemployment, Job Creation, and Job Destruction

The properties of equilibrium unemployment in the extended model with endogenous job destruction are obtained from the simultaneous solution of three of the equations of the model, the job creation condition (2.14), the job destruction condition (2.15), and the Beveridge curve, (2.3). The first two are illustrated in figure 2.1. Unemployment (and vacancies) are obtained from the Beveridge diagram. As we argued in section 2.1, this diagram is now less useful for the analysis of unemployment than it was in the simpler model of chapter 1 because the

Beveridge curve now depends on the endogenous R, but we still use it to illustrate some of the properties of the model.

The Beveridge curve that is obtained from equation (2.3) is drawn, as before, as a downward-sloping curve in vacancy-unemployment space. But the restrictions on the matching function are not now sufficient for the negative slope because higher θ (and so, for given unemployment, more vacancies), on the one hand, imply more job matchings and, on the other hand, imply more job destruction. The former implies a negative slope but the latter a positive one. We assume that the direct effect of θ through the matching function dominates the indirect effect through the reservation productivity, an assumption that we will make every time a similar conflict arises. The justification for it is empirical: Estimated Beveridge curves slope down, and a set of sufficient restrictions on the probability distribution of productivities that ensures that the effect through θ dominates is weak. This conflict was first noted in partial models of search, where the probability of leaving unemployment is the product of a contact probability and an acceptance probability. The relevant literature is cited in the Notes on the Literature at the end of chapter 6.

Under the assumption that the job matching effect of vacancies on unemployment dominates the job destruction effect, the Beveridge diagram has the same shape as before. The solution for θ is still unique and independent of unemployment. Equilibrium vacancies and unemployment are at the intersection of the Beveridge curve with the job creation line, drawn through the origin at an angle θ, obtained from figure 2.1 The Beveridge diagram is not drawn because it is the same as the one in chapter 1, figure 1.2.

The empirical job destruction rate, defined as the ratio of total job destruction to employment, is $\lambda G(R)$, and the job creation rate is, as before, $m(v, u)/(1 - u) = \theta q(\theta)u/(1 - u)$. Although in steady state the two rates are equal, their impact response to productivity and other changes are interesting in their own right (see also section 2.5). R is a sufficient statistic for the behavior of the job destruction rate and θ for the behavior of the job creation rate at given unemployment. The difference between the impact and steady-state effects of a parameter change on the job creation and job destruction rates is due to the behavior of unemployment (or employment). Because the two-equation system (2.14) and (2.15) that determines equilibrium R and θ is independent of unemployment, when a parameter changes, R and θ jump to their new equilibrium values instantaneously. Unemployment starts moving according to (2.2) only if the new job creation and job destruction rates implied by the change in R and θ are not equal. But the job destruction rate, $\lambda G(R)$, is independent of unemployment, so it does not change further in response to any change in unemployment. The job creation rate depends on unemployment; therefore its response is different on impact, for given unemployment, and in steady state, when by definition it is equal to the job destruction rate.

Consider now the influence of productivity on the job creation rate, job destruction rate, and unemployment. Higher general productivities, shown by higher p, shift the job destruction curve in figure 2.1 (for given z) down and to the right. This increases market tightness and reduces the reservation productivity. At given unemployment the job destruction rate decreases, and the job creation rate increases. Unemployment has to decrease until the job creation rate falls down to the level of the lower job destruction rate. So the steady-state effect of higher general productivity is to reduce the job creation and job destruction rates and unemployment.

The effect of productivity on unemployment can also be shown in the Beveridge diagram, where the rise in θ rotates the job creation line anticlockwise and the fall in the reservation productivity shifts the Beveridge curve toward the origin (figure 2.2). Equilibrium moves from point A to point B, where unemployment is lower. The effect on vacancies is ambiguous, though, if we assume that the effect through θ dominates the effect through R, vacancies increase. The fact that empirically vacancies and unemployment move in opposite directions over the business cycle is another reason for making the assumption that the effect through θ always dominates the effect through R, when the two effects conflict with each other.

As in the model of chapter 1, the productivity effects are due to the fact that higher productivity increases the returns from work but has no influence on the return from nonmarket activities, z. It becomes jointly optimal for the firm and the worker to devote more time to work. In decentralized equilibrium this is signaled to firms by a smaller increase in wages than in productivity, because of the fixed z which enters the wage equation. The smaller change in the wage rate increases profits from both job creation and ongoing jobs, increasing job creation and reducing job destruction at given unemployment. As we argued in the

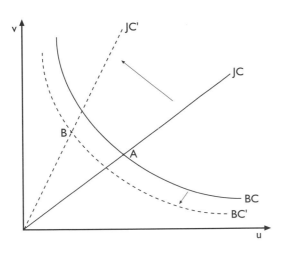

Figure 2.2
Effect of higher productivity on equilibrium vacancies and unemployment

preceding section, if z was proportional to wages, these effects would not materialize.

Because of the property of the model that the level of labor productivity influences job creation and job destruction only to the extent that it influences the ratio z/p, changes in z have the same effect on equilibrium as changes in p but with opposite sign. Thus higher nonmarket income increases wages, reduces job creation at given unemployment, and increases job destruction, leading to higher unemployment in the steady state. These effects still operate if unemployment income is proportional to wages provided that changes in unemployment income are caused by exogenous changes in the replacement rate ρ. This can easily be derived from the pair of equations (2.19) and (2.14) which determine the job creation and job destruction flows in this case.

Now, since all active jobs have productivities in the range pR to p, higher p is equivalent to proportionally higher productivities in all jobs. Two other productivity shifts that are of interest are a translation of the idiosyncratic productivity distribution to the right and a mean-preserving shift in the distribution. The former is another way of analyzing an increase in the productivity of all jobs, but instead of an equal proportional increase it represents an equal absolute increase in all productivities. The mean-preserving shift is a way of representing an increase in the variance of productivity shocks. We will follow a parametric approach to the analysis of these shifts, along the lines suggested by Arrow (1965).

For the analysis of additive shifts, we suppose that all idiosyncratic productivities x depend on an additive shift parameter h, such that

$$x(h) = x + h. \tag{2.20}$$

The influence of h on equilibrium is evaluated by considering the effects of a small displacement of h at the point $h = 0$.

Higher variance in job productivities is similarly represented by a parameter h, which is now multiplicative around the mean of the productivity distribution, $\bar{x}$. It is debatable whether the multiplicative shift should be around the mean of the whole distribution or the mean of the conditional distribution, $E(x \mid x \geq R)$. The latter is the observed mean productivity, since productivities below the reservation R are not taken up. We will assume that the multiplicative shift is around the unconditional mean $\bar{x}$ because it is free of the other parameters of the model, but we will impose the restriction that $z \leq p\bar{x}$, namely that the income of unemployed workers is below mean productivity. This restriction is always satisfied by the conditional productivity mean, $z \leq pE(x \mid x \geq R)$. Imposing this restriction ensures that some active jobs suffer a fall in productivity when there is a multiplicative shock to the distribution. Thus, in examining the effects of a change in the variability of the productivity distribution, we write

$$x(h) = x + h(x - \bar{x}) \tag{2.21}$$

for all x, and evaluate the effects of a small displacement of h at $h = 0$ under the assumption that $z \leq p\bar{x}$.

Consider first the implications of a uniform absolute increase in productivities, shown by the additive shift parameter in (2.20). Reworking the job creation and job destruction conditions (2.14) and (2.15) with $x + h$ replacing x is straightforward. We find that the effect of the additive parameter is to shift the job destruction curve in figure 2.1 down but not move the job creation curve. Therefore the additive shift parameter in the idiosyncratic productivity distribution has the same effect on job creation and job destruction as higher p: It raises market tightness and reduces the reservation productivity. At given unemployment rate the job creation rate rises and the job destruction rate falls, and in equilibrium unemployment also falls.

A multiplicative shift parameter has similarly unambiguous effects on market tightness and the reservation productivity, though their derivation is now less straightforward. Reworking the job creation and job destruction conditions for $x(h)$ as defined in (2.21) gives

$$(1-\beta)(1+h)\frac{1-R}{r+\lambda} = \frac{c}{q(\theta)} \qquad (2.22)$$

and

$$(1+h)R - h\bar{x} + \frac{(1+h)\lambda}{r+\lambda}\int_R^1 (s-R)dG(s) = \frac{z}{p} + \frac{\beta}{1-\beta}c\theta. \qquad (2.23)$$

It is straightforward to see that higher h shifts to the right the job creation curve in figure 2.1, implying more job creation at given R. But the shift in the job destruction curve is ambiguous under our restriction $\bar{x} \geq z/p$ alone (though it would shift it up if the restriction was strengthened to $\bar{x} \geq rU$, the reservation wage of the unemployed). Thus figure 2.1 is not helpful in the analysis of multiplicative shifts.

Differentiation of (2.22) and (2.23) with respect to h, however, shows that at $h = 0$ both market tightness and the reservation productivity rise unambiguously. Differentiation of (2.23) gives

$$\left[1 - \frac{\lambda}{r+\lambda}[1-G(R)]\right]\frac{\partial R}{\partial h} = \bar{x} - R - \frac{\lambda}{r+\lambda}\int_R^1 (s-R)dG(s) + \frac{\beta}{1-\beta}c\frac{\partial\theta}{\partial h}. \qquad (2.24)$$

Differentiation also of (2.22) with respect to h gives

$$\frac{c\eta(\theta)}{\theta q(\theta)}\frac{\partial\theta}{\partial h} = \frac{1-\beta}{r+\lambda}\left[1 - R - \frac{\partial R}{\partial h}\right], \qquad (2.25)$$

where we have used the elasticity notation

$$\eta(\theta) = -\frac{\partial q(\theta)}{\partial\theta}\frac{\theta}{q(\theta)}. \qquad (2.26)$$

As we noted in section 1.1, this elasticity need not be a constant, but it is always a number between 0 and 1. Substitution of $\partial R/\partial h$ from (2.24) into (2.25) reveals that the sign of $\partial\theta/\partial h$ is the same as the sign of

$$\left[1 - \frac{\lambda}{r+\lambda}[1 - G(R)]\right](1 - R) - \bar{x} + R + \frac{\lambda}{r+\lambda}\int_R^1 (s - R)dG(s). \tag{2.27}$$

Collecting terms, we find that the sign of (2.27) is the same as the sign of

$$1 - \bar{x} - \frac{\lambda}{r+\lambda}\int_R^1 (1 - s)dG(s) \tag{2.28}$$

which is unambiguously positive because

$$1 - \bar{x} = \int_0^1 (1 - s)dG(s). \tag{2.29}$$

Hence the effect of higher h on θ is positive. To show that it is also positive on R, we substitute $\partial\theta/\partial h$ from (2.25) into (2.24) and find that the sign of $\partial R/\partial h$ is the same as the sign of

$$\bar{x} - R - \frac{\lambda}{r+\lambda}\int_R^1 (s - R)dG(s) + \frac{\beta\theta q(\theta)}{\eta(\theta)}\frac{1 - R}{r+\lambda}. \tag{2.30}$$

Making use of the job creation condition (2.14) to get rid of $1 - R$ from the last term of this expression, we find that the sign of (2.30) is the same as the sign of

$$\bar{x} - R - \frac{\lambda}{r+\lambda}\int_R^1 (s - R)dG(s) + \frac{\beta}{(1-\beta)\eta(\theta)}c\theta, \tag{2.31}$$

which is unambiguously positive under the restriction $\bar{x} \geq z/p$, given the job destruction condition (2.15) and the fact that $0 \leq \eta(\theta) \leq 1$.

Our analysis of the effects of increased variance of the productivity distribution shows that at given unemployment both the job destruction and job creation rates are higher. Because the job destruction rate is higher, the job reallocation rate, the sum of the job creation and the job destruction rates, is also higher in steady state. But whether unemployment is higher or lower depends on the relative magnitude of the impact effect on each rate. If the parameters are such that the initial increase in the job destruction rate is higher than the initial increase in the job creation rate, unemployment goes up to bring the job creation rate into equality with the job destruction rate, and conversely if the initial increase in the job destruction rate is lower. In terms of the Beveridge diagram, a multiplicative shock shifts the Beveridge curve out and rotates the job creation line up, in contrast to the additive shock, which has the same effect on the job creation line but shifts the Beveridge curve in. This difference has been used by a number of authors to distinguish between aggregative shocks, interpreted as a general increase or decrease in job productivities, and reallocation shocks, interpreted as shocks that increase or decrease the variance of productivities, as causes of the cyclical change in unemployment. Although our analysis has been entirely in terms of steady states, the principles underlying the cyclical analysis and our own are similar.

The reasons that a mean-preserving shift in productivities increases job creation (at given unemployment) are easy to see. The mean-preserving shift makes productivities above the mean better and productivities below the mean worse. The firm and worker, however, do not take up productivities below the reservation value; the distribution of productivities that enters their calculus is truncated at R. Therefore the benefits from the higher productivity of jobs above the mean outweigh the costs from the lower productivity of jobs below the mean.

The multiplicative shift has three effects on the reservation productivity, which are shown by the terms on the right-hand side of (2.24). The first operates directly and pushes the reservation productivity up if $R \leq \bar{x}$, as is likely the case under our restriction that $\bar{x} \geq z/p$, or down otherwise. If $R \leq \bar{x}$, the reservation job yields negative profit after the shift. The second effect always increases the reservation productivity because of the increase in market tightness, which improves the workers' outside options. The final effect increases the option value of the job and so it reduces the reservation productivity. The reason for the increase in option value is the same as the reason for the increase in job creation, the truncation of the productivity distribution at R. The restriction that we have imposed, $z \leq p\bar{x}$, is sufficient to ensure that the negative effects on the profit from the reservation job outweigh the positive, and so get an increase in job destruction after a multiplicative shift. The restriction ensures that the reservation productivity is sufficiently low, when compared with the mean of the distribution, to avoid large increases in the productivity of the reservation job after the shift.

We now consider the influence of the other parameters of the model on the equilibrium job creation and job destruction rates, beginning with the rate of interest. Higher real rate of interest shifts the job creation curve in figure 2.1 to the left and the job destruction curve up. For given reservation productivity, there is less job creation because future profits from new jobs are discounted more heavily. Similarly, for given market tightness, the higher interest rate reduces the option value of the job, and so the reservation productivity is higher. The effect of these shifts on market tightness is unambiguously negative, but it is ambiguous on the reservation productivity. To see this, differentiate (2.14) and (2.15) with respect to r to get

$$\frac{c\eta(\theta)}{\theta q(\theta)}\frac{\partial\theta}{\partial r} = -\frac{1-\beta}{r+\lambda}\left(\frac{1-R}{r+\lambda}+\frac{\partial R}{\partial r}\right), \tag{2.32}$$

$$\left[1-\frac{\lambda}{r+\lambda}[1-G(R)]\right]\frac{\partial R}{\partial r} = \frac{\lambda}{(r+\lambda)^2}\int_R^1 (s-R)dG(s)+\frac{\beta c}{1-\beta}\frac{\partial\theta}{\partial r}. \tag{2.33}$$

Getting rid of the unambiguous $\partial\theta/\partial r$ from these expressions and making use of the original equations (2.14) and (2.15) to simplify the resulting expression, we find that the sign of $\partial R/\partial r$ is the same as the sign of

$$\frac{z}{p}+\frac{\beta c\theta}{1-\beta}-R-\frac{\beta c\theta}{(1-\beta)\eta(\theta)}. \tag{2.34}$$

This expression is generally of ambiguous sign. To see this, suppose that equilibrium is such that θ is close to zero. Then the job destruction condition (2.15) implies that (2.34) is approximately equal to the option value of the job, and so it is positive. In slack markets the higher rate of interest increases job destruction. If market tightness is away from zero, then it is easy to see that sufficiently small elasticity $\eta(\theta)$ can turn (2.34) negative. But even if $\eta(\theta)$ is close to its upper value of 1, (2.34) approximates $z/p - R$, which is not necessarily positive if θ is large.

In contrast, the rate of arrival of idiosyncratic shocks, which in the job creation expression plays the role of a discount rate, has unambiguous effects on job creation and job destruction. Higher rate of arrival of idiosyncratic shocks reduces the expected life of a job, so it reduces job creation, shifting the job creation curve in figure 2.1 to the left. The shorter expected life of a job, however, reduces the reservation productivity because now the option value of the job is higher. The firm is more willing to hold on to labor if it expects a quick arrival of better conditions. The two effects unambiguously imply a lower reservation productivity but as yet undetermined effects on market tightness. Differentiation of the job creation and job destruction conditions, however, yields

$$\frac{c\eta(\theta)}{\theta q(\theta)}\frac{\partial\theta}{\partial\lambda} = -\frac{1-\beta}{(r+\lambda)^2}(1-R) - \frac{1-\beta}{r+\lambda}\frac{\partial R}{\partial\lambda}, \tag{2.35}$$

$$\left[1 - \frac{\lambda}{r+\lambda}[1-G(R)]\right]\frac{\partial R}{\partial\lambda} = -\frac{r}{(r+\lambda)^2}\int_R^1 (s-R)dG(s) + \frac{\beta c}{1-\beta}\frac{\partial\theta}{\partial\lambda}. \tag{2.36}$$

It follows by substitution that

$$\left[\left[1 - \frac{\lambda}{r+\lambda}[1-G(R)]\right]\frac{(r+\lambda)c\eta(\theta)}{(1-\beta)\theta q(\theta)} + \frac{\beta c}{1-\beta}\right]\frac{\partial\theta}{\partial\lambda}$$

$$= \frac{r}{(r+\lambda)^2}\int_R^1 (s-R)dG(s) - \left[1 - \frac{\lambda}{r+\lambda}[1-G(R)]\right]\frac{1-R}{r+\lambda}. \tag{2.37}$$

The right-hand side of this equation is negative because it is equal to

$$-\frac{1-R}{r+\lambda}\left[1 - \frac{\lambda}{r+\lambda}[1-G(R)] - \frac{r}{r+\lambda}\int_R^1 \frac{s-R}{1-R}dG(s)\right], \tag{2.38}$$

and the last two terms in the square brackets are the weighted average of two numbers less than 1.

Thus market tightness falls with λ. At given unemployment, faster arrival of idiosyncratic shocks reduces job creation. The job destruction rate, $\lambda G(R)$, is subject to two opposing influences. On the one hand, it increases because there are now more shocks on average, but on the other hand, it decreases because the firm holds on to jobs longer. If the direct effect dominates, which is the assumption normally (and frequently implicitly) adopted in the literature, the impact effect of faster arrival of idiosyncratic shocks is to increase job destruction and reduce job creation. Unemployment therefore unambiguously increases. In the Beveridge space of figure 1.2, higher λ shifts the Beveridge curve out and rotates the job creation line down.

A related parametric influence to the one just studied is the degree of mismatch. A higher mismatch, as we argued in chapter 1, is represented by a negative shift in the aggregate matching function which reduces the rate of arrival of workers to firms at given market tightness. In figure 2.1 this shifts the job creation curve to the left, reducing both market tightness and the reservation productivity. Job destruction falls and job creation at given unemployment also falls for two reasons, the higher mismatch and the lower degree of market tightness. In the Beveridge diagram this rotates the job creation line clockwise. The Beveridge curve is subject to two influences. The fall in the arrival rate of workers shifts it out, but the fall in the job destruction rate shifts it in. In general, it is not possible to say which effect dominates, but empirically the direct effect of the fall in the matching rate at given tightness is always assumed to be the dominant one. Under this assumption the Beveridge curve shifts out, implying higher equilibrium unemployment.

We consider finally the implications of a higher labor share in the wage bargain, β. Differentiation of (2.15) with respect to β gives,

$$\left[1 - \frac{\lambda}{r+\lambda}[1 - G(R)]\right]\frac{\partial R}{\partial \beta} = \frac{1}{1-\beta}\left[\frac{c\theta}{1-\beta} + \beta c\frac{\partial \theta}{\partial \beta}\right].$$

(2.39)

Differentiation of (2.14) gives

$$\frac{c\eta(\theta)}{\theta q(\theta)}\frac{\partial \theta}{\partial \beta} = -\frac{1-R}{r+\lambda} - \frac{1-\beta}{r+\lambda}\frac{\partial R}{\partial \beta}.$$

(2.40)

The effect of higher labor share is to shift the job destruction curve in figure 2.1 up and the job creation line to the left. Job destruction rises at given market tightness because wages increase and job creation falls for a similar reason. The net effect is to reduce market tightness, and therefore job creation at given unemployment, but it has ambiguous effects on the reservation productivity.

Interestingly substitution of $\partial \theta/\partial \beta$ from (2.40) into (2.39) shows that the sign of $\partial R/\partial \beta$ is the same as the sign of $\eta(\theta) - \beta$. So R reaches a unique maximum at $\beta = \eta(\theta)$. Job destruction increases with labor share at low β and falls at high β because of the nonlinear response of market tightness and the reservation wage to β. We will argue later (chapter 8) that although there is no reason why the two parameters should be equal, even when $\eta(\theta)$ is a constant, the restriction of a constant η equal to β is a natural benchmark to adopt. Under this restriction the reservation productivity is independent of labor's share, and the net effect of labor's share on market tightness becomes

$$\frac{\partial \theta}{\partial \beta} = -\frac{\theta}{(1-\beta)\eta}.$$

(2.41)

In the Beveridge diagram higher labor share rotates the job creation line down and does not shift the Beveridge curve, implying higher equilibrium unemployment and lower vacancies.

2.4 Capital

The introduction of capital into the analysis can take place along the lines discussed in chapter 1, without important changes to the results. Moreover the assumption that there is a perfect second-hand market for capital goods, ensures that the rules governing investment are the same as before and as in other neoclassical models.

In the model of this chapter a job productivity can be anywhere in the range pR to p. We interpret px as the efficiency units of the job, and as before, we define k as the units of capital per efficiency unit of labor and $f(k)$ as the per unit production function. The firm with productivity px then buys capital pxk at the price of output and produces $pxf(k)$. If a shock arrives that changes the productivity of the job to px', the firm sells $p(x - x')k$ of its capital stock if $x' \geq R$ and stays in production; however, if $x' < R$, the firm sells its entire capital stock and closes down. Therefore the value of a job with idiosyncratic productivity parameter x now satisfies

$$r[J(x) + pxk] = px[f(k) - \delta k] - w(x) + \lambda \int_R^1 J(s)\,dG(s) - \lambda J(x). \tag{2.42}$$

Maximization of job value with respect to capital gives the familiar condition

$$f'(k) = r + \delta. \tag{2.43}$$

The other value expressions do not change by the introduction of the capital stock. The value of a vacancy, employment, and unemployment still satisfy (2.7), (2.5), and (2.9), respectively. The wage-sharing rule is still (2.6), and the job creation and job destruction conditions are still given by the two zero-profit requirements, $V = 0$ and $J(R) = 0$.

To derive the job creation and job destruction conditions, we note that the wage-sharing rule gives the wage equation

$$w(x) = (1 - \beta)z + \beta px[f(k) - (r + \delta)k] + \beta pc\theta. \tag{2.44}$$

When this is substituted into (2.42) and use is made of the job destruction condition, we get

$$(r + \lambda)J(x) = (1 - \beta)p(x - R)[f(k) - (r + \delta)k]. \tag{2.45}$$

Therefore (2.42) becomes

$$(r + \lambda)J(x) = (1 - \beta)p[f(k) - (r + \delta)k]\left[x + \frac{\lambda}{r + \lambda}\int_R^1 (s - R)dG(s)\right]$$
$$- (1 - \beta)z - \beta pc\theta. \tag{2.46}$$

With (2.45) and (2.46) in hand, the job creation and job destruction conditions can easily be derived. The job creation condition, which as before satisfies (2.8), is derived from (2.45), and it is

$$(1 - \beta)\frac{1 - R}{r + \lambda}[f(k) - (r + \delta)k] = \frac{c}{q(\theta)}. \tag{2.47}$$

Comparison with the condition without capital, (2.14), shows an obvious generalization.

The job destruction condition is derived from (2.46):

$$[f(k) - (r + \delta)k]\left[R + \frac{\lambda}{r + \lambda}\int_R^1 (s - R)dG(s)\right] = \frac{z}{p} + \frac{\beta}{1 - \beta}c\theta. \tag{2.48}$$

Once again, comparison with (2.15) shows that the only generalization is that productivity is multiplied by $f(k) - (r + \delta)k$.

Equilibrium is now defined by the capital condition (2.43), the job creation and job destruction conditions (2.47) and (2.48), the wage equation (2.44), and the evolution for unemployment (2.2). The equilibrium model is recursive for a given interest rate, with the capital stock for each efficiency unit of labor determined first, the pair θ, R determined next, and wages and unemployment last. Aggregate capital in this economy is

$$K = L(1 - u)pk\int_R^1 xdG(x) \tag{2.49}$$

and aggregate output $F(L(1 - u), K)$, or in per unit terms,

$$Y = L(1 - u)pf(k)\int_R^1 xdG(x). \tag{2.50}$$

Clearly, the properties of the key block of equations, for job creation and job destruction, are still the same as in figure 2.1. The introduction of the capital stock does not alter any of the properties previously described provided that we impose the condition the there is a perfect rental market for capital goods. This justifies our continued use of the model without capital goods to study the properties of job creation and job destruction and those of wages and unemployment.

2.5   Out-of-Steady-State Dynamics

The dynamics of job creation, job destruction and unemployment out of steady state are similar to those studied in chapter 1 but with one important difference. We highlight in this section that difference, discussing the other properties only briefly. We ignore capital and the issues associated with its slow adjustment to equilibrium, for the reasons that we gave in chapter 1.

Recall that in chapter 1 the wage equation and job creation condition gave a unique solution for w and θ, which did not involve any sticky variables. Therefore both w and θ were always at their steady-state values, jumping from any arbitrary initial values to the steady state following unanticipated parametric changes. (Of course, anticipated or preannounced parametric changes can produce nontrivial dynamics in both w and θ, along the lines explored in the rational expectations literature, a question that we do not address in this book.)

We make the same assumptions about job creation and wage determination in the model of this chapter as we did in the model of chapter 1, namely that firms can open and close vacancies without delay and that the wage bargain can be renegotiated at any time. As before, these assumptions imply that the zero-profit condition for new vacancies, $V = 0$, or its equivalent (2.8) hold both in and out of steady state, as does the sharing rule (2.6). In the model of chapter 1, however, the job destruction rate was a constant λ, whereas in the model of this chapter it depends on the reservation productivity R and is given by $\lambda G(R)$. A natural assumption to make is that firms can shut down unprofitable jobs without delay, and so the zero-profit condition satisfied by R, (2.1), holds both in and out of steady state.

Under this assumption, R becomes a jump variable. Because the job destruction condition (2.15) does not depend on sticky variables (and as before, neither the job creation condition (2.14) nor the set of wage equations (2.10) do), in the absence of expected parameter changes all three variables, R, θ and $w(x)$ must be on their steady state at all times. This follows for the same reasons that θ and w were always on their steady state in the model of chapter 1: Jobs are treated as assets with values determined by forward-looking arbitrage equations. Any deviation from the steady state leads to divergence and violates the transversality conditions of the maximization problem underlying the arbitrage equations.

This "instability" can be derived more explicitly from dynamic asset-valuation equations of the kind introduced in section 1.7, an exercise not pursued here.

The out-of-steady-state dynamics of unemployment are given by equation (2.2). As before, unemployment is a sticky variable and is driven by jumps in the two forward-looking variables, R and θ. The equilibrium of the triple, u, R, θ is a saddle, with one stable root (for unemployment) and two unstable ones (one each for R and θ).

The important difference between the dynamics of this version of the model and the model of chapter 1 can now be stated. It is due to the endogeneity of the job destruction rate and the assumption that the firm can shut down jobs without delay. Suppose that a parametric change increases the equilibrium reservation productivity from R to some other value R'. Then the rate of job destruction increases to $\lambda G(R')$, but also by the zero-profit condition satisfied by the reservation productivity, the jobs with idiosyncratic productivity x in the range $R \leq x < R'$ become unprofitable and close down. If initially the economy was in a steady state, the set of jobs that close down has nontrivial mass $[G(R') - G(R)](1 - u)$. The job destruction flow and the unemployment rate immediately increase by this number. Slower dynamic adjustments in unemployment follow this jump, however, according to equation (2.2). The job destruction flow drops to $\lambda G(R')$, where it remains in the absence of further changes in parameters.

The jump in unemployment is asymmetric, in the sense that it does not take place if the reservation productivity falls. If R' falls to R, following a parameter change, firms are now willing to keep in the productivity range (R', R) jobs that were previously destroyed. But they cannot instantly increase employment by $[G(R') - G(R)](1 - u)$ because the hiring of employees is slow, by the restrictions on the matching function, and the arrival of idiosyncratic shocks that pushes productivities in the range (R', R) is also slow. Therefore there are no jumps in unemployment if the reservation productivity falls, the initial value of unemployment remains the same as before the change, and the dynamic adjustment that it follows is smooth throughout the path.

We are now in a position to discuss the dynamic behavior of the job creation and job destruction rates, following parametric changes of the kind discussed in section 2.3. In this discussion we do not make explicit reference to the dynamics of wages, which are driven by the dynamics of

θ; we rather conduct it in terms of the two equations that give θ and R, (2.14) and (2.15).

Consider the two most interesting productivity shocks, a change in common productivity p and a multiplicative shift in the distribution of idiosyncratic productivities, $G(x)$. We saw in section 2.3 that a rise in p decreases the job destruction rate $\lambda G(R)$ and for given unemployment increases the job creation rate $\theta q(\theta)u/(1-u)$, through a downward jump in R and an upward jump in θ. Following the initial changes, unemployment falls smoothly, decreasing the job creation rate until it converges to the new and lower level of the job destruction rate. These adjustments are shown in figure 2.3, panel a. In the figure, initially the job destruction and job creation rates are equal. When the change takes place, the job creation rate jumps from its initial value A to a new value B, and the job destruction rate jumps down from A to C. Eventually unemployment falls until the job creation rate falls down to the level of the job destruction rate when the economy reaches a new steady state.

If common aggregate productivity decreases, R jumps to a higher value and θ to a lower one. The job destruction rate now goes up to $\lambda G(R')$, where R' is the higher value, but also on impact a number of jobs $[G(R') - G(R)](1 - u)$ are destroyed. Hence, as shown on panel b of figure 2.3, the job destruction rate on impact jumps from its initial value A to a new higher value D, but then returns to the value C, which mirrors the one in panel a. The difference between D and C represents the jobs destroyed on impact as a ratio of employment, $G(R') - G(R)$. The job creation rate now falls, but because unemployment rises on impact by $[G(R') - G(R)](1 - u)$, it does not fall by the full amount that would have fallen at given u. After the initial impact of the change, the job creation rate rises to match eventually the higher job destruction rate, at which point a new steady state is reached with higher unemployment.

The analysis of adjustment after a mean-preserving spread in the distribution of productivities follows similar lines. After the spread, both the reservation productivity and market tightness increase. On impact, a mass of jobs is destroyed, causing a jump in the job destruction rate. Following this jump, the job destruction rate falls to a level that is still higher than the initial level, completing its adjustment to the new steady state. The adjustment of the job destruction rate is similar to the one shown in figure 2.3, panel b, for a fall in aggregate productivity. Unlike the path shown in the same diagram, however, the job creation rate first rises, on

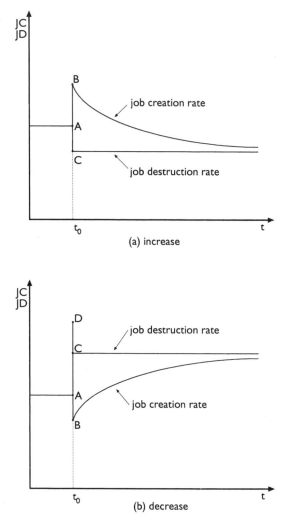

Figure 2.3
Adjustments in the job creation and job destruction rates following a change in aggregate productivity

impact, as shown in panel a of figure 2.3. After the initial rise the job creation rate adjusts gradually to the new level of the job destruction rate, in response to changes in the unemployment rate. It may increase further or decrease depending on whether the initial increase in the job destruction rate is bigger or smaller than the initial rise in the job creation rate. The new steady-state level of unemployment may be higher or lower than in the initial steady state depending on the extent of the change in R and θ. But on impact unemployment rises because the job destruction rate responds faster to the change than the job creation rate does.

If the distribution of idiosyncratic productivities takes a negative mean-preserving spread both the job destruction and job creation rates fall. The job destruction rate falls to its new equilibrium level once for all, along similar lines to the change shown in panel a of figure 2.3. The job creation rate also falls on impact, but whether it rises or falls after the initial change depends again on the relative fall in the two rates.

It follows that the initial change in the job creation rate is negatively correlated with that in the job destruction rate in the case of a uniform change in productivities but positively correlated in the case of a change in the spread of the productivity distribution. In both cases there is an asymmetry in the behavior of the job destruction rate, with a bigger initial jump when the change is positive (i.e., when it increases). Following the initial change, again in both cases, the job creation rate adjusts to the level of the job destruction rate through induced changes in unemployment.

2.6   Notes on the Literature

The model in this chapter is based on Mortensen and Pissarides (1994). The empirical motivation for the model was provided by Davis's and Haltiwanger's (1990, 1992) data for U.S. manufacturing industry. See Davis, Haltiwanger, and Schuh (1996) for more documentation and discussion. Other empirical studies of job flows include Leonard (1987) and Dunne, Roberts, and Samuelson (1989) for the United States; Konings (1995) and Blanchflower and Burgess (1993) for the United Kingdom; Boeri and Cramer (1992) for Germany; Broersma and den Butter (1994) and Gautier (1997) for the Netherlands; Lagarde, Maurin, and Torelli (1994) for France; Albaek and Sorensen (1995) for Denmark; and

Contini et al. (1995) for countries of the European Union. See also the papers collected in OECD (1996) for a discussion of models and data availability for member countries and the OECD *Employment Outlook* for 1994 for comparable data across the OECD. Outside the OECD, job creation and job destruction data for Poland during the transition was reported by Konings, Lehmann, and Schaffer (1996) and for other transition economies by Bilsen and Konings (1998).

The empirical observations of Davis and Haltiwanger and others generated a lot of theoretical interest in job turnover. A variant of the model of Mortensen and Pissarides (1994) was calibrated by Cole and Rogerson (1996) who found that the model accounts for the Davis-Haltiwanger observations provided the pool of nonemployed job seekers is about twice as large as the unemployment rate. This is consistent with evidence presented by Blanchard and Diamond (1990), who found that the flow from out of the labor force to employment justifies the assumption that there are about as many job seekers outside the labor force as there are unemployed. Den Haan, Ramey, and Watson (1997) embedded the model into a real business cycle model and calibrated it. They showed that the model can account for the job creation and job destruction flows and that in addition the labor market frictions magnify and make more persistent the effects of the business cycle shocks.

Other approaches to the modeling of the job creation and job destruction flows include Caballero and Hammour (1994, 1996), Bertola and Caballero (1994), Ramey and Watson (1997), Greenwood, MacDonald, and Zhang (1995), Hopenhayn and Rogerson (1993), and Bertola and Rogerson (1997). In contrast to the approach in Mortensen and Pissarides (1994) and to that in this chapter, which take the match as the unit of analysis, these papers place more emphasis on the firm as the unit of analysis.

The asymmetries in the job creation and job destruction flows, which were a topic of analysis in Mortensen and Pissarides (1993, 1994), have also been analyzed in an alternative framework by Campbell and Fisher (1998). Theoretical explanations of the asymmetry in job turnover take the Davis-Haltiwanger observation of a more volatile job destruction than job creation rate as a fact in need of explanation. Boeri (1996), however, showed that this U.S. fact is not a feature of job reallocation in European countries, with the exception of the United Kingdom. In continental European countries job creation typically shows more cyclical variability. Garibaldi (1998) explained this difference by arguing that in Europe policy restrictions imply that the firm cannot close jobs down without delay, an assumption that is needed to get the asymmetries discussed in this chapter. But even in the United States, Foote (1988) noted that nonmanufacturing exhibits a different asymmetry than manufacturing, with job creation more volatile. He explained it by arguing that declining sectors of the economy exhibit more volatility in job destruction and expanding sectors more in job creation.

The cyclical variability of unemployment was also studied by Gomes, Greenwood and Rebelo (1997), in a model with incomplete markets driven by the decisions of workers who decide each period whether to work or search, given stochastic shocks to the value of their jobs.

The analysis of multiplicative productivity shocks in this chapter (or more generally that of increases in variance) was motivated by the claim, originally made by Lilien (1982), that sectoral shifts in production are a driving force of the cycle. His claim, however, has been disputed. Abraham and Katz (1986) and Blanchard and Diamond (1989) have used the fact that the Beveridge curve responds differently to aggregate and reallocation shocks to differentiate between them, with results favoring aggregate shocks as the predominant driving force. Davis and Haltiwanger and others have attempted to differentiate between the two driving forces by making use of the related prediction that if the driving force is a multiplicative shock, job creation and job destruction should be positively correlated over the cycle. The data presented by Davis, Haltiwanger, and Schuh (1996) showed a strong negative correlation between the job creation and job destruction rates.

In terms of the stylized facts that we discussed in chapter 1, an explanation of the cycle based on multiplicative shifts would produce loops that are too "flat" around the Beveridge curve (i.e., vacancies would not fluctuate enough). It is more likely that structural change takes place in recessions more frequently than it does in booms, which are caused by aggregate shocks, since in recessions the opportunity cost of relocation and production restructuring is less. See Davis (1987) and Caballero and Hammour (1994) for more discussion of this point.

3 Long-Run Equilibrium and Balanced Growth

In this chapter we return first to the model with constant job destruction rate and derive the condition for job creation from a conventional dynamic model of the firm with costs of adjustment. We show that when the model of the firm in chapter 1 is re-expressed in these terms, the only essential departure from the conventional theory of the demand for labor is that in our model there are linear costs of adjustment that depend on the tightness of the market. This correspondence helps to motivate and establish some of the results in this and later chapters.

Following this, we extend the model to a homogeneous long-run equilibrium model that is consistent with the existence of a constant unemployment rate when there is balanced economic growth. In order to achieve this, we change the specification of the value of time to the unemployed worker. We discuss some possibilities, all of which are consistent with the existence of a balanced growth path.

The introduction of growth is important for our analysis because a reasonable equilibrium model of unemployment must be able to accommodate the stylized fact that on a balanced-growth path the rate of unemployment is constant. We introduce growth in two ways. First, we make the assumption that technological progress is disembodied, so labor productivity in existing jobs grows at the exogenous rate of technological progress. We also introduce capital in this model and show that the result is a neoclassical (Solow) growth model with a constant unemployment rate that depends negatively on the rate of growth. The interest rate is treated as an exogenous constant in this analysis. When the interest rate is endogenized, however, by assuming either a constant savings rate or Ramsey consumers, the result may be reversed, with faster growth leading to higher unemployment. The reason is that with the exogenous interest rate the elasticity of the supply of capital is implicitly treated as infinite, whereas when it is endogenized and the supply of capital made to depend on savings, faster growth reduces the amount of capital available to each efficiency unit of labor.

The second way of introducing growth is motivated by Schumpeter's "creative destruction" idea. Technological progress is embodied in new capital, so productivity in existing jobs does not grow. Growth can come about either through job destruction and creation of a new and more productive job or through "restructuring", without (necessarily) job destruction. We model only the case of creative job destruction and give some references in the Notes on the Literature to the alternatives. In this case the rate of job destruction is endogenous and is higher at faster rate of growth. Consequently, and in contrast to the case of disembodied technological progress, faster technological progress is associated with higher steady-state unemployment rate, even with constant interest rate.

3.1 Large Firms

We derived the critical condition for the supply of jobs (1.30) by assuming that each firm has only one job. In this section we derive the same condition again by assuming that the firm employs many workers, and that on average it is large enough to eliminate all uncertainty about the flow of labor. We continue assuming that the wage rate is given by an implicit bargain at the individual level. That is, wages are fixed as if the firm engages in Nash bargains with each employee separately, by taking the wages of all other employees as given. This assumption is clearly the closest one to competitive wage determination in this market environment. In deciding how many jobs to open up the firm anticipates the wage correctly but chooses the number of jobs by taking it as given. This is consistent with profit maximization when there are no long-term contracts and there is a perfect second-hand market for capital goods.

Let K_i and N_i be the capital and employment of firm i, and let $F(K_i, pN_i)$ be a constant returns to scale production function. The parameter p is a labor-augmenting productivity parameter. The firm buys capital equipment K_i at the price of its output and pays workers real wage w, given by (1.31) and taken as given by the firm. We assume that there are no costs of adjustment for capital but adjusting employment involves some linear costs of adjustment.

The firm loses workers at the rate λN_i. In order to recruit workers, it has to open up job vacancies and advertise. Suppose that each vacancy costs the firm pc in recruitment costs and returns a worker at the rate $q(\theta)$, where θ is outside the firm's control. Let V_i be the number of the firm's vacancies. Then the firm's labor force changes according to

$$\dot{N}_i = q(\theta)V_i - \lambda N_i. \tag{3.1}$$

The firm's choice variable in (3.1) is V_i.

The present-discounted value of the firm's expected profit is

$$\Pi_i = \int_0^\infty e^{-rt}\left[F(K_i, pN_i) - wN_i - pcV_i - \dot{K}_i - \delta K_i\right]dt, \tag{3.2}$$

where δ is the rate of depreciation of the capital stock. The firm maximizes (3.2) with respect to K_i and V_i subject to (3.1). Denoting by x the co-state variable associated with (3.1), we get the following Euler conditions, satisfied by the optimal path of K_i and N_i for given paths of p and θ:

$$e^{-rt}[F_1(K_i, pN_i) - \delta] - \frac{d}{dt}(-e^{-rt}) = 0, \tag{3.3}$$

$$e^{-rt}[pF_2(K_i, pN_i) - w] - \lambda x + \frac{dx}{dt} = 0, \tag{3.4}$$

$$-e^{-rt}pc + q(\theta)x = 0. \tag{3.5}$$

For constant p and θ, there is a steady-state solution with constant w, N_i, and K_i satisfying

$$F_1(K_i, pN_i) - \delta - r = 0, \tag{3.6}$$

$$pF_2(K_i, pN_i) - w - \frac{r+\lambda}{q(\theta)}pc = 0. \tag{3.7}$$

The steady-state solution for the firm's vacancies, V_i, is then obtained from the constraint (3.1) for $\dot{N_i} = 0$:

$$V_i = \frac{\lambda N_i}{q(\theta)}. \tag{3.8}$$

Now, because $F(K_i, pN_i)$ is of constant returns to scale, we can re-express $F_1(K_i, pN_i)$ and $F_2(K_i, pN_i)$ as functions of one variable, K_i/pN_i. But then all variables other than K_i/pN_i in both (3.6) and (3.7) are market variables: None is indexed by i. Hence in the steady state all firms will have the same ratio K_i/pN_i, which we denote by k. We define

$$f(k) = \frac{1}{pN_i}F(K_i, pN_i) = F\left(\frac{K_i}{pN_i}, 1\right), \tag{3.9}$$

where $pf(k)$ is output per person employed. Hence

$$F_1(K_i, pN_i) = f'(k), \tag{3.10}$$

$$F_2(K_i, pN_i) = f(k) - kf'(k). \tag{3.11}$$

Substituting from (3.10) into (3.6), we get

$$f'(k) = r + \delta, \tag{3.12}$$

which is condition (1.28). Substituting also from (3.11) into (3.7), we get

$$p[f(k) - kf'(k)] - w - \frac{r + \lambda}{q(\theta)} pc = 0, \tag{3.13}$$

which, noting (3.12), is the job creation condition (1.30).

Condition (3.8) implies that in the steady state all firms choose the same ratio of vacancies to employment, and therefore (3.8) also gives the ratio of all vacancies to total employment. To revert to the notation of chapter 1, let $\Sigma V_i = \theta u L$, where L is the labor force, and $\Sigma N_i = (1 - u)L$, so (3.8) becomes

$$\theta \frac{u}{1 - u} = \frac{\lambda}{q(\theta)}. \tag{3.14}$$

Re-arrangement of (3.14) gives (1.32), the final equilibrium condition of chapter 1.

Inspection of the firm's present-value expression (3.2) shows that the critical new element in this theory of the demand for factors of production is the cost of adjustment for employment $[pc/q(\theta)](\dot{N}_i + \lambda N_i)$. This cost is linear in $\dot{N}_i$, and it has some effect on the level of employment in the steady state. Moreover, since θ stands for labor-market tightness, the cost of adjustment depends on tightness: The firm can adjust employment more cheaply when the market is less tight (lower θ). The congestion externality that we discussed in chapter 1 is due to this new element of the theory. If all firms try to expand employment together, they compete for the pool of unemployed workers by simultaneously opening up more vacancies. This increases market tightness and increases the length of time that a given firm has to wait before a suitable employee arrives. But, if a firm tries to expand employment alone, the waiting time is shorter. Firms follow the same employment policy irrespective of what other firms do, thus ignoring the congestion that their policies create for other firms in the market.

3.2   Unemployment Income

When we analyzed the effects of productivity changes in chapter 1, we saw that the general level of productivity had an influence on employment because of the fixed actual or imputed income during unemployment. The Nash wage equation is a linear combination of unemployment income and labor productivity, and when the former is fixed, productivity changes lead to changes in profitability and job creation. We will now argue that in long-run equilibrium it is more reasonable to allow unemployment income to respond to changes in some of the variables of the model, leading to a proportional relation between wages and the general level of productivity. The responses that we will describe are not derived from explicit maximizing models, but it is easy to see that commonly used models are consistent with them. We omit the derivation to avoid too many digressions from the central theme of the book. Also it will become apparent that the assumption of fixed unemployment income is innocuous in most applications of the model, but it makes a big difference to the analysis of the effects of permanent productivity changes.

Unemployment income consists of actual income received during unemployment and the imputed value of time to unemployed workers. If actual income consists of transfer payments, it is reasonable to assume that it is fixed in terms of the prevailing wage rate, rather than the prevailing price level. For example, unemployment insurance benefits may be indexed to the average wage rate, just as the taxes used to finance them are generally proportional to wage earnings and not lump sum (see also chapter 9). Any income during unemployment other than a transfer payment, like income earned doing odd jobs in a secondary sector of the economy, should also be in fixed proportion to income from work in the primary sector along a steady-state path. Thus the actual-income component of z does not pose any serious problems for the existence of a balanced-growth path with unemployment. It may reasonably be assumed to be proportional to average wages.

This leaves imputed income from leisure activities, which is also part of z. The value of leisure to the worker is computed as the real compensation that the worker requires in order to give up his time for work. If leisure time is a consumption good, the value that a worker puts on it is not independent of market returns. In general, if there is a perfect capital market and workers have a long horizon, the minimum compensation that a worker requires in order to give up a consumption good that he possesses is a function of his wealth. Thus, in a general utility-maximization approach to job search, z is likely to depend on both human and nonhuman wealth.

Human wealth for unemployed workers is equal to U, the "asset value" of the worker during search. Nonhuman wealth has not played a role in our model. Let it be denoted by A. Then, in a general utility-maximization framework, imputed income during unemployment can be approximated by a function of permanent income, the average yield on human and nonhuman wealth:

$$z = \zeta r(A + U), \qquad 0 < \zeta < 1, \tag{3.15}$$

with ζ assumed constant.

Suppose first that we ignore nonhuman wealth; for example, let $A = 0$. Then substitution of z from (3.15) into one of the expressions that we derived for U, such as (1.19), gives

$$rU = \frac{\beta}{(1-\zeta)(1-\beta)} pc\theta, \tag{3.16}$$

so in steady-state

$$z = \frac{\zeta}{1-\zeta} \frac{\beta}{1-\beta} pc\theta. \tag{3.17}$$

Further substitution of z from (3.17) into the wage equation with capital, (1.31), gives

$$w = \beta \left[f(k) - (r+\delta)k + \frac{\zeta}{1-\zeta} c\theta \right] p. \tag{3.18}$$

Thus our assumptions about the worker's imputed unemployment income make wages proportional to the labor-augmenting productivity parameter p. The factor of proportionality depends on the worker's share in the wage bargain, the valuation that the worker places on his leisure time (ζ), the firm's recruitment cost, and market tightness.

Nonhuman wealth makes a difference to this analysis because, if we write $A > 0$ and use (3.15), we get, in place of (3.17),

$$z = \frac{\zeta}{1-\zeta} \left[rA + \frac{\beta}{1-\beta} pc\theta \right]. \tag{3.19}$$

The wage equation then becomes

$$w = \frac{(1-\beta)\zeta}{1-\zeta} rA + \beta \left[f(k) - (r+\delta)k + \frac{\zeta}{1-\zeta} c\theta \right] p. \tag{3.20}$$

Thus wages are again a linear combination of a term that is proportional to productivity and one that is apparently independent of productivity.

As Phelps (1994) argues, however, although it may be reasonable to assume that nonhuman wealth is independent of market outcomes in the short run, in the longer run it adapts to labor-market earnings. A temporary increase in earnings may not have much influence on wealth, but a permanent increase leads to more savings and eventually raises wealth by an amount that reflects the rise in earnings.

If wealth plays an important role in determining reservation wages and the bargaining stand of workers, the slow response of it to long-term changes in labor market conditions could explain persistent effects of productivity changes on unemployment. For example, if wages obey equation (3.20) and ζ is not small, a permanent fall in productivity p (or of its rate of growth) can increase unemployment above its steady state for a long time (for as long as is required for nonhuman wealth to fall to a level consistent with the lower level of productivity and so allow wages to fall).

Such temporary (but potentially long-lived) unemployment responses to long-term productivity changes could be important in the empirical analysis of unemployment, in the light of the long-term productivity changes that took place in industrial countries in the 1970s. In the analysis that follows, however, we will concentrate on the longer-run steady-state properties of equilibrium, when nonhuman wealth, if it matters, has had time to adjust to the labor market equilibrium. Under these circumstances there is no loss of generality if we ignore nonhuman wealth, avoid the modeling of consumption and savings choices, and write the value of imputed income during unemployment as in (3.15), with $A = 0$ and ζ a small positive number. The wage equation is (3.18), so higher valuation of leisure (higher ζ) implies higher wages. Through the higher wages it also implies lower labor market tightness (e.g., see equation (3.13)) and so lower job creation and higher unemployment. These are all intuitive results that need no further discussion.

The key property of the extended model of this section is that wages are proportional to the general productivity parameter p, with the factor of proportionality depending positively on labor-market tightness and the valuation of leisure. Substitution of (3.18) into the job creation condition, (3.13), gives, after making use of (3.12),

$$(1-\beta)[f(k)-kf'(k)] - \frac{\zeta}{1-\zeta}\beta c\theta - \beta\frac{r+\lambda}{q(\theta)}c = 0. \qquad (3.21)$$

Labor-market tightness in the steady state is independent of productivity p.

We note in passing two points about the extended model of this section. First, a very similar but simpler wage equation can be derived by writing $z = \zeta p$. What matters in (3.21) is that the imputed value of leisure is proportional to productivity. Although the simpler restriction $z = \zeta p$ cannot be derived from a utility maximizing model, in many long-run applications of the model it may be a reasonable simplification to make. The approach that we have followed here, of making the imputed value of time depend on permanent income, makes a difference when the shocks to productivity are temporary. For example, a temporary rise in p has only a temporary effect on wages, so the worker's permanent income increases by less than the rise in productivity. This increases expected profits for as long as the productivity remains high, inducing more job creation. If the rise in productivity is perceived to be permanent, this does not happen.

Second, a related point can be made about the firm's recruitment cost, which was assumed from the start to be proportional to general productivity, pc. Intuitively it may be more reasonable to write the recruitment cost as a function of wages, on the ground that recruitment is a labor-intensive activity. Of course, in the latter case, wages would also be proportional to productivity, but in addition they would be proportional to the marginal product of labor, $f(k) - kf'(k)$. Replacing pc by wc, however, is an unnecessary complication for our purposes, and we will not take it up.

The wage equation (3.18) replaces (1.31) in the equilibrium set of equations of chapter 1, (1.29) to (1.32). The unknowns remain the same as before, k, w, θ, and u. The properties of the new system, comprising (1.29), (1.30), (3.18), and (1.32) are qualitatively the same as the properties of (1.29) to (1.32), with one important exception. Now general labor-augmenting productivity shocks are fully absorbed by wages, so equilibrium unemployment does not respond to them. This property makes the new model a more suitable tool for long-run analysis than the model of chapter 1.

3.3 Technological Progress: The Capitalization Effect

We begin our extension of the static labor-market model of chapter 1 to a model of balanced growth by introducing exogenous labor-augmenting technological progress. As in the standard neoclassical model, technological progress is "disembodied," in the sense that all existing and new jobs benefit from the higher labor productivity without the need to replace their capital stock.

Suppose that technological progress is at the rate $g < r$. The interest rate is assumed to be exogenous and the supply of capital infinite, an assumption that is obviously extreme in a model of long-run growth but helpful in the analysis of unemployment. We return to this question in the next section. Let the labor-augmenting productivity parameter be a function of time, and suppose that it grows at the constant rate g:

$$p(t) = e^{gt} p_0, \tag{3.22}$$

where $p_0 > 0$ is some initial productivity level.

It is well-known from the results of growth theory that this is the only form of technological progress that is consistent with balanced growth. The easiest way to derive the implications of growth for equilibrium is to go directly to the Euler equations (3.3) to (3.5), which are obviously still valid, and make p an explicit function of time. In the steady state the ratio θ is constant, but wages grow at the rate g. Therefore the Euler conditions become

$$F_1(K_i, pN_i) - r - \delta = 0, \tag{3.23}$$

$$F_2(K_i, pN_i) - w - \frac{r + \lambda - g}{q(\theta)} pc = 0. \tag{3.24}$$

Defining, as before, k as the ratio K_i/pN_i, we now find a steady state with constant k that satisfies

$$f'(k) - r - \delta = 0 \tag{3.25}$$

and

$$f(k) - kf'(k) - \frac{w}{p} - \frac{r + \lambda - g}{q(\theta)} c = 0. \tag{3.26}$$

The wage equation is, as before, (3.18) which, with constant k, confirms that in the steady state wages grow at the rate g. Substitution of w from (3.18) into (3.26) gives the condition for labor market tightness:

$$(1-\beta)[f(k)-kf'(k)]-\frac{\zeta}{1-\zeta}\beta c\theta-\frac{r+\lambda-g}{q(\theta)}c=0. \tag{3.27}$$

The balanced growth equilibrium is the path for k, θ and w defined by (3.25), (3.26), and (3.18). The path for unemployment in steady state is given as before by the Beveridge condition (3.14).

The rate of technological progress influences equilibrium labor-market tightness. By differentiation we find that at higher g, θ is higher. With higher θ, wages and vacancies are both higher and unemployment lower.

The rate of technological progress influences tightness and unemployment because of the intertemporal element in the firm's employment decisions. Formally, this element is shown in the Euler conditions (3.4) and (3.5). The firm incurs some hiring costs now, in order to acquire workers who will yield some profit in the future. If the firm knows that in the steady state hiring costs rise at the same rate as profits, it can economize on future hiring costs by bringing forward some hiring. So at higher rates of growth, it goes into the market with more vacancies. At lower rates of growth it pays the firm to wait, so it reduces its vacancies.

Thus, with labor-augmenting technological progress, the aggregate capital stock, real wages, and the capital-labor ratio grow in the steady state, but the rates of unemployment and job vacancies are constant. Faster rate of technological progress implies lower rate of unemployment and higher rate of vacancies.

These results depend crucially on the influence of the rate of technological progress on the firm's "effective" rate of discount, $r-g$. Another way of expressing the intuition for the effect of growth that we have derived is to say that at faster rate of technological progress all future income flows are discounted at lower rate. Because the cost of creating a vacancy is borne now, whereas the profits from it accrue in the future, the lower discount rate increases job creation. For this reason Aghion and Howitt (1994) have termed this effect of growth on unemployment the "capitalization effect."

In our model the capitalization effect is present because the interest rate is exogenous. It would also work if the difference $r-g$ decreased in g but not if $r-g$ increased in g. We next give two models of interest rate determination that are consistent with both an increasing and a decreasing $r - g$.

3.4 Endogenous Capital and Interest

In a small open economy with perfect capital mobility, the supply of capital is infinite at the world interest rate. Therefore the growth rate of the small open economy does not influence the interest rate, and the results of the preceding section hold. This may not, however, be the case in a closed economy, or in a large open economy. We consider next two models of the determination of the interest rate, a model with exogenous saving rate, as in the Solow growth model, and one with optimizing savings behavior, as in the Ramsey model. In both models we consider savings by the representative agent; namely we ignore heterogeneity due to differences in labor-market status. This could be justified by the assumption that after labor market status is revealed, agents share the income in large family units, which are a microcosm of the market as a whole. Alternatively, it may be argued that the assumption of a representative consumer is a useful shortcut that avoids the complexity that arises in consumption decisions when income histories have to be traced out.

National income in the steady state is given by $F(K, pN)$, which, in terms of the constant labor force size is equal to $p(1 - u)f(k)$. Both u and k are constant but p is a function of time and grows at rate g. Savings in this economy are given by a constant fraction s of national income. Savings are used to finance additions to the aggregate capital stock and pay for the cost of vacancies. The aggregate capital stock is $K = p(1 - u)k$ and the total cost of vacancies in terms of the labor force is $pcv = pc\theta u$. With a depreciation rate δ we can therefore write

$$
\dot{k} = \frac{\dot{K}}{(1-u)p} + \left(\frac{\dot{u}}{1-u} - g\right)k
$$

$$
= sf(k) - \left(\delta + g - \frac{\dot{u}}{1-u}\right)k - c\theta\frac{u}{1-u}.
$$

(3.28)

In the steady state k and u are constant, so the capital stock is the solution to

$$sf(k) - (g + \delta)k = \frac{u}{1-u}c\theta = \frac{\lambda c}{q(\theta)},$$
(3.29)

where use has been made of the Beveridge equation (3.14).

Equation (3.29) determines the capital stock and (3.25) the interest rate, along the lines of a conventional Solow growth model. Unlike the conventional model, however, (3.29) depends on another unknown, θ. But θ is given, as before, by equation (3.27). With knowledge of θ, unemployment is obtained from the Beveridge equation (3.14).

We investigate the question of the dependence of unemployment on the growth rate by reducing equations (3.29), (3.25) and (3.27) to a block of two equations in two unknowns, k and θ. Substitution of (3.25) into (3.27) gives the job creation condition for an endogenous r:

$$(1-\beta)[f(k) - kf'(k)] - \frac{\zeta}{1-\zeta}\beta c\theta - \frac{f'(k) - \delta + \lambda - g}{q(\theta)}c = 0.$$
(3.30)

Equations (3.29) and (3.30) are solved for the steady-state values of k and θ in terms of the exogenous growth rate.

Consider first equation (3.29) in figure 3.1. If θ is a very small number, the right-hand side of (3.29) is also very small, and in the limit, as θ tends to zero, so does $1/q(\theta)$. Thus, in figure 3.1, k_1 is the limiting capital stock

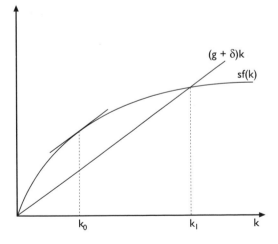

Figure 3.1
Capital market equilibrium

for $\theta = 0$. As θ rises from zero, the right-hand side of (3.29) also rises, and therefore the equilibrium capital stock falls. In figure 3.1 equilibrium points for positive θ lie to the left of k_1 because savings have to exceed capital usage to finance the recruitment cost c. The maximum θ that can be supported in an equilibrium is the one that gives a capital stock k_0 in equation (3.29). If θ were to rise above that level, savings would have to exceed capital usage by more than at k_0, which, from figure 3.1, is not possible. Therefore, in steady-state equilibrium, the capital stock must take a value between k_0 and k_1, defined respectively by

$$sf'(k_0) = g + \delta \tag{3.31}$$

and

$$sf(k_1) = (g + \delta)k_1. \tag{3.32}$$

In this range, $sf'(k) \leq g + \delta$, and so the curve representing (3.29) in θ, k space has negative slope. This line is labeled KE (for capital market equilibrium) in figure 3.2. The second equilibrium relation, (3.30), has a positive slope and is labeled JC. Equilibrium is at the single intersection point of the two curves. With knowledge of θ we then obtain unemployment from the Beveridge curve and with knowledge of k, we obtain the interest rate from the marginal productivity condition (3.25).

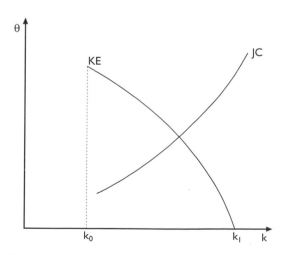

Figure 3.2
Equilibrium capital stock and market tightness with constant savings rate

The exogenous growth rate shifts both curves, the capital market equilibrium condition to the left, and the job creation condition up. For a constant interest rate the capital stock is constant, so θ unambiguously rises. This is the basis of the capitalization effect. But with endogenous r and the implied shift in KE, the capital stock falls, with ambiguous effects on θ. It turns out that the sign of the effect on θ cannot be determined with simple restrictions on parameter values. In the classical case where the KE curve is vertical, the effect of the growth rate on the capital stock is

$$\frac{\partial k}{\partial g} = \frac{k}{sf'(k) - (g + \delta)}, \tag{3.33}$$

which, given that in this case $g + \delta = sf(k)/k$ for a Cobb-Douglas production function, becomes

$$\frac{\partial k}{\partial g} = -\frac{k^{2-\alpha}}{s(1-\alpha)}. \tag{3.34}$$

From (3.25) we then get

$$\frac{\partial r}{\partial g} = -\alpha(1-\alpha)k^{\alpha-2}\frac{\partial k}{\partial g} = \frac{\alpha}{s}. \tag{3.35}$$

The plausible parameter values (e.g., α, the share of capital, is approximately 0.3; s, investment as a fraction of national income, varies across countries but is usually below 0.3) give an effect that exceeds unity, implying that $r - g$ rises when g rises and so θ falls.

More generally, for the model in hand, differentiation of (3.29) and (3.30) gives the result that the sign of the effect of the growth rate on θ for the Cobb-Douglas production function satisfies

$$\text{sign } \frac{\partial \theta}{\partial g} = \text{sign} \left(\frac{\alpha(1-\alpha)k^{\alpha}}{\alpha sk^{\alpha-1} - (g+\delta)} + \frac{\alpha(1-\alpha+s)k^{\alpha-1} - (g+\delta)}{\alpha sk^{\alpha-1} - (g+\delta)} \frac{c}{q(\theta)} \right). \tag{3.36}$$

The first term on the right is negative by the argument made in figure 3.1. The denominator of the second term is also negative, but the numerator may be either positive or negative. Making use of (3.25) to introduce the interest rate in place of k, however, we get

$$\alpha(1-\alpha+s)k^{\alpha-1} - (g+\delta) = (1-\alpha+s)(r+\delta) - (g+\delta). \tag{3.37}$$

A plausible set of values that satisfies (3.31) and (3.32) is $\alpha = 0.3, s = 0.25$, $r = 0.04$, $\delta = 0.07$, and $g = 0.02$. This set of parameter values gives 0.0145 for the sum in (3.37), a positive value. This implies, as in the classical case, that plausible parameter values give a negative effect of growth on job creation and unemployment. A positive effect, however, is within the range of feasible parameter values.

The likely negative effect of growth on unemployment (meaning that unemployment is higher when the growth rate is higher) in the model so far arises from the fact that with exogenous savings rate, the capital stock per efficiency unit of labor falls a lot when growth accelerates, leading to a large increase in the interest rate. As a second model of savings, we consider the model with an optimizing representative household with isoelastic utility function $(C^{1-\gamma} - \gamma)/(1 - \gamma)$, where $\gamma > 0$. C is consumption per head. The labor-market decisions are carried out as before, but now, with capital as the only asset, the household chooses consumption path,

$$\frac{\dot{C}}{C} = \frac{r - \rho}{\gamma}, \tag{3.38}$$

where ρ is the pure rate of time preference. In the steady state, with output per head growing at the exogenous rate g, consumption also has to grow at rate g, so the interest rate satisfies

$$r = \gamma g + \rho. \tag{3.39}$$

With exogenous growth, (3.39) gives a unique solution for the interest rate, and (3.25) then gives the steady-state capital stock:

$$f'(k) = \gamma g + \rho + \delta. \tag{3.40}$$

As before, (3.30) gives θ and the Beveridge curve the unemployment rate.

Now, from (3.39) we immediately get $\partial r/\partial g = \gamma$, and from the job creation condition (3.30), it follows that a sufficient condition for a negative effect of growth on unemployment is $\gamma \geq 1$. More generally, differentiation of (3.30) given (3.40) gives the following effect of growth on job creation:

$$\frac{\partial \theta}{\partial g} = -\frac{(1 - \beta)k\gamma + (\gamma - 1)/q(\theta)}{\zeta\beta c/(1 - \zeta) + (r + \lambda - g)c\eta/\theta q(\theta)}, \tag{3.41}$$

where η is the negative of the elasticity of $q(\theta)$ and is a number between 0 and 1. It is clear from (3.41) that even values of γ below 1 imply a negative effect of growth on job creation. Of course, $\gamma = 1$ gives the logarithmic utility function. So, as in the Solow model with exogenous savings, acceleration of growth in the optimizing model increases unemployment, contrary to the capitalization effect, for a plausible range of the elasticity of intertemporal substitution $1/\gamma$. Small values of γ, however, can give a positive capitalization effect, as in the model with fixed interest rate.

The savings models that we have considered imply that when the interest rate is endogenized, the capitalization effect of growth may be either positive or negative, depending on parameter values. The question is ultimately empirical, but direct evidence on the behavior of the difference $r - g$ when growth varies exogenously is lacking. Indirect evidence, derived by making use of plausible values of the parameters of the structural model, shows that $r - g$ may rise when g rises, offsetting the positive capitalization effect of growth. When g is also endogenized, however, results again vary, a question that we do not pursue here (see the Notes on the Literature for some recent work). Clearly, more work is needed on the question of growth and unemployment before robust results can be derived. We take up one avenue in the next section.

3.5   Creative Job Destruction

Job destruction in the model so far is an exogenous fraction of the level of employment λ. The introduction of idiosyncratic productivity shocks along the lines of the analysis of chapter 2 is, in principle, straightforward under the technology assumptions of the preceding section. If technological progress is of the Solow variety, namely it is disembodied and immediately incorporated into all existing capital equipment, the firm and worker that have a job with idiosyncratic productivity x enjoy appreciation in its value at the rate g, whatever the value of x. For given r, this makes the effective discount rate applied by firms and workers equal to $r - g$. There is no other change to the model of job destruction of chapter 2 brought about by the introduction of disembodied technological progress, apart from the change in the discount rate to $r - g$. We do not describe the model here more fully, to avoid repetition. We note, however, that since the discount rate in the model of chapter 2 reduces job creation but has ambiguous effects on job destruction, the capital-ization effect of technological progress increases job creation but has ambiguous effects on job destruction. If we also take into account the negative effects of the interest rate on the value of wealth, the capital-ization effect of technological progress increases wealth and so increases the value of the imputed value of unemployment. This second effect of the discount rate gives a reason for lower job creation and higher job destruction during periods of fast economic growth.

A more interesting case of job destruction to consider when there is technological progress is job destruction due to obsolescence. Suppose that technology is embodied in new capital equipment; in other words, instead of the disembodied technology of the preceding sections, which benefited all existing jobs, new technology now can benefit only jobs that explicitly invest in new equipment. In reality investment in new equipment can take place in an existing employment relationship, with the existing worker learning how to use the new technology. But there are also new jobs emerging from new technological innova-tions, which make existing jobs obsolete, in the sense that the wages that they pay their employees make a job separation the best available option.

In this section we consider a simplified model where no job can invest in new and more advanced equipment without breaking up the existing employment relationship. Jobs are created at the technological frontier, as in the model of chapter 2, but now keep the same technology until job destruction. Job destruction can take place for one of two reasons. First, because an idiosyncratic shock arrives, an event that as before takes place at the constant rate λ, and second, because, as wages and costs grow in new jobs, existing jobs become obsolete. Following Aghion and Howitt (1994), we refer to the latter reason for job destruction by the Shumpeterian term "creative job destruction."

Our analysis is further simplified by ignoring the explicit reference to capital and assuming instead that a new job produces exogenous output p, a parameter that grows at the constant rate $g < r$. The interest rate is exogenous and constant. Once a job is created, its output remains con-stant at the value that it acquired at creation time. In order to make this fact explicit, we need to distinguish some variables both by current time and by the job's creation time. Let these be, respectively, t and τ. At time t the output of a job created at time $\tau \leq t$ is $p(\tau)$, but wages generally change with time. Wages are renegotiated continually and are denoted by $w(\tau, t)$. The creation time τ is the *vintage* of the job.

The expected present discounted value of future profit J and wage income W for a given job-worker match depend on the job's vintage and the current date. These value functions solve the following asset pricing equations:

$$rJ(\tau, t) = p(\tau) - w(\tau, t) - \lambda J(\tau, t) + \dot{J}(\tau, t), \tag{3.42}$$

$$rW(\tau, t) = w(\tau, t) - \lambda[W(\tau, t) - U(t)] + \dot{W}(\tau, t), \tag{3.43}$$

where as before $U(t)$ is the value of unemployed search in t. Note that both firms and workers make capital gains in the steady state from changes in the value of the job, denoted in (3.42) and (3.43) as time derivatives. Implicit in the value expressions is an optimal choice of a life for the job because the job destruction event in this context is not exogenous.

The value of creating a vacancy, $V(t)$, is zero in equilibrium, namely

$$rV(t) = -cp(t) + q(\theta)J(t, t) = 0. \tag{3.44}$$

The value of a new job to the firm, $J(t, t)$, is obtained from (3.42) by noting that new jobs are created on the technological frontier; that is, the output of a job created at t, when the worker arrives, is $p(t)$. Finally the value of unemployment solves the asset pricing equation

$$rU(t) = z(t) + \theta q(\theta)[W(t, t) - U(t)] + \dot{U}(t) \tag{3.45}$$

with $z(t)$ given, as before, by (3.17).

The wage bargain maximizes the Nash product at each and every t,

$$w(\tau, t) = \arg \max [W(\tau, t) - U(t)]^{\beta} [J(\tau, t) - V(t)]^{1-\beta}, \tag{3.46}$$

so, as before, with $V(t) = 0$ wages are set to satisfy

$$\beta J(\tau, t) = (1 - \beta)[W(\tau, t) - U(t)], \tag{3.47}$$

where β represents the worker's share. We first substitute $J(\tau, t)$, $W(\tau, t)$, and $U(t)$, respectively, from (3.42), (3.43), and (3.45), into (3.47) by noting that the sharing rule in (3.47) also holds for the capital gain terms. Next we substitute $z(t)$ from (3.17) out of the resulting wage equation, to get

$$w(\tau, t) = \beta p(\tau) + \frac{\zeta}{1-\zeta} \beta c\theta p(t). \tag{3.48}$$

Comparing with the wage equation in the case of disembodied technological progress, (3.18), we find that as before, wages are a sum of two
terms, one representing job product and one representing the outside
options. But whereas in this case the outside options grow at the rate of
technological progress, because all new jobs are created on the technological frontier, the product of the job remains fixed at the output at
creation time, $p(\tau)$. This contrasts with the case of disembodied progress,
where the product of the job also grew at the rate of technological
progress. Therefore with embodied progress, wages grow during the life
of the job but at a slower rate than wages in new jobs. This implies, first,
that eventually profits will become negative and the job will be
destroyed, and second, that when the worker who becomes unemployed
finds another job his wages will take a jump that will make up for their
slower growth during his previous job.

By substituting from the wage equation into (3.42), we obtain,

$$(r+\lambda)J(\tau,t) = (1-\beta)p(\tau) - \frac{\zeta}{1-\zeta}\beta c\theta p(t) + \dot{J}(\tau,t). \tag{3.49}$$

The firm chooses the life of the job to maximize its value. The choice is
dynamically consistent, in the sense that the optimal life chosen at the
time that the job is created is also the optimal life at subsequent times,
and it coincides with the time that the value of the job drops to zero. To
derive this formally, let T be the optimal life of the job, and integrate
(3.49) from the current time to $\tau + T$, which is the time when the job is
destroyed. Then the optimal value of the job at any time t satisfies

$$J(\tau,t) = \max_{T}\left\{\int_{t}^{\tau+T}\left[(1-\beta)p(\tau) - \beta\frac{\zeta}{1-\zeta}c\theta p(s)\right]e^{-(r+\lambda)(s-t)}ds\right\}. \tag{3.50}$$

The first-order condition for the maximization problem is

$$(1-\beta)p(\tau) - \beta\frac{\zeta}{1-\zeta}c\theta p(\tau+T) = 0; \tag{3.51}$$

that is, the life of the job is chosen such that the firm's share of the
product is equal to the costs at the end of the horizon. Substitution of
the first-order condition into (3.50) clearly shows that $J(\tau, \tau + T) = 0$,
which says that jobs are destroyed at the point where their value drops
to zero. Substitution also of (3.51) into the wage equation (3.48) shows
that at the time that the job is destroyed, $w(\tau, \tau + T) = p(\tau)$, which says

that the wage rate has risen up to the value of total product. Continuation of the employment relationship beyond $\tau + T$ would push wages above the value of total product because of the competition from new jobs.

Condition (3.51) can be simplified to,

$$1 - \beta - \frac{\zeta}{1-\zeta} \beta c \theta e^{gT} = 0, \tag{3.52}$$

giving the optimal life T in terms of market tightness θ. From this we immediately find that the life of the job falls with tightness because wages are higher in more tight markets, and as a result jobs become obsolete faster. Also, for given tightness, the optimal life is shorter when the rate of growth is higher, again because wages (but also other costs) rise faster, and when the value of leisure and the worker's share in the wage bargain are higher, also because wages are higher.

Now, to complete the description of equilibrium, we need an equation for market tightness and one for unemployment. The equation for tightness comes, as before, from the job creation condition and the equation for unemployment is a generalization of the Beveridge curve.

Job creation takes place until the vale of a new vacancy drops to zero. From (3.44) this implies that

$$J(t,t) = \frac{c}{q(\theta)} p(t). \tag{3.53}$$

The value equation (3.50) for $t = \tau$ and an optimal T implies that

$$J(t,t) = p(t) \int_t^{t+T} \left[1 - \beta - \frac{\zeta}{1-\zeta} \beta c \theta e^{gs} \right] e^{-(r+\lambda)s} ds. \tag{3.54}$$

Let the value of the integral be denoted by $J^0(\theta, g)$, with the other parameters suppressed from the notation. J^0 is (locally) independent of T by the envelope theorem. It decreases in θ, since higher θ implies higher wages, and decreases also in the growth rate, since wages and other costs rise faster at higher g. With the new notation the job creation condition (3.53) becomes

$$J^0(\theta, g) = \frac{c}{q(\theta)}. \tag{3.55}$$

Conditions (3.52) and (3.55) are uniquely solved for the optimal life of a job and market tightness. In horizon-tightness space, (3.52) slopes down and (3.55) is vertical (figure 3.3). The condition for optimal horizon is denoted *JD* because it is the condition that determines the incidence of creative destruction. A higher *T* indicates lower job destruction.

We have already seen that for given tightness, higher rate of growth decreases the optimal horizon. Thus the job destruction curve in figure 3.3 shifts down and to the left. In (3.55), higher rate of growth implies lower θ, so when *g* is higher, the job creation line in figure 3.3 shifts to the left. These effects are shown in figure 3.4. Market tightness (and so job creation) unambiguously falls. The effect on the optimal horizon cannot be signed from the diagram alone, but we can easily show that it will also be negative. Substitute

$$\frac{\zeta}{1-\zeta}\beta c\theta = (1-\beta)e^{-gT} \tag{3.56}$$

from (3.52) into (3.54) and then into (3.55) to get

$$(1-\beta)\int_0^T \left(1-e^{-g(T-s)}\right)e^{-(r+\lambda)s}ds = \frac{c}{q(\theta)}. \tag{3.57}$$

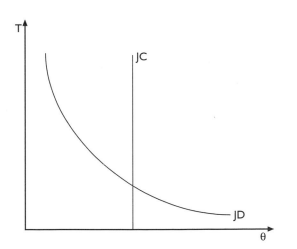

Figure 3.3
Equilibrium job obsolescence and market tightness

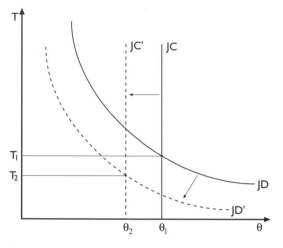

Figure 3.4
Implications of faster technological progress for equilibrium

The left-hand side is increasing in T and g, the right-hand side is increasing in θ, and so the effect of g on T must be negative.

These results contrast with those derived for the case of disembodied technological progress, where for given r market tightness is higher at the higher rate of technological progress. The reason is that whereas in the case of disembodied progress both revenue and costs rise faster when there is more technological progress, in the case of embodied progress only costs rise in existing jobs. Thus the capitalization effect in the latter case works against job creation, since revenues are received at a flat rate but costs are paid at an increasing rate, in contrast to the former case. Also in this model there is more job destruction at a faster rate of technological progress because optimal horizons are shorter and more obsolescence takes place, in contrast to the case of disembodied progress where the adoption of new technology does not require job destruction.

To derive the implications of the analysis for unemployment and job flows, first note that job creation at time t is

$$C(t) = \theta q(\theta) u(t), \tag{3.58}$$

where $u(t)$ is the unemployment rate. Job destruction is equal to the flow of jobs that attain the age of optimal obsolescence plus the flow of all jobs that experience exogenous destruction. Since the fraction of jobs of each cohort that survives to age T is $e^{-\lambda T}$, given the exogenous destruction rate λ, the total job destruction flow at time t is

$$D(t) = e^{-\lambda T} C(t - T) + \lambda[1 - u(t)]. \tag{3.59}$$

In the steady state both θ and unemployment are constant. Hence the steady-state unemployment rate that equates job creation and job destruction flows is

$$u = \frac{\lambda}{\lambda + (1 - e^{-\lambda T})\theta q(\theta)}. \tag{3.60}$$

Equation (3.60) is a generalization of the Beveridge equation. The higher rate of obsolescence, shown by lower T, shifts this curve to the right; it increases unemployment at given market tightness. Therefore the faster rate of technological progress is unambiguously associated with higher unemployment: Creative job destruction is higher, shifting the Beveridge curve to the right, and market tightness is lower, rotating the job creation line clockwise. The diagrammatic analysis is the same as that for once-for-all productivity gains, shown in figure 2.2, only now the shifts of the curves is in the opposite direction. In terms of the diagram, an economy with faster rate of growth lies on point A, in contrast to one with lower rate of growth which lies on point B.

3.6   Notes on the Literature

The idea that the equilibrium derived in the symmetric job-matching model can be re-expressed as a standard problem of the firm with variable costs of employment adjustment was first formalized in the first edition of this book. However, Mortensen (1970) modeled the firm in his search model as a profit maximizer with adjustment costs, and the main difference between his model and ours is in the wage equation and the specification of equilibrium, not in the modeling of the firm.

The introduction of balanced growth in the search-equilibrium model was also new in the first edition. The respecification of labor's threat point in the wage bargain, which is necessary for balanced growth, was discussed in Pissarides (1987), where the difference between the effects of permanent and temporary productivity shocks was also pointed out. The growth effect highlighted in the first edition of this book is the one that Aghion and Howitt (1994) subsequently termed the capitalization effect. In their study Aghion and Howitt (1994) emphasize, in addition, the creative destruction effect in a model that is similar to the one of this chapter, except that there are no stochastic elements. The discussion of the creative destruction effect in this chapter draws on Mortensen and Pissarides (1998). In the latter paper there is also discussion of a more general model that allows the firm to implement the new technology at a cost. It is shown that as the implementation cost goes to zero, the capitalization effect dominates, and as the implementation cost becomes large, the creative destruction effect dominates. Consequently there is a critical cost at which the effect of growth on unemployment reverses from negative to positive.

The interest rate in all papers mentioned so far is assumed to be exogenous and constant. Eriksson (1997) considered the capitalization effect of growth in an optimizing (Ramsey) model with endogenous interest rate and showed that reasonable parameter values may give the opposite effects from the ones in this chapter, for the reasons explained in the text. The analysis of the Ramsey model in this chapter draws from his paper. He also shows, however, that if growth is endogenous the positive association between growth and employment is restored, a point also made by Falkinger and Zweimuller (1998). The idea that the difficulties of modeling consumption for agents with heterogeneous histories by making the assumption that all agents belong to large family units is due to Merz (1995), though Andolfatto (1996) used a similar "insurance" assumption in his model. It is clearly the case that, though convenient, this assumption can hide a wealth of new results when capital markets are imperfect and the unemployed cannot borrow without collateral, a research agenda not yet taken up in the context of search models.

The job destruction effects of faster growth were also examined by Caballero and Hammour (1994), in a model that bears some similarities to the model of Aghion and Howitt (1994), and by Cohen and Saint-Paul (1994) in a two-sector model with alternating productivity-improving shocks. See also the discussion in Aghion and Howitt (1998, ch. 4). Evidence for the effect of productivity growth on unemployment was examined by Wilson (1995), who found that although on impact a positive shock to productivity growth increases unemployment, in the long run the effect disappears.

King and Welling (1995) examined a model similar to the Lucas-Prescott (1974) model, where a capitalization effect of growth operates on workers, rather than firms, as in the model of this chapter. They find that higher growth increases search activity. Other search models with growth effects can be found in Laing, Palivos, and Wang (1995), Bean and Pissarides (1993), and Acemoglu (1997). Laing et al. (1995) explore endogenous growth propelled by education investments that take place before search, so the parameters of the search model influence growth through workers' education choices. Bean and Pissarides (1993) examine the effect of unemployment on growth by claiming that higher unemployment (1) erodes workers' skills and (2) it reduces savings, both of which are bad for growth. Acemoglu (1997) claims that when workers of different skills compete for the same jobs in markets with search frictions, skilled workers work with less physical capital than in Walrasian markets. This implies that there is less wage inequality and lower rate of return to capital. The latter reduces investment and growth. Jones and Newman (1995) considered the conflict between faster growth and efficiency of matching in a model similar to the one in this chapter, on the assumption that matching efficiency improves with the expected duration of a job.

The idea that productivity growth effects can have a long-lasting, though still temporary, impact on unemployment, because of the dependence of the imputed value of leisure on nonhuman wealth, is due to Phelps. See Phelps (1994, ch. 15) and Phelps and Hoon (1998).

II FURTHER ANALYSIS OF THE LABOR MARKET

4 Labor Turnover and On-the-Job Search

The rate of labor turnover has so far been assumed to be identically equal to the rate of job turnover. This assumption is factually incorrect. Firms replace a large number of quitting employees, consistent with the observation that labor turnover is much larger than job turnover. The implication for our model is that there are reasons other than the arrival of negative productivity shocks that make workers leave their jobs. The empirical literature has identified several reasons, which include retirements from the labor force and new entry, quitting into unemployment, and job-to-job quitting.

In this chapter we generalize the model of chapter 2 to account for these other reasons for labor turnover. The main theme of the chapter is the study of labor market equilibrium when there is search on the job and job-to-job quitting without intervening unemployment. The search and quitting decisions are the outcome of optimal choices by workers. We also study briefly the implications of retirements, new entry and quitting into unemployment, which, however, we assume to be exogenous. We return to the study of optimal participation decisions in chapter 7.

The model that we use to study these issues is the model of chapter 2, with jobs entering at maximum productivity but then moving within the range $(R, 1)$ because of idiosyncratic productivity shocks. We ignore growth effects and obsolescence. We also ignore learning about the job and accumulation of human capital during employment, both of which have been identified by the empirical literature as important factors in quitting decisions.

4.1 Exogenous Labor Turnover

We begin by introducing three new labor flows into the job creation and job destruction model of chapter 2, which are modeled as jump processes with constant exogenous rate: entry into the labor force taking place at rate b (for births), exit from the labor force at rate d (for deaths), and quitting into unemployment to look for another job at rate λ_0.

We assume that all new entrants enter, in the first instance, unemployment to look for a job. Retirements (or deaths) are drawn randomly from the sets of employed and unemployed workers. Although the model does not have an explanation for these flows, the underlying assumption is that they are due to demographic changes. The final flow modeled, quitting into unemployment, is also exogenous. For example, some workers may decide to leave their job to look for another in another area, which necessitates a move to the new area prior to search. Or there might be exogenous shocks to tastes that make workers leave their jobs to look for another while unemployed, caused, for example, by changes in family life or in relations with colleagues in the previous job. As with new entry and retirements, we do not model the reasons for such quitting. We investigate instead the implications of such flows for unemployment and wages. Although endogenous reasons for quitting into unemployment have been suggested in the literature, in particular learning about the nonpecuniary characteristics of the job, we do not model them here. As before, we continue assuming that there are no differences in job qualities.

The retirements and exogenous quitting processes analyzed here, as well as the endogenous job-to-job quitting introduced in the next section, are reasons for job separations unrelated to the idiosyncratic shock process that explained job destruction and job separations in the model of chapter 2. In our model, however, they do not give rise to more labor turnover than job turnover, because of the simplifying assumptions used in the analysis of job destruction. Once a worker leaves, the firm has the option of either closing the job down and reopening another one, or re-advertising it and recruiting another worker to it. In the absence of job destruction and job creation (setup) costs, it is obviously to the firm's advantage to close the job down and create a new one, since by assumption new jobs can be created at maximum productivity. If the old job is re-advertised, productivity will be at the lower level than it was before the worker quit. This is reflected in the formula for the value of an occupied job (e.g., equation (2.4) or (2.11)) where the option value from a job is due entirely to the existence of a worker in the job.

It follows that without further assumptions about job creation and job destruction costs, quitting in this model leads to job destruction. For the sake of expositional clarity we will not introduce new costs in the model, so, as in the model of the preceding chapters, the (theoretical) job turnover and labor turnover rates in the model of this chapter are identical with each other. The empirical literature, however, does not normally classify the replacement of a quitting employee by another, even if in the meantime there is an updating of technology, as separate job destruction and job creation events. In the data it would show up as labor turnover in a continuing job and only changes in employment will show up as job creation or job destruction. Thus, despite the strict interpretation of the model of this chapter as one where there is no distinction between job turnover and labor turnover, the correct empirical interpretation of the model is one where the job separations due to idiosyncratic productivity shocks lead to job turnover, whereas the job separations due to quitting (in the absence of productivity shocks) cause labor turnover without job turnover.

As before, we assume that there is a jump process that shocks idiosyncratic productivity at rate λ. This leads to job destruction and a flow into unemployment of $\lambda G(R)(1 - u)L$ workers, with L denoting the total labor force. In addition there is now a flow of new entrants bL into unemployment and quits $\lambda_0(1 - u)L$. The exits from unemployment are the retirements, duL, and the total matches of unemployed workers with vacant jobs which we write, as previously, as $q(\theta)\theta uL$ Total unemployment is given by uL, so its evolution is given by

$$\frac{d}{dt}uL = [\lambda G(R) + \lambda_0](1 - u)L + bL - duL - q(\theta)\theta uL. \tag{4.1}$$

Using the dot notation for time derivatives, we derive the evolution of the unemployment *rate* (the ratio of total unemployment to the labor force) as

$$\dot{u} = [\lambda G(R) + \lambda_0](1 - u) + b - du - q(\theta)\theta u - \frac{u\dot{L}}{L}. \tag{4.2}$$

The rate of growth of the labor force, $\dot{L}/L$, is given by total entry less total exit, $b - d$, so substitution into (4.2) gives the following equation for the evolution of the rate of unemployment:

$$\dot{u} = [\lambda G(R) + \lambda_0 + b](1 - u) - q(\theta)\theta u. \tag{4.3}$$

The steady-state level of unemployment derived from (4.3) is

$$u = \frac{\lambda G(R) + \lambda_0 + b}{\lambda G(R) + \lambda_0 + b + q(\theta)\theta}. \tag{4.4}$$

Equation (4.4) is the Beveridge curve when there is labor turnover over and above the rate of job turnover. The rate of quitting into unemployment and the entry rate shift the Beveridge curve to the right. The retirement rate has no influence on the curve. Hence, other things equal, population groups or countries with higher entry rates or quitting rates should have higher equilibrium unemployment rates than other groups or countries. We will see that these predictions generalize (with some caveats) when we consider the endogenous determination of job creation and job destruction.

The retirement rate does not influence the Beveridge curve because of our assumption that retirements are at the same rate from both unemployment and employment. If the rate of retirements from unemployment is higher than the rate of retirements from employment, the average retirement rate shifts the Beveridge curve to the left, implying lower equilibrium unemployment rate at given vacancy rate.

Consider now the determination of the job creation and job destruction flows with the exogenous quit rates. The value of a vacant job is given, as before, by

$$rV = -pc + q(\theta)[J(1) - V], \tag{4.5}$$

so the zero-profit condition that determines the creation of job vacancies, $V = 0$, implies that

$$J(1) = \frac{pc}{q(\theta)}. \tag{4.6}$$

As before, the value of a filled job is distinguished by the idiosyncratic productivity of the job and new jobs are created at maximum productivity.

The equation that gives the value of a filled job now changes to reflect the fact that a job may be terminated for one of three reasons, the arrival of idiosyncratic productivity shocks, λ, the quitting of the holder of the job, λ_0, and the retirement of the holder, d. Only the first of these may move the value of the job to another positive value, the other two leading to zero returns with probability 1. Hence, for any idiosyncratic productivity x, $J(x)$ satisfies

$$rJ(x) = px - w(x) + \lambda \int_R^1 J(s)dG(s) - (\lambda + \lambda_0 + d)J(x). \tag{4.7}$$

Capital is ignored throughout under the assumption that there is a perfect market in second-hand capital. The wage rate is determined as before by the Nash solution to the wage bargain, so for the moment is shown as a general function of productivity. Under the assumption that profit is monotonically increasing in productivity, job destruction satisfies the reservation rule, which is implicit in (4.7).

The worker's returns from holding a job with productivity x are given by

$$rW(x) = w(x) + \lambda \int_R^1 W(s)dG(s) - (\lambda + \lambda_0 + d)W(x) + [\lambda G(R) + \lambda_0]U. \quad (4.8)$$

We have assumed that exit from the labor force due to retirement has no utility. The returns from the state of unemployment under the same assumptions satisfy

$$rU = z + \theta q(\theta)[W(1) - U] - dU, \quad (4.9)$$

where as before z is unemployment income.

By straightforward substitutions, we find that the Nash wage equation once again shares the job surplus in fixed proportions, with fraction β going to the worker. Hence, for all x, and given the zero-profit condition for vacancy creation,

$$W(x) - U = \frac{\beta}{1 - \beta} J(x), \quad (4.10)$$

and therefore

$$w(x) = (1 - \beta)z + \beta p(x + c\theta). \quad (4.11)$$

It remains to derive the job creation and job destruction conditions with the wage equation in (4.11). We proceed as in the model of chapter 2. Substitution of the wage equation into the condition for job value, (4.7), gives

$$(r + \lambda + \lambda_0 + d)J(x) = (1 - \beta)(px - z) - \beta pc\theta + \lambda \int_R^1 J(s)dG(s). \quad (4.12)$$

As expected, the value of the job is monotonically increasing in x. Therefore job destruction satisfies the same reservation property as in the model of chapter 2. Jobs with idiosyncratic productivity $x < R$ are destroyed, with R satisfying $J(R) = 0$. Making use of this property in (4.12), we get, after calculating $J(x) - J(R)$,

$$J(x) = (1 - \beta)\frac{p(x - R)}{r + \lambda + \lambda_0 + d}. \tag{4.13}$$

From this expression we derive the job creation and job destruction conditions, as we did before for the model of chapter 2.

Substitution of $J(x)$ for $x = 1$ from (4.13) into (4.6) gives the new job creation condition

$$(1 - \beta)\frac{1 - R}{r + \lambda + \lambda_0 + d} = \frac{c}{q(\theta)}. \tag{4.14}$$

This equation generalizes equation (2.14) of the model without exogenous labor turnover. To derive the generalization of the job destruction condition, (2.15), we make use of (4.13) and (4.12) to get

$$R - \frac{z}{p} - \frac{\beta c}{1 - \beta}\theta + \frac{\lambda}{r + \lambda + \lambda_0 + d}\int_R^1 (s - R)dG(s) = 0. \tag{4.15}$$

This completes the description of equilibrium of the model. Equations (4.14) and (4.15) give the equilibrium market tightness and reservation productivity. With knowledge of market tightness, equation (4.11) gives the wage rate in each job, and with knowledge of both market tightness and reservation productivity, the Beveridge equation gives equilibrium unemployment.

The effect of the three new turnover rates on equilibrium, the entry rate b, the exit rate d, and the turnover rate λ_0, is found by investigating their role in this system of four equations. The entry rate and exit rate are the easiest rates to analyze. The entry rate shifts only the Beveridge curve and has no influence elsewhere. Therefore it does not change the job creation and job destruction rates, and also has no influence on wages, but increases both unemployment and vacancies by the same proportion. Market tightness is unaffected. The reason for this is simple. The higher entry rate simply means that more people are joining the unemployment pool from outside the labor force. Because of the search externalities and constant returns to scale in the matching and production functions, more vacancies also enter the market, to match the higher number of workers. Wages and profits from existing or new jobs are unaffected. Of course, implicit in this is the assumption that capital increases to match the increase in labor, so the equilibrium described is a long-run equilibrium.

The exit rate d does not shift the Beveridge curve but influences both the job creation and job destruction conditions. Inspection of the two equations (4.14) and (4.15) shows that the exit rate is added to the rate of discount. The reason is that higher exit rate increases the probability that the job will terminate sooner. It therefore reduces market tightness at given reservation productivity by reducing the expected duration of the job, and increases the reservation productivity at given tightness because the option value of the job becomes lower. As with the analysis of higher interest rate in chapter 2, the overall effect on tightness is negative but the effect on the reservation productivity is ambiguous because the fall in tightness pushes the reservation productivity in the opposite direction. If, however, the effect through tightness (and job creation) dominates, the influence of higher exit rate on unemployment is negative.

Higher labor turnover rate λ_0 influences the equilibrium set of equations through both previous channels by shifting the Beveridge curve to the right as the entry rate does, and by increasing the effective discount rate as the exit rate does. The reason is that a higher turnover rate does two things: It increases the flow into unemployment and reduces the expected duration of jobs. The overall effect of the higher rate of quitting into unemployment on job creation, job destruction, and unemployment is shown in figure 4.1. Higher λ_0 shifts the job creation curve to the left and the job destruction curve up (panel a). The effect on market tightness is negative but the effect on the reservation productivity is ambiguous (shown in figure 4.1 as a rise). The rate of interest and rate of retirement have similar effects on job creation and job destruction.

In the Beveridge diagram (panel b) the job creation line rotates clockwise, but the Beveridge curve, which is influenced by R, may or may not shift out. It is pushed outward by the direct influence of λ_0 (see equation (4.4)), which is an effect similar to that of a rise in the birth rate. In addition it shifts either to the right or to the left depending on whether R rises or falls, an effect that is absent when the birth rate rises. In the diagram it is shown as an outward shift, implying an increase in unemployment and either a rise or a fall in vacancies.

It is now clear from the analysis that the effect of different rates of growth of the labor force on equilibrium depend on whether the differences are due to higher birth rate or lower death rate. If it is due to a

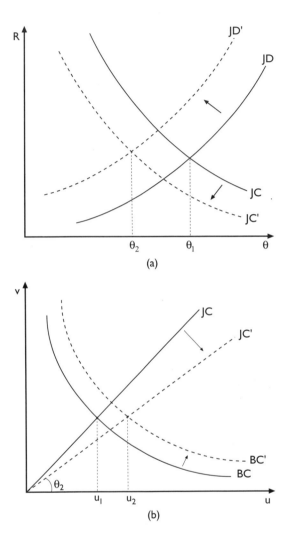

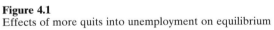

Figure 4.1
Effects of more quits into unemployment on equilibrium

combination of the two, the lower death rate has the same effect in the job creation and job destruction diagram (figure 4.1, panel a) as a lower λ_0; that is, it increases market tightness and has ambiguous effects on the reservation productivity. The higher birth rate does not influence the job creation–job destruction diagram but shifts the Beveridge curve out. So, if the change in R in panel a is small and can be ignored, the higher rate of growth of the labor force shifts the Beveridge curve out through the higher birth rate and rotates the job creation line counterclockwise through the lower death rate. The number of vacancies and market tightness both go up, but unemployment does not rise unless the changes through the birth rate dominate those through the death rate.

4.2 Search on the Job

We now turn to the main theme of this chapter, the analysis of search on the job and job-to-job movements. For the sake of simplicity, we ignore other reasons for labor turnover, so the three turnover rates of the preceding section are now set to zero. Consistent with our assumptions that there is perfect foresight, including full knowledge of each side's actual and expected returns and the transition probabilities for each, we assume that when the worker is searching on the job, the firm knows it and that the Nash bargain that determines wages takes it into account. This implies, in general, that the wages for job seekers are different from the wages of those that do not search on the job. We will see that the optimal search strategy is determined by a reservation rule. As before, there is a reservation productivity R such that jobs with idiosyncratic productivities below R are destroyed. But now there is also a second reservation productivity S, such that workers in jobs with idiosyncratic productivities between R and S search on the job. Workers in jobs with productivities above S do not search.

The rates at which employed and unemployed workers move into new jobs are, as before, derived from an aggregate matching function. For simplicity, we do not distinguish between employed and unemployed job seekers in the aggregate matching function. If unemployment is again u, vacancies v and the number of employed job seekers is denoted by $e \leq 1 - u$, we write the aggregate matching function as

$$m = m(v, u + e). \tag{4.16}$$

Under the assumption of constant returns to scale, the rate at which workers arrive to vacancies is a function of the ratio of vacancies to all job seekers. We use the same notation as before,

$$q(\theta) \equiv m\left(1, \frac{u+e}{v}\right), \tag{4.17}$$

but with θ now denoting the ratio $v/(u + e)$.

We have already implicitly assumed that employed and unemployed workers search with the same intensity and that they are equally good at finding jobs. Therefore jobs arrive to each searching worker at the same rate which, as before, is equal to $\theta q(\theta)$. Thus the quitting probability for employed job seekers is $\theta q(\theta)$ as is the transition rate for unemployed workers. As with the exogenous quit rate of the preceding section, when a worker quits to take another job, the returns to the firm drop from $J(x)$ to zero. The returns from the new job to the worker are, however, always $W(1)$ because all job vacancies enjoy the highest productivity. The Nash sharing rules that we have been using require that the worker compensate the firm, through appropriate wage adjustments, for this asymmetry in expected returns after a quit. So, for given job productivity, the wage rate for a worker who searches on the job should be lower than the wage rate for a worker not searching.

Suppose that on-the-job search costs a fixed amount $\sigma \geq 0$. We will see that even at zero search cost not all employed workers below productivity 1 will search. Workers in jobs with productivity 1, of course, will not search because they are earning the highest wage in the market. Variable search costs are not introduced to avoid complicating the problem, but we will return to this question in chapter 5 when we consider variable search intensity by unemployed job seekers.

The approach that we follow in order to find the optimal search strategy is to calculate the worker's returns for each productivity x when he is and when he is not searching on the job. Let the former be $W^s(x)$ and the latter $W^{ns}(x)$. Then search on the job takes place at productivity x when $W^s(x) \geq W^{ns}(x)$. Trivially, at maximum productivity, search on the job is not optimal,

$$W^s(1) \leq W^{ns}(1). \tag{4.18}$$

The reservation productivity, if it exists, satisfies

$$W^s(S) = W^{ns}(S).\tag{4.19}$$

The existence of a reservation rule for search on the job requires first that the difference $W^s(x) - W^{ns}(x)$ decreases in x; that is, as the job's productivity decreases, the worker's net gain from search on the job increases. In addition it requires that the crossing point S be above R because the search on the job takes place at all $x < S$ and only jobs with productivities $x \geq R$ are active.

Whether the latter is satisfied or not depends on the cost of search, which we have assumed to be exogenous and constant. To avoid trivial outcomes for search on the job, we assume that the cost σ is sufficiently small to imply that if there is a reservation rule defined by S, then $S > R$. But first we need to demonstrate that the reservation rule exists, namely that $W^s(x) - W^{ns}(x)$ decreases in x.

The expected returns of the employed worker when he does and when he does not search respectively satisfy

$$rW^s(x) = w^s(x) - \sigma + \lambda \int_R^1 \max(W^{ns}(s), W^s(s))dG(s) + \lambda G(R)U$$
$$- \lambda W^s(x) + \theta q(\theta)[W^{ns}(1) - W^s(x)]\tag{4.20}$$

and

$$rW^{ns}(x) = w^{ns}(x) + \lambda \int_R^1 \max(W^{ns}(s), W^s(s))dG(s) + \lambda G(R)U - \lambda W^{ns}(x).\tag{4.21}$$

Wages are distinguished by superscripts to emphasize the fact that the Nash bargain solution gives a different wage outcome when there is and when there is no search on the job. Equation (4.21) does not need much explanation because it is the same as the expression that we had before in the model of chapter 2. Equation (4.20) includes in addition the cost of search and the capital gain that is enjoyed when the worker finds another job and makes the transition without intervening unemployment.

Search on the job at productivity x takes place when $W^s(x) \geq W^{ns}(x)$, which, from (4.20) and (4.21), requires

$$\theta q(\theta)[W^{ns}(1) - W^s(x)] \geq w^{ns}(x) - w^s(x) + \sigma.\tag{4.22}$$

The left-hand side of (4.22) shows the expected return from on-the-job search, the gain in expected returns from the change of job multiplied by the probability of making that gain. The right-hand side is the total cost of search on the job, the wage reduction that takes place when the worker searches on the job plus the direct cost of search.

Wages share the surplus created by the job match, so for job seekers,

$$W^s(x) - U = \frac{\beta}{1-\beta} J^s(x), \tag{4.23}$$

and a similar expression is satisfied for nonseekers. Because β is a constant between 0 and 1, it follows that if it is optimal for the worker employed at productivity x to search on the job, then the firm is also made better off by the worker's search, namely $J^s(x) \geq J^{ns}(x)$. The value of a filled job to the employer therefore satisfies

$$rJ^s(x) = px - w^s(x) + \lambda \int_R^1 \max(J^s(s), J^{ns}(s)) dG(s) - [\lambda + \theta q(\theta)] J^s(x) \tag{4.24}$$

when there is search on the job, and when there is no search,

$$rJ^{ns}(x) = px - w^{ns}(x) + \lambda \int_R^1 \max(J^s(s), J^{ns}(s)) dG(s) - \lambda J^{ns}(x). \tag{4.25}$$

Note that in (4.24) we have taken into account the fact that the job may be destroyed for two reasons, the arrival of a bad productivity shock and the quit of the worker.

The zero-profit condition on vacancy creation is, once again, (4.6). The expected returns from unemployment still satisfy (4.9), with $d = 0$. Therefore, given the Nash sharing rule applied to new jobs,

$$rU = z + \frac{\beta}{1-\beta} pc\theta. \tag{4.26}$$

With knowledge of the value expressions for occupied and filled jobs, we can now proceed as in chapter 2 and derive the wage equations by substituting from the value expressions into the Nash sharing rules (4.23). For jobs where there is no search on the job, the wage equation is the same as before,

$$w^{ns}(x) = (1-\beta)z + \beta p(x + c\theta). \tag{4.27}$$

For jobs where it is optimal to search, the derived wage equation implies that the wage rate increases by a fraction $(1 - \beta)$ of the direct cost of search, σ, but falls by the same fraction of the expected return from search, $\beta pc\theta/(1 - \beta)$:

$$w^s(x) = (1 - \beta)(z + \sigma) + \beta px. \tag{4.28}$$

The wage equation for job seekers reflects the fact that the cost of search is borne by the worker and that the benefits also accrue to the worker. Because the wage bargain shares the costs and benefits from on-the-job search according to the parameter β, the firm compensates the worker for a fraction $(1 - \beta)$ of the costs and takes from the worker a fraction $(1 - \beta)$ of the expected returns from search.

That the wage rate without on-the-job search is the same as before is not surprising. What is surprising is that the wage rate of those searching for another job is independent of outside market conditions. It depends only on the worker's income when unemployed, his cost of search, and his productivity. The difference between the two wages at given x is

$$w^{ns}(x) - w^s(x) = (1 - \beta)\left(\frac{\beta}{1 - \beta} pc\theta - \sigma\right), \tag{4.29}$$

which is unambiguously positive. Noting that $\beta pc\theta/(1 - \beta)$ is, in equilibrium, equal to the expected return from search, this property should be obvious. But we can also show it more formally. Substitution of the two wage equations into the condition for the optimality of search, (4.22), gives the result that search on the job takes place at productivity x when

$$W^{ns}(1) - W^s(x) \geq \beta \frac{pc}{q(\theta)} + \beta \frac{\sigma}{\theta q(\theta)}. \tag{4.30}$$

Rearrangement of (4.30) gives

$$W^{ns}(1) - U - \beta \frac{pc}{q(\theta)} \geq \beta \frac{\sigma}{\theta q(\theta)} + W^s(x) - U, \tag{4.31}$$

and application of the sharing rules (4.23) and zero-profit condition (4.6) gives

$$\frac{\beta}{1 - \beta} pc\theta \geq \sigma + \frac{\theta q(\theta)}{1 - \beta} J^s(x). \tag{4.32}$$

Since for all active jobs, $J^s(x) \geq 0$, (4.32) gives the required result, $\beta pc\theta/(1 - \beta) \geq \sigma$. Thus the wage rate received by job seekers is a lower fraction of their productivity than the wage rate received by workers who do not search on the job.

Condition (4.30) establishes two further important properties of search on the job. First, search on the job satisfies the reservation property. With the wage equation given by (4.28), it trivially follows that $W^{s\prime}(x) \geq 0$. The left-hand side of (4.30) decreases monotonically in x, whereas the right-hand side is independent of it. Therefore there is a reservation productivity S such that in jobs with productivity below S the worker searches on the job and in jobs with productivity above it there is no search. (We have assumed that the parameters are such that $S > R$.)

Second, the gain from search on the job has to be strictly positive even if the direct cost of search, σ, is zero; otherwise, no search is undertaken. That is, $S < 1$ at all $\sigma \geq 0$. The reason for this is that when the worker finds another job and quits, he imposes costs on his current employer for which he has to compensate him when employed. The cost to the employer is the loss of the job value $J^s(x)$. The gain that the worker is able to extract from his new employer is only a fraction β of total revenue because of the nature of the Nash bargain. Therefore at zero search cost the profit from the current job has to be less than a fraction β of the profit from the new job if search is to be undertaken. The new job has idiosyncratic productivity $x = 1$. Search on the job at zero cost does not take place in jobs with high idiosyncratic productivities, where profits are higher than a fraction β of profits at $x = 1$.

To derive this more formally, we use the Nash sharing rules and the zero-profit condition for vacancies in (4.30) to re-write it in the more convenient form:

$$J^s(x) \leq \beta J^{ns}(1) - (1 - \beta)\frac{\sigma}{\theta q(\theta)}. \tag{4.33}$$

Note that $1/\theta q(\theta)$ is the expected duration of search, so the last term in (4.33) is the fraction of the expected cost of search borne by the employer. $\beta J^{ns}(1)$ is the worker's share of profits from a new job after a quit, whereas $J^s(x)$ is the cost of the quit to the current employer. As claimed, even with $\sigma = 0$, the profit from the current job needs to be less than a fraction β of the profit from the new job if search is to take place. Of course this cannot be socially optimal. Social optimality requires that search on the job should take place at all x that satisfy

$$W^s(x) + J^s(x) \leq W^{ns}(1) + J^{ns}(1) - \frac{\sigma}{\theta q(\theta)}. \tag{4.34}$$

By the Nash sharing rules, (4.34) implies that

$$J^s(x) \leq J^{ns}(1) - (1-\beta)\frac{\sigma}{\theta q(\theta)}. \tag{4.35}$$

Comparison with (4.33) shows that there is too little search. The worker, who chooses whether to search or not, ignores the benefits that will accrue to his new employer from his search. For example, if the cost of search is zero, all workers in jobs below maximum productivity should search. But if $\beta < 1$, as it must be if there is a nontrivial equilibrium, there are some workers with productivity strictly below maximum that do not search.

4.3 Equilibrium

An equilibrium is a pair of reservation productivities R, S, a value for labor market tightness θ, a wage rate for each productivity $w(x)$, and a path for unemployment. Note that in this model θ is the ratio of vacancies to all job seekers, so if we want to know the equilibrium rate of vacancies, we need to know the equilibrium rate of both unemployment and employed job seekers. With knowledge of R and S, the number of employed job seekers is given by all workers employed in jobs with idiosyncratic productivities in the range $[R, S]$. Changes in the number of employed job seekers come from productivity shocks that move jobs in and out of the relevant range and from employed job seekers who find jobs. Following the arrival of a productivity shock, the sum of new entry into the range $[R, S]$ and re-entry by jobs already in the range is $\lambda(1-u)[G(S) - G(R)]$. The number of jobs in the range that get a shock is λe, and the number of jobs that exit because the worker employed in them found another job is $\theta q(\theta)e$. Therefore the evolution of the number of employed job seekers, e, is given by

$$\dot{e} = \lambda(1-u)[G(S) - G(R)] - \lambda e - \theta q(\theta)e. \tag{4.36}$$

In the steady state

$$e = \frac{\lambda[G(S) - G(R)]}{\lambda + \theta q(\theta)}(1 - u). \tag{4.37}$$

The evolution of unemployment is given as before by

$$\dot{u} = \lambda G(R)(1 - u) - q(\theta)\theta u, \tag{4.38}$$

so, as in the model of chapter 2, we need know only θ and R to solve for it. The existence of on-the-job search influences unemployment only to the extent that it influences the equilibrium values of θ and R. With knowledge of e from (4.36) and u from (4.38), vacancies are given by

$$v = \theta(u + e). \tag{4.39}$$

We have already shown that the wage rate is given by (4.28) when $R \le x \le S$ and by (4.27) when $S \le x \le 1$. Therefore the wage equations can be obtained with knowledge of $R, S,$ and θ. So the key block of equations in this model is the one that gives the simultaneous solution for R, S, and θ. Once we know the solutions to this block, we can get the evolution of employment, unemployment, employed job seekers, vacancies, and wages.

To derive the block of equations that determines R, S, and θ, we rewrite the expressions for the expected profit from a filled job when there is and when there is no on-the-job search, (4.24) and (4.25), by substituting into them the wage equations, (4.28) and (4.27). The results are

$$(r + \lambda)J^{ns}(x) = (1 - \beta)(px - z) - \beta pc\theta + \lambda \int_R^1 \max(J^{ns}(s), J^s(s))dG(s) \tag{4.40}$$

and

$$(r + \lambda + \theta q(\theta))J^s(x) = (1 - \beta)(px - z - \sigma) + \lambda \int_R^1 \max(J^{ns}(s), J^s(s))dG(s). \tag{4.41}$$

It follows trivially from these expressions that both $J^{ns}(x)$ and $J^s(x)$ are increasing in x, confirming the fact that the reservation properties hold for both S and R.

The expected profit from the job with the reservation productivity S has the property that $J^{ns}(S) = J^s(S) \equiv J(S)$. Hence (4.40) and (4.41) imply (consistent with (4.32)) that

$$J(S) = \beta \frac{pc}{q(\theta)} - (1 - \beta)\frac{\sigma}{\theta q(\theta)}. \tag{4.42}$$

But as before, $J^s(R) = 0$, so (4.41) implies that for all x in the range $[R, S]$,

$$J^s(x) = (1 - \beta)\frac{p(x - R)}{r + \lambda + \theta q(\theta)}. \tag{4.43}$$

Combining (4.42) and (4.43) for $x = S$, we get the first equation of the block that solves R, S, and θ, the one for the search reservation threshold S:

$$\frac{S - R}{r + \lambda + \theta q(\theta)} = \frac{\beta}{1 - \beta}\frac{c}{q(\theta)} - \frac{\sigma/p}{\theta q(\theta)}. \tag{4.44}$$

The condition for job creation is derived from the expression for the initial job value, $J^{ns}(1)$, and the zero-profit condition for job vacancies. From (4.40) we get that

$$(r + \lambda)[J^{ns}(1) - J(S)] = (1 - \beta)p(1 - S). \tag{4.45}$$

Making use of (4.42) and the free entry condition $J^{ns}(1) = pc/q(\theta)$, we derive

$$\frac{1 - S}{r + \lambda} = \frac{c}{q(\theta)} + \frac{\sigma/p}{\theta q(\theta)}. \tag{4.46}$$

This is the second equation of the key block that solves for R, S, and θ. It can be turned into a more familiar form by making use of the search condition (4.44) to write it as

$$(1 - \beta)\frac{1 - R}{r + \lambda} = \frac{c}{q(\theta)} + \frac{\beta c\theta - (1 - \beta)\sigma/p}{r + \lambda}. \tag{4.47}$$

This form of the job creation condition can be compared more easily with the corresponding condition without on-the-job search, (2.14), or (4.14). The existence of on-the-job search adds the last term of the right side of (4.47), which represents the gain from on-the-job search going to the firm. Since this gain is always positive, condition (4.47) states that the expected productivity gain from a new job (the left-hand side of the equation) net of the gain from on-the-job search has to compensate the firm for the expected job creation cost.

To derive the final equation, for the reservation R we impose the job destruction condition $J^s(R) = 0$ in (4.41). To simplify the notation, we denote the option value of the job by Λ and write

$$\Lambda = \lambda \int_R^1 \max(J^{ns}(s), J^s(s)) dG(s)$$
$$= \lambda \int_R^S J^s(s) dG(s) + \lambda \int_S^1 J^{ns}(s) dG(s). \tag{4.48}$$

Making use of (4.43) and a similar expression for $J^{ns}(x)$ derived from (4.40),

$$J^{ns}(x) = \frac{1-\beta}{r+\lambda} p(x - R) - \frac{1-\beta}{r+\lambda} \left(\frac{\beta}{1-\beta} pc\theta - \sigma \right), \tag{4.49}$$

we re-write the option value of the job as

$$\Lambda = \lambda(1-\beta)p \left(\frac{1}{r+\lambda+\theta q(\theta)} \int_R^S (s - R) dG(s) + \frac{1}{r+\lambda} \int_S^1 (s - R) dG(s) \right)$$
$$- \frac{\lambda(1-\beta)p}{r+\lambda} \left(\frac{\beta}{1-\beta} c\theta - \frac{\sigma}{p} \right)(1 - G(S)). \tag{4.50}$$

Noting (4.44), we establish that $\Lambda(.)$ is locally independent of S, by the envelope theorem. So we can simplify (4.50) to

$$\Lambda = \lambda(1-\beta)p\Lambda(R, \theta, \sigma), \tag{4.51}$$

with

$$\frac{\partial \Lambda}{\partial \theta} < 0 \tag{4.52}$$

and

$$\frac{\partial \Lambda}{\partial R} = -\frac{1-G(S)}{r+\lambda} - \frac{G(S)-G(R)}{r+\lambda+\theta q(\theta)} < 0. \tag{4.53}$$

Also trivially

$$\frac{\partial \Lambda}{\partial \sigma} = \frac{1-G(S)}{r+\lambda} \frac{1}{p} > 0. \tag{4.54}$$

Making use now of (4.41) and (4.51), we re-write the job destruction condition $J^s(R) = 0$ as

$$R + \lambda\Lambda(R, \theta, \sigma) = \frac{z + \sigma}{p}. \tag{4.55}$$

As in the model without on-the-job search, the reservation productivity covers the worker's costs net of the option value of the job. The option value now is lower, however, by an amount that depends on the returns from on-the-job search. The intuition is that since now the job match can be dissolved because of on-the-job search, the value of keeping it open is less.

Equations (4.44), (4.47), and (4.55) jointly determine R, S, and θ. We analyze their properties with the help of diagrams of the kind that we used before.

The job creation condition (4.47) gives a negatively sloped curve in R, θ space, for reasons similar to the ones in the model without on-the-job search. For given R, however, the curve now lies to the left of the one without on-the-job search, namely at given R, market tightness is everywhere less, because the existence of on-the-job search implies on average a shorter job duration. Also the curve is now steeper because higher θ now increases the expected returns from search, reducing expected job durations further.

The job destruction condition (4.55) is upward-sloping because by substitution,

$$1 + \lambda\frac{\partial\Lambda}{\partial R} > 0. \tag{4.56}$$

Of course, the job destruction curve without on-the-job search also had positive slope (see figure 2.1). The reasons for the positive slope now, however, are different from the ones in the model without on-the-job search. In the model without on-the-job search, higher θ implied more job destruction because of the effect of θ on wages, whereas when there is on-the-job search higher θ reduces the option value of the job. The option value falls for two reasons. First, higher θ implies that a given amount of job search is more likely to lead to faster job destruction because the worker is more likely to find another job and quit. Second, when θ is higher, more search is undertaken. This again implies higher R, because the job is more likely to be destroyed within a given time interval.

Our discussion of job creation and job destruction leads to the conclusion that the R, θ pair is uniquely determined in a diagram similar to figure 2.1. With knowledge of R and θ, the reservation productivity for search on the job is determined from (4.44). Wages are given by (4.28) for productivities in the range $[R, S]$ and by (4.27) for jobs with productivities above S. Finally the path of unemployment is given by (4.38) and the path of the stock of workers who search on the job by (4.36).

4.4   The Implications of On-the-Job Search for Equilibrium

What are the properties of the equilibrium with search on the job, and how does the equilibrium with search compare with the equilibrium without search? We take up these questions in this and the next section. We investigate only the properties of the steady-state equilibrium, by studying the implications of higher or lower search costs for equilibrium. Since the model without on-the-job search can be interpreted as a special case of the model of this chapter, with search costs sufficiently high, our approach is general. Then, as we did in the model without search on the job, we study in the next section the effects of higher common productivity p, which by the structure of the model are the same as the effects of lower unemployment income z.

Before beginning the comparison, we note that market tightness, θ, has common definition in the two models, to the extent that it is the ratio of job vacancies to job seekers. But since in the model without on-the-job search only the unemployed search, the ratio of vacancies to unemployment in the two models is likely to behave differently, even if θ behaves similarly. We refer to θ as market tightness in both models and return to the behavior of the ratio of vacancies to unemployment later in this section. We will show that the more general definition of θ in this model has some interesting implications for the Beveridge curve.

The key block of equations that determine equilibrium in both models are the equations that determine the pair R, θ. We saw that in both models equilibrium job creation can be represented by a downward-sloping curve in R, θ space and equilibrium job destruction by an upward-sloping curve. The job creation curve is steeper when there is search on the job, but we will ignore such differences in slopes in the discussion that follows.

The behavior of the reservation productivity for search decisions is obtained from (4.44), which gives the productivity range over which there is search on the job. With knowledge of R, S, and θ, we can derive the following stocks and flows in steady-state equilibrium.

The rate of unemployment is given, as before, by

$$u = \frac{\lambda G(R)}{\lambda G(R) + \theta q(\theta)}. \tag{4.57}$$

The fraction of employed workers who search is obtained from (4.37), and it is

$$\frac{e}{1-u} = \frac{\lambda[G(S) - G(R)]}{\lambda + \theta q(\theta)}. \tag{4.58}$$

The number of job-to-job quits is $e\theta q(\theta)$, so the quit rate is

$$\frac{e}{1-u}\theta q(\theta) = \lambda[G(S) - G(R)]\frac{\theta q(\theta)}{\lambda + \theta q(\theta)}. \tag{4.59}$$

Finally, as before, the job destruction rate is $\lambda G(R)$, and the job creation rate $u\theta q(\theta)/(1-u)$. For future reference we use (4.57) to substitute θ out of (4.58) and write the quit rate in terms of the reservation productivities and unemployment only:

$$\frac{e}{1-u} = \frac{[G(S) - G(R)]u}{u + (1-u)G(R)}. \tag{4.60}$$

Consider first the role of the cost of search, σ, in the equilibrium just described. For given R the job creation condition (4.47) implies that θ is higher when σ is higher. The reason is that when the cost of search is higher, the expected returns from search are lower, and so, for given R, fewer workers search on the job. The expected duration of a job is then higher, implying more job creation. In figure 4.2 higher σ shifts the job creation line to the right, from JC to JC'.

The cost of search also enters the job destruction curve, (4.55). By (4.54), (4.55), and (4.56) higher σ raises the reservation productivity, implying more job destruction at given market tightness. Inspection of (4.55) shows that the reason for this effect is that the firm has to pay some of the cost of search through higher wages. In figure 4.2, σ shifts the job destruction curve up, from JD to JD'.

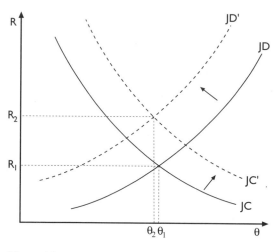

Figure 4.2
Implications of less search on the job (higher search cost) for reservation productivity and market tightness

The reservation productivity is unambiguously higher when the two shifts are combined, implying more job destruction. Differentiation of (4.44), (4.47), and (4.55) with respect to σ establishes that higher σ also implies lower θ and so less job creation (both for given unemployment). The most intuitive way to understand these results is to think of the job match as a joint venture between firm and worker which offers, in addition to the production possibilities, the opportunity to search on the job for a more productive match. A higher cost of search reduces the expected rewards from search and so makes the job less rewarding for the firm-worker pair. The job is therefore more likely to be destroyed when negative shocks arrive and fewer jobs are created.

To find the effect of search costs on search on the job, we differentiate (4.44) with respect to σ to get

$$\frac{\partial S}{\partial \sigma} - \frac{\partial R}{\partial \sigma} = \frac{\partial S}{\partial \theta}\frac{\partial \theta}{\partial \sigma} - \frac{r + \lambda + \theta q(\theta)}{\theta q(\theta)}\frac{1}{p}, \tag{4.61}$$

where

$$\frac{\partial S}{\partial \theta} = \frac{\beta c}{1 - \beta}\left(1 + \eta\frac{r + \lambda}{\theta q(\theta)}\right) + \frac{(1 - \eta)(r + \lambda)\sigma/p}{\theta^2 q(\theta)} > 0 \tag{4.62}$$

and η is, as before, the elasticity of $q(\theta)$. Therefore (4.61) implies that the gap between S and R, when σ is higher, narrows for two reasons: First, because of the direct effects of search costs on search activity on the job, which is negative, and second because with lower tightness, the expected arrival of job offers during search is lower.

Now, because R increases in σ, we do not know if S rises or falls in response to a higher σ. But this is not a serious shortcoming. The interesting question is whether S rises or falls in relation to R, since it is the gap between R and S that determines how much search on the job is taking place. We have shown that this gap narrows, so search on the job takes place over a smaller productivity range when search costs are higher.

Unemployment is higher at higher search costs, by (4.57), because R is higher and θ lower: The higher rate of job destruction and lower rate of job creation at given initial unemployment bring about a rise in the equilibrium unemployment rate. The number of employees who search on the job, e, is lower at higher cost, by virtue of (4.57) and (4.58). But we cannot in general tell how the fraction of employed workers who search on the job responds, since both employment and the number of workers who search on the job are lower (see (4.57); the ambiguity arises because both $G(S) - G(R)$ and θ are lower). But (4.60) implies that for given unemployment, the fraction of workers who search is lower because the difference $G(S) - G(R)$ is lower and the job destruction range $G(R)$ higher. Finally, and crucially, the job-to-job quit rate, given by (4.59), is lower.

To summarize the most important implications of more search on the job for equilibrium, we have shown that lower search costs imply lower job destruction and higher job creation rates at given unemployment rate, and so lower unemployment in equilibrium and more job-to-job quitting. The implications of on-the-job search for wages are easily obtained from (4.27) and (4.28). When search costs are lower, wages in productivities $x \geq S$, where there is no search, rise because of the rise in market tightness. But wages in the productivity range $R \leq x < S$ are lower by a fraction of the search cost. Thus wage inequality is higher when search costs are lower and more workers search on the job.

The existence of on-the-job search has some interesting implications for the Beveridge curve. Without on-the-job search, the Beveridge curve has the form shown in figure 2.2. Equilibrium vacancies and unemployment are given by the intersection of the Beveridge curve, which slopes downward and is convex to the origin, and by a straight line through the origin. With on-the-job search, vacancies are given by $v = (u + e)\theta$, which is again a straight line but has a positive intercept and shifts when the number of employed job seekers, e, changes. The reason for this shift is that the number of vacancies that come into the market depend on the number of all job seekers, not only of the unemployed ones, through the search externalities. The Beveridge curve, represented by equation (4.57) with $\theta = v/(u + e)$, is still convex to the origin by the properties of the matching function but shifts when e changes. Higher e shifts the Beveridge curve out because the entry of more employed job seekers in the matching process causes congestion for the unemployed.

Now lower search costs raise θ, so, in figure 4.3, they shift the job creation line up and make it steeper; they reduce R, so they shift the Beveridge curve in; and they increase e, so they shift the Beveridge curve back out and the job creation line further up. Figure 4.3 shows the effect on the job creation line, which unambiguously shifts up, and on the Beveridge curve, which is shown to shift to the left, though the net effect of the lower R and higher e could well be an outward shift. Equilibrium

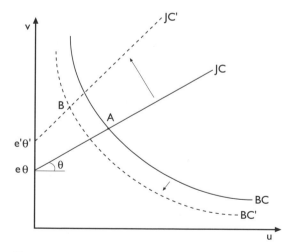

Figure 4.3
Implications of more search on the job (lower search cost) for equilibrium vacancies and unemployment

moves from A to B, where unemployment is lower and vacancies higher. Note that whatever the shift in the Beveridge curve, unemployment is unambiguously lower when search costs are lower, despite the rise in e.

4.5   The Implications of Higher Labor Productivity

How is the equilibrium with on-the-job search influenced by different, say, higher levels of productivity p or lower unemployment income z?

Inspection of the equations for S, θ, and R, respectively (4.44), (4.47), and (4.55), shows that the general level of productivity influences equilibrium through two channels. First, as in the model without on-the-job search, it influences the gap between income from work and unemployment income and shifts the job destruction curve (4.55). Second, it influences the relative cost of search and shifts all three equilibrium relations. For $\sigma = 0$, the influence of productivity on equilibrium is the same as in the model without on-the-job search. It is also the same as the influence of unemployment income z, but in the opposite direction. For $\sigma > 0$, productivity has in addition an influence through σ, which is the same as the one that we analyzed for σ but in the opposite direction.

We therefore discuss first the implications of higher productivity or lower unemployment income by holding σ/p constant (or, without loss of generality, by setting $\sigma = 0$). We subsequently combine the effects obtained with those obtained above for lower σ.

For $\sigma = 0$, either higher p or lower z shifts the job destruction line (4.55) down and to the right (figure 4.2). Equilibrium R is lower, implying lower job destruction rate, and equilibrium θ is higher, implying more job creation at given unemployment. Unemployment therefore falls and wages in high productivity jobs, $x \geq S$, rise (but not if the changes were due to lower z). From (4.44) we also find that the range of productivities over which search is taking place widens because of the rise in θ and the implied increase in the rate of arrival of jobs. Therefore, from (4.57), (4.58), and (4.59), both the number of workers who search on the job and the job-to-job quit rate increase. Because the rate of employment, $1 - u$, increases, the number of employed job seekers and the quit rate must also be higher. Therefore in the Beveridge curve diagram (figure 4.3) higher general productivities shift the job creation and Beveridge curves in the same direction as the one shown for lower search costs.

We note also that because (4.47) and (4.55) are locally independent of S, the increased search activity by the employed that follows the rise in p does not influence the final effect on unemployment (which is fully determined by R and θ). It obviously influences the effect that p has on vacancies, because $v = \theta(e + u)$. So the increased congestion caused by the additional search by the employed on unemployed job seekers is exactly offset by the additional vacancies that firms create (the latter effect is sometimes known in the literature as "vacancy chains"). There may, however, be effects on the dynamic adjustment path of unemployment and a slowing down of the speed of adjustment caused by congestion, since, by (4.60), the rise in the fraction of employed job seekers is higher at given initial unemployment than it is after unemployment starts to decline. We do not take up this point here (see the Notes on the Literature at the end of this chapter).

To summarize, when $\sigma = 0$ higher general productivity or lower unemployment income imply lower job destruction, more search on the job and job-to-job quitting, and lower unemployment. In addition higher productivity implies higher wages everywhere, with wages in high productivity jobs increasing by more. But these results are qualitatively the same as the results obtained earlier for lower search costs. Therefore, when $\sigma > 0$ and the higher productivity reduces the search costs relative to the rewards from work, the results described here are reinforced. Generally, and in accordance with intuition, an economy that is "booming," in the sense of higher rewards from production than from nonmarket activities, is one where there is less job destruction and a smaller flow into unemployment but more on-the-job search and job-to-job quitting.

4.6   Notes on the Literature

Empirically most job acceptances are by workers who are not unemployed. This fact led early critics of search theory to reject it as a good model of unemployment because it ignored on-the-job search. See, for example, Tobin (1972). However, although some influential empirical studies of job-to-job mobility were published, such as Parsons (1973), it was not until much later that theoretical and empirical models of unemployment with search on the job appeared in the literature.

The fact that when there is search on the job the optimal policy can be described by two reservation wages was first noted in a partial context by Burdett (1978). The early literature is surveyed by Mortensen (1986). Mortensen (1994) introduces and calibrates job-to-job mobility in the job creation and job destruction model of chapter 2. His numerical results confirm the results derived here.

Empirical studies of on-the-job search were provided, among others, by Barron and McCafferty (1977), Black (1981), Kahn and Low (1984), Holzer (1987) and Parsons (1991) for the United States; Arellano and Meghir (1992), Hughes and McCormick (1994) and Pissarides and Wadsworth (1994) for the United Kingdom; and Belzil (1994) for Canada. Data on worker flows were reported and analyzed by Blanchard and Diamond (1990) for the United States; Burda and Wyplosz (1994) for large European countries; Burgess, Lane, and Stevens (1994) for a large U.S. firm-level panel data set; Broersma and den Butter (1994) and Gautier and Broersma (1994) for the Netherlands; and Albaek and Sorensen (1998) for all manufacturing plants in Denmark. Contini and Revelli (1997) study the relation between job flows and worker flows for several countries, and Gautier (1997) discusses models and data of both job flows and worker flows with applications to the Netherlands.

The probability of quitting in the model of this chapter is constant at all job tenures. Empirically there is a strong correlation between job tenure and quitting, with quitting much more likely at shorter job tenures. This property is attributed to learning on the job, either of the nonpecuniary features of the job or of job-specific skills. For a model of the former mechanism, see Wilde (1979). Jovanovic's (1979) model of turnover uses the latter mechanism and is built into an equilibrium search model in Jovanovic (1984). See Farber (1994) for an empirical evaluation of that model. A theoretical model of search equilibrium with on-the-job search that explores the implications of learning can be found in Pissarides (1994), where there are two types of jobs, good and bad; no productivity shocks; and search on the job eventually ceases because of learning on the job. That paper also summarizes some of the evidence on job-to-job quitting.

The implications of search on-the-job for the empirical behavior of unemployment have been studied by Burgess (1993), who has shown that employed job seekers cause congestion for unemployed job seekers, especially when good aggregate shocks first arrive, thus increasing the persistence of unemployment. A similar persistence effect is present in Pissarides (1994). Kennes (1994) also derives the implications of on-the-job search for unemployment dynamics and shows how the initial jump in market tightness is influenced by the search behavior of employed workers. Fuentes (1998) shows that changes in search activity by the employed can and has shifted outward the British Beveridge curve.

Vacancy chains caused by quitting are studied by Contini and Revelli (1997) and Akerlof, Rose, and Yellen (1998). For other models of search equilibrium that study the implications of search on the job, see Abbring (1997, ch. 3), where the implications of search on the job for wage determination are studied, and Barlevy (1998), where the fact that in recession on-the-job search activity drops is shown to contribute to the creation of low-quality jobs.

5 Search Intensity and Job Advertising

In the model of chapters 1 through 3 the supply of labor has only an indirect influence on the equilibrium outcome. Variables traditionally associated with the supply of labor, such as the value of leisure, influence the equilibrium outcome only through their effect on the wage rate. This may well be an important channel for labor supply effects in a modern economy. But there are also other channels, and this is where we turn our attention in this chapter and the next two. For this analysis we extend the labor-market model of chapter 1 in several directions.

Growth is not important in this analysis, so for simplicity we assume that it is zero. More important for a full description of equilibrium is the issue of endogenous job destruction and labor turnover, addressed in chapters 2 and 4. Introducing the labor supply influences that we will study in this and the next two chapters in the full model of chapter 2 (and even more so in the model of chapter 4) complicates the analysis considerably, with no obvious gain in the generality of the new results. We therefore study the influence of labor supply on equilibrium by concentrating on the simpler model of chapter 1 and the job creation margin. It will become apparent, as we introduce the new influences, that the job creation margin is the more important one for the transmission of the new effects. Search intensity by the unemployed, rejection of poor job matches by unemployed job seekers, and participation decisions are not likely to have a big influence on the separation choices of matched firms and workers. The existence of search on the job is also not likely to have a big influence on the way that the labor supply issues discussed in these chapters influence job creation provided that the costs of on-the-job search are higher than the costs of unemployed search. If the costs were the same, the unemployed would simply accept the first job offer that comes along and continue searching on the job (with reduced intensity because of the income gain) until they find a job that is sufficiently good to keep until job destruction.

Workers can influence the equilibrium outcome through their choice of search intensity, by deciding whether or not to accept a job they have located and by moving in and out of the labor force. We examine the implications of these decisions for equilibrium unemployment and (in part III) for efficiency. In this analysis we ignore capital, on the ground argued in chapter 1: With a perfect second-hand market for capital goods, it does not influence the search equilibrium outcome in the steady state.

In this chapter we examine the implications of search intensity. For symmetry we also examine the implications of variable intensity by hiring firms, which for the sake of brevity we call *job advertising*. We will show, however, that job advertising does not have an important role to play in the model. The choice of job vacancies, which played a critical role in the macroeconomic model of part I, makes the choice of job advertising redundant.

5.1   The Matching Technology with Variable Intensity

Search intensity and job advertising can be thought of as "technical change" parameters in the job-matching technology. We saw that the inputs into job matching are the number of unemployed workers and the number of job vacancies. The output is the number of job matches that form within a given period of time. If now unemployed workers or vacant firms search more intensely for a match, the number of job matches for given unemployment and job vacancies rises. It is as if there has been an improvement in the technology of job matching. Our formalization of the effects of variable intensities on job matching draws heavily on what we know about technical change in production technologies.

It is well known that general technical change, where a technical change parameter is entered as a factor of production in a production function, yields ambiguous results in production theory. The same is true of search intensity. Regardless of the ambiguity of the results, it is not even clear what the meaning of a general unrestricted technical change parameter would be in a production process. Technical change in production technologies is invariably defined as input-augmenting, and we will follow the same convention in our approach to job matching with variable intensities.

Thus, let s be a variable measuring the intensity of search by workers, and let a be a variable measuring job advertising. Define the efficiency units of searching workers as su, where u is, as before, the rate of unemployment. Define also the efficiency units of job vacancies as av. In discrete-time analysis we may think of s and a as the fraction of the period during which the worker and firm, respectively, are actively searching. In continuous time the interpretation is analogous. We can think of it as the fraction of unemployed workers who search during a small interval of time. Hence we write the job matching technology as

$$m = m(su, av). \tag{5.1}$$

As before, we assume that $m(., .)$ is of constant returns to scale with positive first-order and negative second-order partial derivatives.

The variables s and a in (5.1) are market averages; that is, they are, respectively, the intensity of search of the representative unemployed worker and the level of job advertising of the representative hiring firm. Individual workers and firms choose their own intensities by taking the intensities of the representative agents as given. In equilibrium no agent will find it advantageous to change his or her intensity, given that all other agents are in equilibrium.

To derive the transition probabilities of workers and firms, we need to look at the difference between individual search intensities and market averages. Thus let s_i be the intensity of search of worker i. During search this worker is worth s_i efficiency search units. For each efficiency unit supplied, there is a Poisson process transferring workers from unemployment to employment at the rate $m(su, av)/su$. Hence the transition probability of worker i in unit time is given by

$$q_i^w = \frac{s_i}{su} m(su, av). \tag{5.2}$$

Worker i chooses s_i during search by taking all the other arguments of q_i^w as given. In general, we can write q_i^w as $q^w(s_i; s, a\theta)$, where as before $\theta = v/u$.

The firm is faced with a similar transition probability. The process that transfers a job from a vacant state to a filled one for each efficiency unit of advertising supplied is Poisson with rate $m(su, av)/av$. Firm j supplies a_j efficiency units for each vacancy. Hence each vacancy's transition probability in unit time is

$$q_j = \frac{a_j}{av} m(su, av). \tag{5.3}$$

As with q_i^w, q_j is a function of a_j, s, a, and θ.

In symmetric Nash equilibrium all workers choose the same intensity and all firms choose the same level of advertising. Thus $s_i = s$ and $a_j = a$

in (5.2) and (5.3), respectively, give the transition rates for the representative worker and firm:

$$q^w = \frac{m(su, av)}{u} = m(s, a\theta).\tag{5.4}$$

$$q = \frac{m(su, av)}{v} = m\left(\frac{s}{\theta}, a\right).\tag{5.5}$$

As before, q^w and q are related by

$$q^w(s, a, \theta) = \theta q(s, a, \theta),\tag{5.6}$$

with q^w increasing in the three arguments s, a, and θ and q increasing in s and a but decreasing in θ. The elasticity of $1/q$ with respect to θ, η, is given by

$$\eta = \frac{sum_1(su, av)}{m(su, av)},\tag{5.7}$$

and it lies between 0 and 1. It is a function of s and the product $a\theta$, though if the extended matching function in (5.1) satisfies the Cobb-Douglas restrictions, it is a constant.

The equilibrium condition for unemployment, the Beveridge curve, is given, as before, by

$$u = \frac{\lambda}{\lambda + \theta q(s, a, \theta)},\tag{5.8}$$

where λ is the rate at which job destruction shocks arrive. Equation (5.8) gives the rate of unemployment that equates the flows into unemployment with the flows out of it when there is no growth in the labor force. Search intensity and job advertising become shift variables in the relation between unemployment and vacancies. Thus, to describe the full equilibrium of the model, we now need two more equations, one to determine s and the other to determine a.

5.2 The Choice of Search Intensity

Search intensity is chosen by unemployed workers to maximize the present-discounted value of their expected income during search. We assume that raising search intensity is costly and that the cost increases on average as well as at the margin. Also the cost of search may be partly subjective, so it may depend on the worker's actual or imputed income during unemployment. In general, we assume that the cost of s_i units of search is σ_i, where

$$\sigma_i = \sigma(s_i, z), \quad \sigma_s(s_i, z) > 0, \quad \sigma_{ss}(s_i, z) \geq 0, \quad \sigma_z(s_i, z) \geq 0. \tag{5.9}$$

The worker's net income during unemployment is given by the difference $z - \sigma_i$, which may have any sign. The cost of search depends positively on income during unemployment on the ground that some of the cost of search is forgone leisure and z includes the imputed value of leisure. We return to this point later in this chapter.

The present-discounted value of the unemployed worker's income is as in the model of chapter 1, equation (1.10), except that now income during unemployment is $z - \sigma(s_i, z)$ and the transition probability is given by q_i^w, defined in (5.2). Hence present-discounted value U_i satisfies

$$rU_i = z - \sigma(s_i, z) + q^w(s_i; .)(W - U_i). \tag{5.10}$$

The present-discounted value from employment, W, is common to all workers, so we omit the subscript. Also we assume that z is exogenous, but we return to this question at the end of this chapter.

The worker chooses the intensity of search s_i to maximize U_i, taking s and the other market variables as given. The optimal s_i satisfies

$$-\sigma_s(s_i, z) + \frac{\partial q_i^w}{\partial s_i}(W - U_i) = 0, \tag{5.11}$$

where U_i is evaluated at the optimal s_i.

From the definition of q_i^w in (5.2), we find that a single individual's s_i increases in the efficiency units of search supplied by firms, av, but decreases in the efficiency units supplied by other workers, su. These properties follow from the congestion externalities that characterize the matching technology, and they are discussed again below. Our main interest here is not in the behavior of a single individual, given the behavior of all others, but in the behavior of the representative worker.

We consider only symmetric equilibria where all unemployed workers choose the same search intensity s_i. To obtain an equation that describes the behavior of the average s, we write $s_i = s$ in (5.11) and evaluate all expressions at the s that satisfy (5.11).

From (5.2) and (5.4), $\partial q_i^w / \partial s_i$ at $s_i = s$ satisfies

$$\left. \frac{\partial q_i^w}{\partial s_i} \right|_{s_i = s} = \frac{q^w(s, a, \theta)}{s}. \tag{5.12}$$

Hence (5.11) implies that the contribution of one efficiency unit to expected net worth, $(W - U)q^w(s, a, \theta)/s$, is equal to the marginal cost of an efficiency unit. Our specification of the transition probability in (5.2) implies constant returns to efficiency units of search. The optimum in (5.11) is unique because the cost of efficiency units is increasing at the margin. From (1.12) and (1.13) the optimal U and W imply that

$$W - U = \frac{w - z + \sigma(s, z)}{r + \lambda + q^w(s, a, \theta)}, \tag{5.13}$$

where, as before, w is the equilibrium wage rate. Hence the equation satisfied by the optimal search intensity, obtained by substituting (5.12) and (5.13) into (5.11), is

$$-\sigma_s(s, z) + \frac{w - z + \sigma(s, z)}{r + \lambda + q^w(s, a, \theta)} \frac{q^w(s, a, \theta)}{s} = 0. \tag{5.14}$$

Although equation (5.14) looks complicated, the properties of the optimal s are easy to obtain because of the restrictions satisfied by $q^w(.)$ and derived from (5.4). The comparative static properties of the optimal s, holding all other endogenous variables constant, are briefly as follows.

An increase in the wage increases search intensity because the relative income from work is now higher. An increase in unemployment income has the opposite effect, for similar reasons (under the assumption $\sigma_{sz}(.) \geq 0$; see below). Also an increase in either the rate of discount or the rate of job loss reduces the expected future returns from a job, and so reduces search intensity.

The effects of labor market tightness and job advertising, although partial, are of special interest. An increase in labor-market tightness increases the intensity of search. Workers search more intensely when the ratio of jobs to workers goes up, since the chances that they will locate a job improve. This is an example of the discouraged-worker effect (in this particular example operating in reverse). It implies that when the unemployment rate is higher, for any given number of job vacancies, workers come into the market less frequently to look for the job vacancies.

The effect of job advertising on intensity has a similar interpretation. When the level of job advertising is higher, unemployed workers are more likely to come across a vacant job. They respond by increasing their search intensity, that is, by coming more frequently into the market to look for the jobs.

The effects of labor-market tightness and job advertising on intensity are the result of the positive trading externality that exists in our model. An increase in either the number of traders, or the frequency with which they are willing to trade on one side of the market, induces an increase in the frequency with which traders on the other side of the market are willing to trade. This externality has some implications for the equilibrium and efficiency of the model that we will study in this chapter and in chapter 8.

5.3   The Choice of Job Advertising

Firms choose the level of advertising for each vacancy to maximize the present-discounted value of profits. As with the choice of vacancies, the firm's optimal policy can be derived from the single-job model of chapter 1 or from the cost-of-adjustment model of chapter 3. The results are identical, and the choice of model is a matter of convenience. We follow the single-job approach here.

In chapter 1 we assumed that the cost of a vacancy, pc, is out of the control of the firm. Here we assume that the cost depends on the level of advertising that the firm chooses for the job. We write

$$c = c(a_j), \ c'(a_j) > 0, \ c''(a_j) \geq 0, \tag{5.15}$$

where a_j is the level of advertising for job j.

The firm's expected profit from one more job vacancy is, from (1.6),

$$rV_j = -pc(a_j) + q(a_j; \, .)(J - V_j), \tag{5.16}$$

where $q(a_j; \, .)$ is given by (5.3). The firm chooses a_j to maximize V_j. The first-order condition is given by

$$-pc'(a_j)+\frac{\partial q_i}{\partial a_j}(J-V_j)=0,\tag{5.17}$$

where V_j is evaluated at the optimal s_j. From (5.3),

$$\frac{\partial q_i}{\partial a_j}=\frac{q(s,\ a,\ \theta)}{a},\tag{5.18}$$

so (5.17) becomes

$$-pc'(a_j)+\frac{q(s,\ a,\ \theta)}{a}(J-V_j)=0.\tag{5.19}$$

We are interested in the symmetric Nash equilibrium outcome where all firms choose the same intensity, a. For this we substitute $a_j = a$ in (5.19) and treat the resulting relation as an equation in the market equilibrium level of advertising.

Consider first the partial-equilibrium condition for a, with θ taken as given. That is, the equilibrium level that would be chosen by the firm had the number of jobs been exogenously fixed. This yields an equilibrium condition very similar to the condition for search intensity, (5.14). By using (5.16) and the expression for the asset value for a job derived in chapter 1, (1.8), we rewrite (5.19) as

$$-pc'(a)+\frac{p-w+pc(a)}{r+\lambda+q(s,\ a,\ \theta)}\frac{q(s,\ a,\ \theta)}{a}=0.\tag{5.20}$$

The partial equilibrium properties of job advertising are simple to obtain and intuitive.

An increase in the marginal product of labor, p, a decrease in the wage rate, a decrease in the interest rate, and a decrease in the rate of job separation increase job advertising because they increase the expected profit from the job. The effect of search intensity is due to the positive trading externality that we discussed in the preceding section. If unemployed workers come into the market more frequently to look for jobs, firms respond by advertising their jobs more. Labor-market tightness has a negative effect, which is also due to trading externalities working in the opposite direction. If the market is more tight, there are more jobs for each unemployed worker, so a typical firm's chances that it will find a worker drop. The firm responds by advertising less, a kind of discouraged-jobs effect.

The partial equilibrium properties of job advertising are not particularly interesting, since they depend on the assumption that the firm holds the number of jobs fixed when varying its level of job advertising. But the firm will never find it optimal to do so. If we use the equilibrium condition for the number of jobs to simplify (5.20), the equation determining job advertising changes dramatically.

Recall that profit maximization with respect to the number of jobs corresponds to a zero-profit condition for V_j in equation (5.16). But if we set $V_j = 0$ in (5.16), we get

$$J = \frac{pc(a_j)}{q(a_j; \, .)} \tag{5.21}$$

for all optimal a_j. Hence (5.19) implies, for $a_j = a$, that

$$\frac{c'(a)a}{c(a)} = 1. \tag{5.22}$$

When the number of jobs is optimized, the level of advertising is chosen such that the elasticity of the cost of advertising is equal to 1.

There is a close (formal) connection between condition (5.22) and the similar elasticity condition found in efficiency-wage models, where the firm can control both the effort supplied by each worker and the number of workers. In efficiency wage models the firms uses the number of employees to control the labor input and the wage rate as an instrument to ensure that each unit of effort from each worker is supplied at minimum cost. Similarly here the firm uses its vacancy rate as an instrument for attracting workers, and its level of advertising in order to minimize the cost of each vacancy. The optimum level of advertising is independent of market variables, and it depends only on the properties of the cost function.

5.4 Equilibrium

We consider now the steady-state equilibrium of the economy when search intensity and job advertising are determined by their respective equations, (5.14) and (5.22). The equation for unemployment is (5.8). To complete the description of equilibrium, we need two more equations, one for wages and one for the number of jobs.

The derivation of these equations is straightforward and proceeds as before. The equation for wages is (1.23) but with unemployment income $z - \sigma(c, z)$. Thus wages are given by

$$w = (1 - \beta)[z - \sigma(s, z)] + \beta p(1 + c\theta). \tag{5.23}$$

The equation for job creation is again (1.22), except that now q depends also on search intensity and job advertising.

The equation for search intensity, (5.14), can be simplified considerably by using a method similar to the one we used to derive the equation for advertising, (5.22). Thus we know that the Nash wage equation satisfies

$$W - U = \frac{\beta}{1 - \beta} J. \tag{5.24}$$

In equilibrium (5.11) and (5.12) imply that

$$W - U = \frac{\sigma_s(s, z)s}{\theta q(s, a, \theta)}, \tag{5.25}$$

whereas J is equal to $pc/q(s, a, \theta)$. Hence, combining (5.24) and (5.25), we get

$$s\sigma_s(s, z) = \frac{\beta}{1 - \beta} pc\theta. \tag{5.26}$$

Equation (5.26) replaces (5.14) in the equilibrium set of equations. We note that (5.26) is not a behavioral equation for search intensity but a relation between intensity and labor-market tightness that holds in equilibrium. The behavioral equation for intensity is (5.14). Another way of deriving (5.26) is by substituting equilibrium wages and the firm's condition for the optimal supply of jobs into (5.14).

We rewrite the set of equilibrium relations here, except for the wage equation (5.23), after substituting wages from (5.23) into the condition for the supply of jobs, (1.22):

$$u = \frac{\lambda}{\lambda + \theta q(s, a, \theta)}, \tag{5.27}$$

$$(1 - \beta)[p - z + \sigma(s, z)] - \beta pc(a)\theta - \frac{r + \lambda}{q(s, a, \theta)} pc(a) = 0, \tag{5.28}$$

$$s\sigma_s(s, z) = \frac{\beta}{1-\beta} pc(a)\theta, \tag{5.29}$$

$$\frac{c'(a)a}{c(a)} = 1. \tag{5.30}$$

The model is, as before, recursive for given real interest rate. Equation (5.30) gives the equilibrium level of job advertising. With knowledge of a, equations (5.29) and (5.28) give the solutions for search intensity and labor-market tightness. And finally, with a, c, and θ known, (5.27) gives equilibrium unemployment and (5.23) gives equilibrium wages. The key to the system is the intensity-tightness block (5.29) and (5.28). Compared with the model of chapter 1, the only nontrivial new equation is (5.29).

On inspection, it is not immediately clear that (5.29) and (5.28) yield unique solutions for s and θ. The search externalities make s a rising function of θ (for given z), and θ a rising function of s, so there may be more than one equilibrium (see figure 5.1). The possibility of nonuniqueness arises because, if (e.g., by chance) not many jobs come into the market, unemployed workers search less, justifying firms' decisions not to bring many jobs into the market. If many jobs come in and workers respond by searching more, again firms' decisions to open the additional jobs may be justified. But two restrictions satisfied by our model ensure the uniqueness of equilibrium. First, the job-matching technology has constant returns to scale, and second, search intensity enters the matching technology multiplicatively, like input-augmenting technical progress. With these restrictions and with the axes as in figure 5.1, the curve for the intensity of search (5.29) is everywhere steeper than the curve for the number of jobs (5.28), so their intersection is unique. The curves are respectively labeled $s(\theta)$ and $\theta(s)$ in figure 5.1.

Whether or not the two restrictions on the matching technology are reasonable is an empirical matter. In this book we accept both restrictions as plausible, and we do not venture into an analysis of the same problems when they do not hold. The lessons learned from growth theory suggest that constant returns and input-augmenting technical change may be necessary assumptions for well-behaved long-run results. In the growth model of chapter 3, increasing returns in the matching technology would imply ever decreasing unemployment rate. This is contradicted by the facts. If increasing returns are considered plausible in the

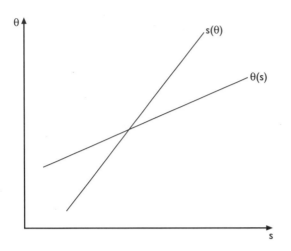

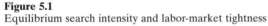

Figure 5.1
Equilibrium search intensity and labor-market tightness

short run, even if in the long run there are constant returns, it is necessary to explain why short-run matching technologies may differ from
long-run ones. The reasons for any differences are not obvious, given that
in a matching technology there are unlikely to be inputs that are fixed
in the short run but variable in the long run, and vice versa. Existing
empirical evidence supports the assumption of constant returns in the
matching technology (see the Notes on the Literature at the end of
chapter 1). Other authors, however, prefer not to impose the restrictions
that we have imposed on the matching technology and sometimes derive
different results.

Of the two restrictions satisfied by our matching technology the important one for uniqueness is constant returns. With increasing returns multiplicity is possible, a point made by Peter Diamond in a number of
papers. We discuss briefly his main result and compare it with ours. The
second restriction satisfied by our matching technology is more relevant
for some results that have been obtained regarding the efficiency of equilibrium, so we postpone discussion until chapter 8.

In Peter Diamond's (1982a) coconut model, an increase in the rate at
which people participate on one side of the market, increases the rate at
which people want to participate on the other side of the market. This
complementarity is similar to the positive dependence that we obtained
here between search intensity on the one hand and the number of job

vacancies on the other. Equilibrium in Diamond's model is described by a diagram like the one shown in figure 5.1. But Diamond's main proposition, that aggregate demand management may permanently shift the economy onto a potentially more efficient equilibrium, relies on nonuniqueness of equilibrium. That is, it relies on more than one crossing point in figure 5.1. We saw that with constant returns the two curves in figure 5.1 can intersect only once. In later work with the same model, for example, in Diamond (1984a), it is shown that multiplicity requires increasing returns to scale in the matching technology. The matching technology in Diamond (1982a) satisfies increasing returns.

It is also possible to get multiple equilibria in our model if the matching technology has increasing returns to scale. With increasing returns, a rise in the scale of trading for given ratios increases the probability that each trading participant will succeed to trade, because the number of job matchings increases faster than the inputs into search. In figure 5.1 the scale of trading becomes higher as we move away from the origin, since then both the intensity of search and the number of job vacancies rise. Thus, with increasing returns, the trading probabilities of both firms and workers rise faster as we move away from the origin, so both search intensity and the number of job vacancies should also rise faster than shown in figure 5.1. Hence the $s(\theta)$ curve becomes flatter and the $\theta(s)$ curve steeper the further away from the origin we are, giving rise to the possibility of a second intersection at higher levels of s and θ.

Of course, increasing returns is a necessary but not sufficient condition for multiple equilibria. The significance of multiple equilibria in this setup is that if they exist, temporary policy measures may move the economy permanently from an equilibrium with high unemployment to one with lower unemployment. Under our assumptions policy does not have such effects on the economy. Although it can influence the equilibrium unemployment outcome, permanent policy change is needed for permanently lower unemployment (see chapter 9).

5.5   Unemployment and Search Intensity

Equation (5.27) suggests that search intensity has a potentially important role to play in the determination of equilibrium unemployment. Intensity and job advertising enter the relation between vacancies and unemployment as shift variables, so they can influence unemployment independently of the number of jobs in the economy. However, in equilibrium several of the partial effects previously discussed disappear. Also the role of search intensity in the determination of unemployment depends crucially on the assumptions that we make about the nature of the cost of search to the worker. Unfortunately, neither theory nor empirical evidence can help very much in the specification of the cost of search, beyond the restrictions in (5.9).

The important difference between the partial effects on search intensity and the equilibrium ones is that in the former wages are held fixed, whereas in the latter they respond to changes in the average intensity of search. The number of jobs is also held fixed in the former and allowed to vary in the latter, but its role in this respect is less important than the role of wages. From equation (5.29) we conclude that the responses of wages and of the number of jobs to changes in search intensity are such that the direct effects of all exogenous variables on intensity disappear, except for those that influence the marginal cost of search, the cost of hiring, and the share of labor in the wage bargain.

The role of job advertising in equilibrium is even more restricted; as we saw above, the only determinant of optimal advertising is the shape of the cost function. Here the critical variable that offsets the partial effects in equilibrium is the number of jobs. Firms use their vacancy rate to attract workers and do not vary their advertising for each vacant job according to their hiring needs.

The parameters of the cost functions for search and advertising, $\sigma(.)$ and $c(.)$, are shift variables in the relation between vacancies and unemployment. However, they are not likely to vary much either secularly or over the cycle, and they are not interesting parameters for our purposes. The only interesting variables that may influence intensity through the cost functions are unemployment income and job productivity, which may influence, respectively, the marginal cost of search and the cost of hiring. But our assumption that the influence of productivity on the cost of advertising is multiplicative removes any influence that it may have on the key elasticity in (5.30). This leaves only the influence of unemployment income, z, on the marginal cost of search, a point that we discuss below.

The share of labor, β, is also a shift variable in the relation between vacancies and unemployment. In the model we described in chapter 1, β

is a constant, and exogenous changes in it are difficult to justify. Changes in bargaining strength are reflected in changes in the worker's and firm's threat points, not in their share of the surplus from the job match. In the Nash bargaining solution β is normally taken to equal $\frac{1}{2}$. But we will see in chapter 9 that the relative share $\beta/(1 - \beta)$ may be affected by some policy parameters. If that is the case, the appearance of $\beta/(1 - \beta)$ as a shift factor in the relation between vacancies and unemployment introduces policy parameters into the analysis as new shift variables.

The sign with which actual or imputed unemployment income influences search intensity in equilibrium, independently of any effect that it may have on it through labor-market tightness, depends on the sign of the cross-partial $\sigma_{sz}(s, z)$, that is, on how changes in unemployment income influence the marginal cost of search. If the cost of search is separable both from actual and imputed unemployment income, the latter does not influence search intensity independently, so z is not a shift variable in the Beveridge curve. In this case a rise in z shifts the Beveridge curve to the right only in a partial model, with wages held fixed. But separability may not be a good assumption, and in any case, a realistic specification of the marginal cost of search should imply that s does not change during balanced growth. We now consider a plausible specification of the cost of search that has this property.

Suppose that search requires time and that in order to generate s efficiency units of search, a worker needs to devote $h(s)$ hours to search. If workers start searching first the more accessible employers, it is reasonable to assume that $h'(s) > 0$ and $h''(s) \geq 0$. The cost of search to the worker is the cost of $h(s)$ hours. Results hinge critically on what we assume about the imputed value of time to the worker and what unemployment income z represents.

If z represents entirely the imputed value of leisure, then net income during unemployment, $z - \sigma(s, z)$, has to be recalculated as the imputed value of total hours net of the hours of search, $h(s)$. If the total number of hours available in unit time is normalized to unity, the leisure time available to the unemployed worker who searches with intensity s is $1 - h(s)$. Then a reasonable specification of imputed income during unemployment is $z[1 - h(s)]$, implying that the cost of search is

$$\sigma(s, z) = zh(s). \tag{5.31}$$

A more general specification could make the imputed income during unemployment a concave function of total hours $1 - h(s)$, instead of linear, on the assumption that the utility of leisure is diminishing at the margin. Nothing is gained, however, from this generalization in the present context.

In the linear case of (5.31) the marginal cost of search is $\sigma_s(s, z) = zh'(s)$, and so the condition for equilibrium intensity, (5.29), becomes

$$zsh'(s) = \frac{\beta}{1-\beta}pc\theta. \tag{5.32}$$

By differentiation we establish that equilibrium search intensity rises in general productivity p, in the share of wages in the wage bargain, β, but falls in unemployment income, z.

If z includes some actual unemployment income, such as unemployment compensation, the specification in (5.31) is difficult to justify under our risk neutrality assumptions. Actual unemployment income should not influence the cost of search under these conditions, and so the equilibrium condition (5.32) should be independent of any actual income included in z. Actual income does not shift the Beveridge curve through search disincentive effects.

The result just obtained is unsatisfactory, since intuition and some evidence support the view that unemployment income has disincentive effects on search. The next chapter demonstrates that such effects can be obtained even with risk neutrality when there are stochastic job matchings, which imply that some job matches are rejected through the optimal choice of reservation rules. They can also be obtained in the model of this chapter either from the assumption of risk aversion, which would make the cost function in (5.31) nonlinear in actual income, or indirectly through the assumption that the imputed value of leisure depends on the wage rate. As we argued in chapters 1 and 3, the assumption that z is proportional to either wages or wealth is a natural one to make, especially in a growing economy. In the present context it ensures that if there is growth, the optimal s is constant, and so a balanced growth path for output with constant unemployment can be derived.

To demonstrate that actual unemployment income influences intensity in the latter case, suppose that $z = \rho w$, as in the model of chapter 1, but that there is now unemployment compensation $b_0 = bw$, where b is a policy parameter. Then the marginal cost of search is $\rho w h'(s)$ and from (5.23) wages are given by

$$w = \frac{\beta(1+c\theta)}{1-(1-\beta)[b+\rho(1-h(s))]}p. \tag{5.33}$$

The equilibrium condition for search intensity then becomes

$$\frac{\rho s(1+c\theta)h'(s)}{1-(1-\beta)[b+\rho(1-h(s))]} = \frac{c\theta}{1-\beta}. \tag{5.34}$$

This version of equilibrium is general enough to have both types of unemployment income as shift variables. Without further restrictions on functional forms, however, results are ambiguous. Higher s implies, on the one hand, higher marginal cost of time, $h'(s)$, but on the other hand, more time devoted to search and therefore lower imputed income during search and lower wages in equilibrium. The lower wage rate reduces the imputed cost of time, working in this way against the direct effect of higher s on the marginal cost of time. This conflict can clearly be seen in (5.34), where both the numerator and denominator of the left-hand fraction increase in s.

Rather than work with the more general specification in (5.33) and (5.34), with or without further restrictions, we return to the simpler specification of the cost of search in (5.31), and use the equilibrium condition (5.32) to study the effects of higher p/z on equilibrium, namely the effects of either higher productivity or lower unemployment income on wages, unemployment, and vacancies. For concreteness, and to make comparisons with similar exercises discussed in part I, we refer only to the effects of higher p in the discussion that follows.

From the equilibrium condition for search intensity, (5.32), we already know that for given θ, higher p implies higher s. Therefore, in figure 5.1, the $s(\theta)$ line shifts to the right. But the condition for market tightness, (5.28), immediately gives that for given s, higher p also implies higher θ. The $\theta(s)$ line in figure 5.1 shifts up. The shifts are shown in figure 5.2. Equilibrium s and θ both increase and there is a multiplier effect in operation because of the complementarity between search intensity and job creation: When productivity is higher, firms open up more vacancies, workers respond by searching more intensely, and firms respond, in their turn, by opening up more vacancies.

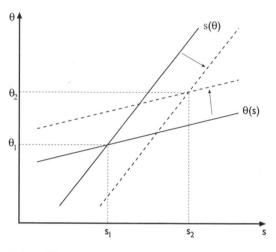

Figure 5.2
Effect of higher productivity on search intensity and market tightness

There are two offsetting effects on wages from these changes. The higher market tightness increases wages, but the higher search intensity reduces them, through its negative effect on income during unemployment. Of course, the direct effect on wages from the higher productivity is positive, and it interacts with the positive tightness effect to give a bigger upward push to wages. Although the overall effect is of indeterminate sign, it is likely to be strongly positive.

Unemployment decreases both because of the higher market tightness and because of the higher search intensity. We show this in the Beveridge diagram, figure 5.3. The job creation line rotates anticlockwise because of the rise in θ. The Beveridge curve shifts in because the higher intensity increases the rate at which job matches form. Unemployment unambiguously falls, but the effect on job vacancies is generally ambiguous. The introduction of variable search intensity in this diagram rotates the job creation line by more than otherwise and shifts the Beveridge curve inward. Thus the effect on unemployment due to variable intensity is in the same direction as the effect with fixed intensity, when only the job creation line rotates (discussed in chapter 1). The additional effects on vacancies is made up of a positive component, due to the higher rise in θ, and a negative one, due to the shift in the Beveridge curve. Which one dominates depends on parameter values.

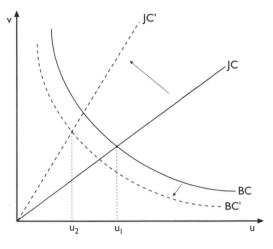

Figure 5.3
Effect of higher productivity on unemployment and vacancies

What has the introduction of search intensity added to the theory of unemployment of the model of chapter 1? First, a lesson learned is that many of the partial effects of search intensity disappear once wages are endogenized and the model solved for market equilibrium. But, second, some effects do remain, and these effects shift the Beveridge curve. Most notable among them is income during unemployment (or the subjective valuation of leisure) and the share of labor in the wage bargain. Empirically the Beveridge curve has shifted in a way that the model of chapter 1 cannot reconcile (see the Notes in the Literature that follow this section). Variable search intensity may provide one of the reasons behind the shifts. Finally, with variable search intensity, the effect of changes in productivity and the valuation of leisure on unemployment is enhanced and on vacancies is mitigated. This may be a factor behind the fact that unemployment seems to change by more than vacancies, at least in postwar European data.

5.6 Notes on the Literature

The effects of variable search intensities were discussed by a number of authors in the early search literature, but it was not until the early 1980s that a two-sided model with variable search intensities was considered.

The first equilibrium models that also discussed efficiency questions were by Mortensen (1982a) and Pissarides (1984b). We discuss the efficiency analysis in these models in chapter 8. For another model along similar lines, see Howitt and McAfee (1987).

The idea of modeling variable intensity as input-augmenting technical progress in an aggregate matching function is new, though it is closely related to an idea in Hosios (1990) and a little more distantly to the ideas in Mortensen (1982a).

The idea that when inputs into trade are variable on both sides of the market equilibrium is given by the intersection of two similarly sloped curves was first explored by Diamond (1982a). Diamond argued that multiple intersections cannot be ruled out, though in later work (Diamond 1984a, b) he stated that a necessary condition for multiple intersections is increasing returns to scale in the job-matching technology. Increasing returns also give rise to the possibility of multiple equilibria in the model of Howitt and McAfee (1987).

Some of the very early work with Beveridge curves in the United Kingdom—for example, Dow and Dicks-Mireaux (1958) and Lipsey (1960, 1974)—assumed (without verification) what was effectively increasing returns in job matching (though they also postulated uniqueness of equilibrium). More recent evidence, however, largely supports constant returns (see the Notes on the Literature at the end of chapter 1).

The literature has not paid much attention to the specification of the cost of search, and generally the assumption made is that the cost function is exogenous and increasing at the margin. The assumption that hours of search should increase at the margin was justified by Seater (1979).

The importance of variable intensity in the empirical analysis of unemployment in Britain, as a shift variable in the Beveridge curve, was emphasized by Jackman, Layard, and Pissarides (1989). Starting from the observation that in Britain vacancies since the early 1970s have been a cyclical variable without trend but unemployment has trended up, they concluded that the Beveridge curve has shifted to the right because of a fall in search intensity associated with higher and more generally available unemployment income.

Our way of analyzing intensity is not the only one in the literature. Benhabib and Bull (1983) define intensity differently, as the number of firms a worker decides to search during a period before making up his mind whether or not to accept the best offer observed. However, the differences between their approach and ours are superficial rather than real, since "sample size" in Benhabib and Bull's terminology could be given the interpretation of "efficiency units of search" supplied during a small time interval in our terminology.

Other partial utility-based approaches to intensity, such as Siven's (1974), Seater's (1977), and Burdett's (1979), could potentially be used to derive plausible expressions for the subjective cost of search in equilibrium, but they have not generally been applied to this purpose. This group of models considers a general problem of the allocation of time to work and search, but it has not led to important and usable results.

6 Stochastic Job Matchings

The idea formalized in this chapter is that jobs and workers have many unobservable characteristics that can influence the productivity of a job match. Two vacant jobs may look the same to a worker before he searches the firms offering them; two workers may look the same to a firm before it screens them. But when the jobs and workers are brought together, one pair may be more productive than the other.

The model we use to formalize this idea is a simple extension of the model of earlier chapters with constant job destruction rate. Searching firms and workers are indistinguishable from other firms and other workers, respectively, and they are brought together by a job-matching technology. But in contrast to the model of chapter 1, the productivity of job-worker matches varies according to parameters that are specific to the match. Formally the productivity of a job-worker pair is a drawing from a known probability distribution, and its realization becomes known only after the firm and worker meet.

Thus two features of the model of previous chapters are retained, the ex ante homogeneity of firms and workers and the ex post resolution of all uncertainty. The new feature now introduced is the ex post match-specific heterogeneity. We refer to this extension of the model as *stochastic job matchings*.

Low realizations of the match productivity may be rejected because of the prospect of a better job match in the future. Thus the new question in this chapter is which job matches are accepted and which are rejected. Although the question is remarkably similar to the question asked by the very first models of job search, the equilibrium nature of our model introduces an entirely new dimension into the analysis. The equilibrium analysis shares some features with the analysis of job destruction in chapter 2. As in the model of chapter 2, the firm and worker follow the same reservation rule when deciding whether to accept or reject a match, because of the equilibrium nature of the model. We ignore job destruction decisions in this chapter for the reasons given in the preceding chapter. The decision margins that we analyze here are about job acceptance, so their main influence on equilibrium outcomes is through job creation.

We also ignore on-the-job search. The key requirement in the model of this chapter is that the state of unemployment has some option value to the worker; otherwise, all jobs that paid at least as much as the level of unemployment income would be accepted. Assuming that search on the job is not possible gives this option value to unemployment—the unemployed worker can take advantage of other job offers in a way that the employed worker cannot. Assuming that on-the-job search is possible but more costly than unemployed search also implies an option value for unemployment, at the cost of much analytical complexity. Also, assuming that job change is costly, even if search is equally costly for all workers, implies an option value for unemployment because high-wage jobs can be accepted without having to pay the costs of multiple job changes. The assumptions that we are making, of zero cost of job change and no on-the-job search, are the easiest ones and the ones most commonly made in the literature.

6.1 Job Matching

We first need to define precisely what we mean by productivity differences. Our definition is a natural extension of labor-augmenting technological differences to job-specific situations.

We assume that the output of each job match j can be written as the output of α_j efficiency units of labor. Each job-worker match has its own parameter α, known both to the worker and to the firm when they make contact and specific to the job match. There is a distribution function $G(\alpha)$ of the productivity parameters, known to all, with finite range normalized to $0 \leq \alpha \leq 1$. Our assumptions about productivity differences in this model are therefore similar to those that we made in the analysis of job destruction in the model of chapter 2. (Of course, the distribution function in the two cases is not generally the same, though we use the same notation $G(.)$ for convenience.) But whereas in the model of chapter 2 the firm and worker started the employment relationship at maximum productivity, and they moved elsewhere according to an exogenous process, in the model of this chapter the firm and worker start at some randomly drawn productivity α and remain there until job destruction. Because of this difference, in the model of chapter 2 the reservation rule determined whether the job should continue or not after a shock. In the model of this chapter the reservation rule determines whether the job should start or not after a meeting.

In the more general model with capital, when the firm and worker meet and discover that their productivity is α, the firm hires k units of capital for each efficiency unit of labor. With the existence of a perfect second-hand market for capital goods, taking into account the invest-ment decision does not influence the choice of reservation rule, for the reasons explained in chapter 2. Hence we will ignore capital in this chapter and concentrate instead on the choice available to firms and workers when they meet and discover that their match-specific produc-tivity is some constant parameter α.

Because of the existence of a productivity distribution for new matches, not all job matches are acceptable to firms and workers. In equi-librium the Nash sharing rule for wages implies that firms and workers always agree on which job matches to accept and which to reject. There is some common reservation productivity, α_r, below which neither the firm nor the worker will want to trade. Although the existence of this equilibrium reservation will not be demonstrated until later in the chapter, we will set up the model conditional on its existence.

Let again u be the aggregate unemployment rate and v the aggregate vacancy rate. We ignore search intensity and job advertising because nothing new is added, either to the analysis of job rejection or to the choice of intensity, by considering them together. Then the rate of job *contacts* is given by

$$m = m(u, v). \tag{6.1}$$

Equation (6.1) is like the matching technology of earlier chapters and satisfies the same properties. The difference now is that not all job con-tacts will lead to job matches, since some job matches are not produc-tive enough. Because all firms and workers are ex ante identical, the reservation productivity α_r is common to all job-worker pairs. So if all productivities $\alpha \geq \alpha_r$ are accepted, the fraction of acceptable job contacts is

$$\int_{\alpha_r}^{1} dG(\alpha) = 1 - G(\alpha_r). \tag{6.2}$$

The rate of job matching now is $[1 - G(\alpha_r)]m$. Converting this to indi-vidual transitions, a worker arrives to a job vacancy at rate

$$q = [1 - G(\alpha_r)]\frac{m(u, v)}{v} = [1 - G(\alpha_r)]q(\theta), \tag{6.3}$$

and workers move from unemployment to employment at the rate

$$q^w = [1 - G(\alpha_r)]\frac{m(u, v)}{u} = [1 - G(\alpha_r)]\theta q(\theta). \tag{6.4}$$

These transitions are both market averages (i.e., the transitions of the representative worker and the representative job) and individual transitions. Because the probability density of productivities is independent of the number of workers, the number of jobs, and the reservation productivity chosen by the representative agent, any single job-worker pair that chooses the reservation productivity α_r will have individual transitions given by (6.3) and (6.4). This contrasts, for example, with the case of variable search intensity, because the intensity of search influences the contact rate between firms and workers, and not whether the firm and worker form the match after they meet. With variable search intensity the representative agent's intensity enters the job-matching technology and influences a given individual's transition probability.

As before, the firm's and worker's transition rates satisfy the simple relationship, $q^w = \theta q$. The equilibrium condition for unemployment is also the same as before, except that now the flow out of unemployment depends on the reservation productivity

$$u = \frac{\lambda}{\lambda + \theta q(\theta)[1 - G(\alpha_r)]}. \tag{6.5}$$

An exogenous rise in the reservation productivity increases $G(\alpha_r)$, the rejection rate, so it increases unemployment at given vacancies. Diagrammatically, the exogenous rise in α_r shifts the Beveridge curve out.

6.2   The Choice of Reservation Wage

An unemployed worker chooses which jobs to reject and which to accept on the basis of the wages that he observes when he makes contact with a firm. In general, the wage rate offered will depend on the productivity of the job match,

$$w_j = w(\alpha_j). \tag{6.6}$$

We show later that $w'(\alpha) \geq 0$. The worker chooses a reservation wage w_r and accepts all jobs offering $w \geq w_r$. Search stops when the first job offering at least as much as w_r is found. By (6.6) we can write

$$w_r = w(\alpha_r), \tag{6.7}$$

so we can re-express the worker's reservation wage in terms of a reservation productivity. We will do this when we discuss equilibrium later in the chapter. Here we derive the optimal reservation wage from a partial model.

We derive the reservation wage under the assumption that firms will not reject a worker who wants to accept a job with them. This assumption is satisfied in equilibrium. Then, if a worker i has the reservation wage w_{ri}, his transition from unemployment to employment follows a Poisson process with rate

$$q_i^w = \theta q(\theta)[1 - G(\alpha_{ri})], \tag{6.8}$$

where α_{ri} is obtained from (6.7) by setting $w_r = w_{ri}$.

Now let U_i be the unemployed worker's returns from search and W_j the present-discounted value from employment when the job pays wage w_j. If the worker accepts the wage w_j, his net worth is W_j; if he rejects it and searches optimally for another job, his net worth is U_i (evaluated at the optimal w_{ri}). Hence, he accepts w_j if (and only if)

$$W_j \geq U_i. \tag{6.9}$$

Since, as we show below, $\partial W_j/\partial w_j \geq 0$ and $\partial U_i/\partial w_j = 0$, there is a reservation wage w_{ri}, satisfying

$$W_{ri} = U_i, \tag{6.10}$$

such that all jobs paying $w_j \geq w_{ri}$ are accepted.

If a worker finds a job during search, he will earn a wage that is as yet unknown to him. But he knows that the wage will be at least as high as w_{ri}, and the net worth from the job will be at least as much as W_{ri}. We define the conditional expectation

$$W_i^e = E(W_j \mid W_j \geq W_{ri}). \tag{6.11}$$

$E(.)$ is the expectations operator and the superscript e will have the same meaning throughout this chapter. It denotes the conditional mean of a variable, and it corresponds to the mean value of the variable that would be observed in the market by an independent observer. W_i^e is subscripted by i to emphasize that it depends on the reservation wage of worker i.

In equilibrium all workers are equally productive ex ante, so W_i^e and U_i will be common to all workers.

Let again z denote unemployment income and λ the rate at which negative productivity jobs arrive and jobs are destroyed. The net worth of unemployed worker i satisfies

$$rU_i = z + q_i^w(W_i^e - U_i),\tag{6.12}$$

with q_i^w given by (6.8). It is immediate that U_i is independent of any particular wage offer w_j. The net worth from accepting a wage w_j satisfies

$$rW_j = w_j + \lambda(U_i - W_j),\tag{6.13}$$

where, trivially, $\partial W_j/\partial w_j > 0$. Hence the reservation wage rule in (6.10) exists and gives a unique reservation wage. To find the reservation wage, we substitute w_{ri} for w_j in (6.13) and use condition (6.10) to eliminate W_{ri}. This gives

$$w_{ri} = rU_i.\tag{6.14}$$

Equation (6.14) makes good intuitive sense. rU_i is the permanent income of unemployed worker i. The worker is willing to accept all jobs that compensate him for his loss of permanent income. Anything he earns over and above his reservation wage is pure economic rent.

To write equation (6.14) in terms of wages and the other variables, we take conditional expectations of (6.13) and substitute W_i^e out of (6.12). The reservation wage then becomes

$$w_{ri} = \frac{(r+\lambda)z + q_i^w w_i^e}{r+\lambda+q_i^w}.\tag{6.15}$$

Since all workers are alike during search, they will all choose the same reservation wage. The common choice of reservation wage w_r satisfies

$$w_r = \frac{(r+\lambda)z + q^w w^e}{r+\lambda+q^w},\tag{6.16}$$

where q^w is given by equation (6.4) and w^e is the conditional mean of the wage rate $E(w \mid w \geq w_r)$.

The partial comparative statics of the reservation wage are easy to derive. Higher average productivity increases the reservation wage because it increases the expected wage w^e. Higher dispersion of the productivity distribution, represented, for example, as in the analysis in chapter 2 by a mean-preserving multiplicative shift parameter, also increases the reservation wage. The reason is that following the spreading out of the distribution, the prospect of finding a job at the top end of the range is now more rewarding, since these jobs pay more. The prospect of finding a job at the lower end of the range is not any worse, since the worker was planning to reject those jobs in any case. Hence, on average, the worker is made better off by the increased dispersion, and he requires higher compensation to give up search.

Higher unemployment income reduces the cost of holding out for a better-paying offer, so reservation wages again rise. Higher interest rate or rate of job separation reduce the present-discounted value of a job, the former because future wages are discounted more heavily and the latter because jobs last on average less. Job seekers are made worse off, so their reservation wages fall. Finally a higher ratio of vacancies to unemployment (labor-market tightness) improves the chances that the worker will make a job contact, so it leads to an increase in the reservation wage.

The effect of labor-market tightness on the reservation wage is another example of the trading externality that we discussed in earlier chapters. The acceptance decision of a worker who has located a job depends on how many other workers and jobs are engaged in search. As before, this externality has some implications for the efficiency of equilibrium, which we will discuss in chapter 8. But it also has some implications for equilibrium that are different from the ones we discussed before. If, say, the number of jobs increases, workers increase their reservation wage: The former reduces unemployment by increasing the number of job contacts; the latter increases it by reducing the fraction of job contacts that are accepted. This contrasts with the implications of the trading externality when search intensity is variable, where both the increase in the number of jobs and the increase in search intensity reduce unemployment. Moreover, with stochastic job matchings, variations in the number of workers and jobs engaged in search can be brought about through the job acceptance decision. This becomes another source of externalities. We take these points up again later in this chapter, when we discuss equilibrium.

6.3   The Choice of Hiring Standards

The firm, like the worker, will not want to take on all workers who apply
for a job. As with job advertising, it makes a big difference in the derivation of the firm's acceptance policy if the number of jobs is held fixed or
if it is allowed to vary optimally. In the former case the reservation productivity of the firm behaves predictably, since the problem is similar to
the one facing the worker choosing his reservation wage. The properties
of the reservation hiring standard need not be derived, to avoid repetition. Higher mean or dispersion of the productivity distribution increases
the reservation hiring standard. Higher interest rate, rate of job destruction, and cost of vacancy advertising, all decrease the hiring standard for
obvious reasons. Finally the externality now is also negative, since higher
labor-market tightness implies that firms find it harder to recruit and so
become less choosey about whom they hire.

   If the number of jobs is allowed to vary optimally when the firm is
considering whether to accept or reject a worker, the problem is different. With no restrictions on the number of jobs, a worker recruited to a
particular job does not deprive the firm of the chance to offer a job to
another worker who may come along after him. Thus the only requirement for recruitment is that the worker should be able to cover the (variable) cost of production: All workers whose marginal product is at least
as high as the wage rate are hired. If the number of jobs is held fixed,
the firm's hiring standard is higher because the worker taken on will have
to compensate the firm for the loss of a scarce job slot. We consider now
the case where the number of jobs is variable and optimally set by the
firm.

   The firm considers hiring workers to jobs whose productivities are distributed according to $G(\alpha)$, where α is, as before, the number of efficiency units of each job match. If it applies a hiring standard α_f, the
expected productivity of a new job match is α_f^e, where

$$\alpha_f^e = E(\alpha \mid \alpha \geq \alpha_f). \tag{6.17}$$

Hence the expected value of production is $p\alpha_f^e$, where, as before, p is a
general productivity parameter. The expected profit from a new job
match therefore satisfies

$$rJ_f^e = p\alpha_f^e - w_f^e - \lambda J_f^e, \tag{6.18}$$

where J_f^e is the conditional expectation of the job's net worth, w_f^e is the expected wage of an acceptable job and λ the job destruction rate that leads to the job's closure.

The uncertainty about the job's productivity is resolved when the firm and worker meet. For any job-specific parameter α_j, the job's net worth satisfies

$$rJ_j = p\alpha_j - w(\alpha_j) - \lambda J_j. \tag{6.19}$$

The net worth of a vacancy is, as before, denoted by V, and it satisfies,

$$rV = -pc + q_f(J_f^e - V). \tag{6.20}$$

q_f is the rate at which vacant jobs become filled, and it is given by

$$q_f = q(\theta)[1 - G(\alpha_f)]. \tag{6.21}$$

In profit-maximizing equilibrium $V = 0$, so

$$J_f^e = \frac{pc}{q_f}. \tag{6.22}$$

Now consider a firm with a vacancy, which is in contact with a worker with productivity α_j. If the firm accepts the worker, its return will be $J_j = J(\alpha_j)$, given by (6.19). If it rejects him, its return will be V, which in equilibrium is 0. Hence, if the number of jobs is in equilibrium, all workers that yield nonnegative profit are accepted. If $J(\alpha)$ is a monotonically increasing function of α, which as we show below it is, there is a reservation productivity α_f such that all $\alpha_j \geq \alpha_f$ are accepted. α_f is defined by the condition

$$J(\alpha_f) = 0, \tag{6.23}$$

so from (6.19) it satisfies

$$p\alpha_f - w(\alpha_f) = 0. \tag{6.24}$$

The similarity between condition (6.23) and the condition for the optimal reservation productivity in the job destruction model of chapter 2 is obvious. Once contact between the firm and the worker is established, the marginal worker just covers the cost of his employment. The cost of his hiring is "sunk," and in equilibrium it is covered by the intramarginal workers, who yield economic rents to the firm. Condition (6.24) equates marginal product to the wage rate.

The job creation condition for given wages is (6.22). With knowledge of the conditional expectation of jobs from (6.18), this becomes

$$p\alpha_f^e - w_f^e - (r + \lambda)\frac{pc}{q_f} = 0. \tag{6.25}$$

The job creation condition (6.25) depends on the choice of the firm's hiring standard, α_f. But, since in equilibrium all firms choose the same hiring standard, (6.25) is also a market condition for job creation. It is the natural extension of the condition that we derived in previous chapters, for example, (1.22), to the case of stochastic job matchings. The number of jobs is such that the firm expects the average marginal product of labor to cover the wage and hiring costs for the average job.

6.4   Wage Determination

Wages are determined as before by the meeting firm and worker. Suppose that a firm and a worker meet and discover that their match productivity is α_j. If they form the match, the worker enjoys net worth W_j and the firm J_j, given, respectively, by (6.13) and (6.19). If they do not form it, the worker has net worth U and the firm V. The wage rate w_j is chosen to maximize the product

$$(W_j - U)^{\beta}(J_j - V)^{1-\beta}, \tag{6.26}$$

so it solves

$$W_j - U = \frac{\beta}{1 - \beta}(J_j - V). \tag{6.27}$$

Condition (6.27) immediately implies that the firm and the worker will agree on which job matches to form and which to reject. Workers accept all jobs that satisfy $W_j \geq U$, and firms accept all matches that satisfy $J_j \geq V$. Hence there is a common reservation productivity, and both agree to reject all job matches with productivity $\alpha_j < \alpha_r$. The common α_r satisfies both the reservation wage formula (6.16)—given the wage function (6.7)—and the hiring standard formula, (6.24).

To derive the wage equation, we proceed as in chapter 1 and substitute into (6.27) the net worths from (6.12), (6.13), and (6.19), noting that in equilibrium $V = 0$. The result is, perhaps surprisingly,

$$w_j = (1 - \beta)z + \beta p(\alpha_j + c\theta). \tag{6.28}$$

What is surprising in (6.28) is that despite the stochastic job matchings and the fact that the searching worker is confronted with a wage offer distribution, the wage equation is the same as before. Wages are a linear function of unemployment income, own productivity, and labor-market tightness. If market conditions are different when there are stochastic job matchings, wages are affected only if labor-market tightness is affected.

Since $\beta < 1$, we find from (6.19) and (6.28) that $\partial J_j/\partial\alpha_j > 0$, confirming the existence of a reservation productivity for the firm. Productivity differences are job specific, so the gains from a more productive job are shared between the firm and the worker. To derive the equilibrium equation for the reservation productivity, which by construction satisfies also the reservation wage formula (6.16), we substitute the wage rate from (6.28) into (6.24). We use α_r to denote the reservation productivity in place of α_f in order to emphasize the equilibrium nature of the equation:

$$\alpha_r = \frac{z}{p} + \frac{\beta}{1 - \beta}c\theta. \tag{6.29}$$

Before discussing some of the properties of this equation, we note that it is economically interesting mainly because unemployment has an option value for the worker. From (6.24) and (6.14) we derive

$$rU = p\alpha_r = z + \frac{\beta}{1 - \beta}pc\theta, \tag{6.30}$$

which confirms a similar expression derived in earlier chapters for the equilibrium value of unemployment. If unemployment had no option value, the unemployed worker's net worth would be simply z/r, the present discounted value of income. In this case the reservation productivity $p\alpha_r$ would be z, an exogenous constant. It is because of the option value of unemployment, in equilibrium given by $\beta pc\theta/(1 - \beta)$, that there are interesting questions to discuss about job acceptance.

Our assumptions that the option value derives form the fact that the employed cannot search imply that as in the case of search intensity, the reservation productivity in equilibrium is a linear function of labor-market tightness. Comparison of the equation for search intensity (5.29) with (6.29) shows that the same function of θ enters both equations. The main difference between the two equations is that the net unemployment income during search, z, enters the expression for the reservation productivity directly. The reason is that unlike search intensity, the reservation productivity has to cover the worker's loss of income when accepting a job. If firms and workers share the surplus from a job equally ($\beta = \frac{1}{2}$), then the reservation productivity just covers the loss of income of the worker and the firm's average hiring cost for each unemployed worker. For given market tightness, the common reservation productivity increases in unemployment income, the firm's recruitment costs, the share of labor in the wage bargain, and in tightness itself. It decreases in average productivity p. But in equilibrium θ is also influenced by these parameters, so the equilibrium effect of the parameters on job acceptance may well turn out to be different from the partial effect on reservation productivity.

6.5 Equilibrium

We now have all the equilibrium equations of the model with stochastic job matchings except one, the equation for average wages. But this is simply found by taking the conditional expectation of (6.28):

$$w^e = (1 - \beta)z + \beta p(\alpha^e + c\theta). \tag{6.31}$$

We give here all the equilibrium conditions, after substituting wages from (6.31) into the condition for jobs creation, (6.25):

$$u = \frac{\lambda}{\lambda + \theta q(\theta)[1 - G(\alpha_r)]}, \tag{6.32}$$

$$\alpha_r = \frac{z}{p} + \frac{\beta}{1 - \beta} c\theta, \tag{6.33}$$

$$(1 - \beta)\left(\alpha^e - \frac{z}{p}\right) - \beta c\theta - \frac{(r + \lambda)c}{q(\theta)[1 - G(\alpha_r)]} = 0. \tag{6.34}$$

The system is, as before, recursive. By differentiating equation (6.34) with respect to the reservation productivity, we find that the two effects that α_r has on it, through α^e and through $G(\alpha_r)$, cancel each other out, so (6.34) is independent of α_r (an envelope property implied by the optimality of α_r). Hence, with knowledge of r, (6.34) can be solved uniquely for θ, as in chapter 1. Then, with knowledge of θ, equation (6.33) gives

the reservation productivity, and with knowledge of θ and α_r, equation
(6.32) gives the equilibrium rate of unemployment. The wage rate for
each job is determined by (6.28) with knowledge of θ, and the average
wage rate from (6.31) with knowledge of both θ and α_r.

We study in the remainder of this section the equilibrium properties
of the two-equation block (6.33) and (6.34), which uniquely determines
the reservation productivity and market tightness. In the next section we
use the results to study the properties of unemployment, vacancies, and
wages.

The two-equation block is shown graphically in figure 6.1. The equation for the reservation productivity, (6.33), is linear with intercept z/p.
It is denoted by RP. The equation for tightness, (6.34), is a vertical line,
by virtue of the envelope property that it satisfies. Equilibrium is given
by the intersection of the two lines and is unique (contrast this with the
equivalent diagram with variable search intensity, figure 5.1; the difference arises from the fact that the choice of reservation productivity
jointly maximizes the firm's and worker's payoffs, in contrast to the
choice of search intensity, which maximizes the worker's payoffs before
contact is made with the firm).

The interesting parameters are, as before, unemployment income z
and general productivity p, which enter in ratio form and have a

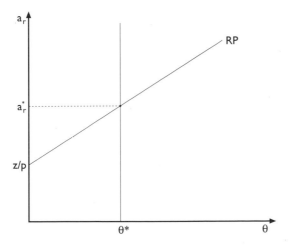

Figure 6.1
Equilibrium reservation productivity and market tightness

similar—but with opposite sign—influence, and the share of labor in wages. But now shifts in the distribution of productivities, $G(\alpha)$, can also influence the equilibrium, and for completeness we will also briefly consider the influence of the other parameters of the model.

Higher ratio of unemployment income to productivity, z/p, shifts the *RP* line in figure 6.1 up and the θ line to the left (figure 6.2). Although market tightness falls, the effect on the reservation productivity is ambiguous from the diagram alone. However, differentiation of equations (6.33) and (6.34) easily establishes that

$$\frac{\partial \alpha_r}{\partial z/p} = \frac{(r+\lambda)\eta(\theta)}{(r+\lambda)\eta(\theta)+\beta\theta q(\theta)[1-G(\alpha_r)]},\tag{6.35}$$

where $\eta(\theta)$ is the (negative of) the elasticity of $q(\theta)$ and is a number between 0 and 1. Hence the reservation productivity increases. Of course, if unemployment income was proportional to average productivity, through a proportional dependence on wages, both these effects would disappear.

The intuition behind these results is straightforward. Higher unemployment income relative to productivity implies both higher reservation wages and higher actual wages. The latter reduces job creation,

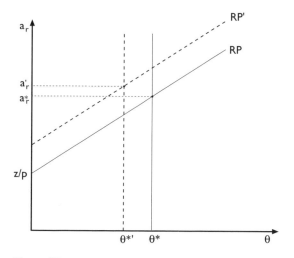

Figure 6.2
Influence of higher unemployment income or lower productivity on equilibrium

explaining the fall in market tightness. The former increases the reservation productivity, reducing job acceptance, despite the negative influence on it from the fall in tightness.

Additive shifts in the distribution of productivities $G(\alpha)$ increase the expected productivity α^e in (6.34) and so shift the θ line in figure 6.2 to the right. This increases both market tightness and, through it, the reservation productivity. More interesting, however, are mean-preserving spreads in $G(\alpha)$. A mean-preserving spread in $G(\alpha)$ indicates increased job-specific heterogeneity. Because (6.34) is independent of α_r, the mean-preserving spread in $G(\alpha)$ influences the equilibrium θ only through the (conditional) productivity, α^e. In the calculation of α^e the distribution of productivities is truncated to the left, so a mean-preserving spread increases it: The small α that would offset the effect of the large α on the mean of the distribution are not taken into account in calculating α^e. Hence the effect of a mean-preserving spread on θ is the same as the effect of an exogenous increase in α^e. The θ line in figure 6.1 shifts to the right, increasing both labor-market tightness and the reservation productivity.

The implications of higher labor share in the wage bargain, β, are more complex but similar to those that we derived for the labor share in the model with endogenous job destruction (chapter 2). Higher β shifts the θ line in figure 6.1 to the left, unambiguously reducing market tightness. But it also shifts the RP line up, resulting in ambiguous effects on the reservation productivity.

Intuitively, higher labor share implies higher wages at every productivity level, so job creation falls, justifying the fall in tightness. Lower tightness implies a fall in the reservation productivity but against this, higher wages elsewhere make workers who meet up with a firm more choosey about the firm's offer. To find out the net effect, we differentiate (6.33) and (6.34) with respect to β to find

$$\frac{\partial \alpha_r}{\partial \beta} = \frac{(r+\lambda)c\theta}{(1-\beta)^2} \frac{\eta(\theta) - \beta}{\beta\theta q(\theta)[1 - G(\alpha_r)] + (r+\lambda)\eta(\theta)}. \tag{6.36}$$

So, as with the reservation productivity in the job destruction model, the reservation productivity with stochastic job matchings reaches a maximum at the point $\beta = \eta(\theta)$. As we pointed out in chapter 2, there is no reason to expect that the share of labor in the wage bargain should equal the elasticity of the matching function with respect to unemployment, though the assumption of a constant η and a $\beta = \eta$ is a useful benchmark in many exercises with endogenous reservation rules (see also chapter 8).

Higher recruitment costs for firms shift the θ line to the left and the *RP* line up, with ambiguous effects on the reservation productivity. Higher interest rate or job destruction rate shifts only the θ line to the left, giving rise to a fall in both θ and the reservation productivity. With higher r or λ the present discounted value of profits from the job are lower, explaining the fall in θ. The fall in the reservation productivity is due to the fall in job availability caused by the lower θ.

6.6   Unemployment and Vacancies with Stochastic Job Matchings

The relation between unemployment and vacancies (the Beveridge curve) is given by equation (6.32). When comparing this curve with the simpler case discussed in chapter 1, we find that the only difference is that now the probability of leaving unemployment is multiplied by $1 - G(\alpha_r)$. The slope of the Beveridge curve at any point is monotonically related to the slope of the probability of leaving unemployment with respect to θ. Substituting α_r from (6.33) into $G(\alpha_r)$ and differentiating with respect to θ, we find the slope of the probability of leaving unemployment,

$$\frac{\partial q^w}{\partial \theta} = q(\theta)(1-\eta)[1-G(\alpha_r)] - \theta q(\theta)g(\alpha_r)\frac{\beta c}{1-\beta}, \tag{6.37}$$

where η is, as before, the negative of the elasticity of $q(\theta)$ and $g(\alpha_r) = G'(\alpha_r)$.

It is apparent from (6.37) that the slope of the Beveridge curve now has ambiguous sign. This ambiguity is common in models of search where the probability of leaving unemployment is the product of the probability of making a contact with a job and the probability of finding the job acceptable. We have already discussed briefly this ambiguity, when we derived the optimal reservation wage. Although our model is a market-equilibrium one and partial results on reservation wages do not always carry over, a simple way of giving the intuition for the ambiguity is to think in terms of a partial model and decompose the effect of a parameter on unemployment into a job-offer effect and a reservation-wage effect. The job-offer effect operates through the probability of making contact: If vacancies increase at given unemployment, the number of contacts between unemployed workers and firms with job vacancies increases. But, if a worker expects to make contact with a job with higher probability, he increases his reservation wage: The reservation-wage effect leads to more job rejection. The net effect on exit from unemployment is ambiguous because after the parameter change the acceptable jobs are a smaller fraction of a bigger pool of contacts.

The resolution of the ambiguity in (6.37) is empirical, since it is not possible to appeal to theoretical restrictions to compare the distribution of productivities (and wage offers) with the elasticity of the contact probability. The usual assumption made in the literature is that the job-offer effect (which in the case of a variable search intensity is reinforced) dominates the reservation-wage effect, and the Beveridge curve slopes down. Although the models that have been used to examine this question are partial-equilibrium ones, this assumption is plausible and available empirical evidence strongly supports it (see also the Notes on the Literature at the end of this chapter).

In light of this, what is the contribution of stochastic job matchings to the theory of unemployment? It is twofold. First, unemployment income and some other exogenous variables become shift variables in the relation between unemployment and vacancies. This is important for the empirical analysis of unemployment, especially when we consider the effects of policy in chapter 9, and we consider it below with the help of the Beveridge diagram. Second, the effect of every other exogenous change on unemployment is mitigated, since the reservation-wage effect offsets some of the demand-side effects that work through job offers.

There is, however, another and perhaps more important contribution of stochastic job matchings to our understanding of labor markets. This concerns the question of whether workers are efficiently allocated to jobs. In the analysis of the preceding chapters this question could not be raised, since jobs were identical to each other. Only questions about the determination of total employment could be raised. The interesting question now is whether the reservation productivity α_r achieves an efficient allocation of workers to jobs. We take up this question in chapter 8, when we consider the efficiency of equilibrium in each of the models that we have studied.

Now, the condition for the optimal reservation productivity (6.33) implies that there are some new shift variables in the relation between vacancies and unemployment: labor productivity, unemployment income, the share of labor in the wage bargain, and the cost of hiring. Armed with the results of the preceding section, it is easy to derive the effects of changes in these parameters on vacancies and unemployment.

Before we briefly discuss the role of the most important of these parameters, we note that the Beveridge diagram is not changed in a fundamental way by the introduction of stochastic job matchings. The Beveridge curve still slopes down (by assumption) though it is steeper than the curve without stochastic job matchings. Equilibrium job creation is still shown by a straight line through the origin, at the equilibrium θ obtained in figure 6.2. Consider now some parameter changes.

Higher unemployment income z rotates clockwise as before the job creation line (see figure 6.3). But it now also shifts the Beveridge curve out because of its effect on reservation productivity (see figure 6.2). Unemployment unambiguously increases, but the effect on vacancies is in general ambiguous. The effect on wages is ambiguous because of three opposing influences, the direct effect of z, which is positive, the indirect effect through market tightness, which is negative, and for mean wages there is also a second positive effect through the loss of some low-wage

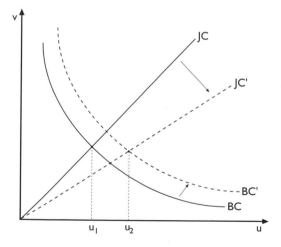

Figure 6.3
Effect of higher unemployment income on unemployment and vacancies

jobs following the rise in the reservation wage. It is, however, likely that the direct effect through the wage bargain dominates, since the reason that tightness falls is that the workers' outside opportunities improve when z is higher.

Higher general productivity p has the opposite effects on vacancies and unemployment. It rotates the job creation line counterclockwise and shifts the Beveridge curve toward the origin, reducing unemployment. The effect on vacancies is, as with changes in unemployment income, ambiguous. Wages now are unambiguously higher, since both the direct effect through p and the indirect effect through tightness are positive.

Higher labor share in the wage bargain has similar effects on job creation to those of higher unemployment income. The job creation line rotates clockwise. From equation (6.36), for given θ the reservation productivity may increase or decrease, so the shift in the Beveridge curve is ambiguous. Differentiation of the equilibrium relations, however, establishes that unemployment is always higher at higher labor share. To see this, recall that the influence of β on unemployment has the opposite sign from the effect of β on the probability of leaving unemployment. The latter is given by (6.4). Substitution of α_r from (6.33) into (6.4) and differentiation with respect to β gives

$$\frac{\partial q^w}{\partial \beta} = \frac{\partial q^w}{\partial \theta} \frac{\partial \theta}{\partial \beta} - \theta q(\theta) g(\alpha_r) \frac{c\theta}{(1-\beta)^2}. \qquad (6.38)$$

Now the partial with respect to θ has been assumed to be positive in (6.37) in order for us to get the negative slope in the Beveridge curve. The effect of β on θ is always negative, so the first term on the right-hand side of (6.38) is negative. The second term is also negative, implying that the probability of leaving unemployment is always lower at higher labor share. Unemployment is therefore always higher.

The discussion in this section shows that the introduction of stochastic job matchings and the rejection of low-productivity job offers enriches the analysis of unemployment in one important direction: It can explain more shifts in the Beveridge curve in full steady-state equilibrium than was possible in the models examined in earlier chapters, and it introduces a richer set of parameters in the reduced-form unemployment equation. Since empirically the Beveridge curve frequently shifts, stochastic job matchings and job rejection may well turn out to be important in empirical applications of the model.

6.7   Notes on the Literature

Stochastic job matchings were first analyzed by Jovanovic (1979) in a partial model of labor turnover. The early models of search were also partial, and most of them had reservation wage rules that were not too different from the partial reservation wage rules derived in this chapter. See, for example, McCall (1970), Holt (1970), and Gronau (1971). Following the criticisms of Rothschild (1973), several authors have tried to derive a distribution of wage offers from otherwise homogeneous labor; see, for example, Stiglitz (1985) and Salop (1973). These models are not generally simple to implement, and they have not led to important new results. The idea of appealing to stochastic job matchings to generate a distribution of wages in equilibrium has largely superceded them.

More recently, however, the question of the existence of jobs with different wages for workers with similar skills has been reconsidered by some authors within the framework of equilibrium models. This line of research derives equilibrium wage distributions by giving up the assumption that wages are determined by bargaining games and assuming instead that they are posted by the firm. Wage distributions then arise if there is a positive probability that the worker will simultaneously have the choice between two or more wage offers. For an early attempt, see Albrecht and Axell (1984). In the model of Burdett and Mortensen (1998) workers search on the job. When they locate a wage offer, they have the choice between their own wage and the new one that they have found. It is then shown that a robust wage distribution arises under the assumption that firms set wages to maximize profit. See Mortensen (1990) for a discussion of this line of research.

Hiring standards and reservation wages were analyzed in a partial framework in some detail in Pissarides (1976b).

The ambiguity regarding unemployment when both job contacts and reservation wages are variable is present in every model that addressed the issue. See, for example, Barron (1975) and Feinberg (1977). Burdett (1981) looked at the conditions needed for one effect to dominate the other and derived a sufficient condition for the dominance of the job-contact effect. His condition is not necessarily satisfied by all "reasonable" statistical distributions. The empirical evidence, however, strongly favors the job-contact effect. See Barron (1975) and Pissarides (1986). In the latter there is a strong positive effect of labor-market tightness

(v/u ratio) on the probability of leaving unemployment. Thus all exogenous variables that raise the reservation wage by increasing the v/u ratio raise also the probability of leaving unemployment, so the Beveridge curve slopes down. If the reservation-wage effect dominated, the Beveridge curve would slope up. Also none of the more recent empirical studies listed in the notes to chapter 1 have found a positive slope for the Beveridge curve, indirectly confirming the assumptions made here.

Evidence that the Beveridge curve has shifted recently in several countries is given in the empirical papers cited in the notes to chapter 1. The property explored in Jackman et al. (1989) is that a rise in unemployment income raises unemployment but has conflicting effects on vacancies, as shown in the final section of this chapter. Other evidence of earlier shifts was given by Gujarati (1972) and discussed by a number of authors.

The related empirical question of the effect of unemployment income and other parameters on reservation wages and the probability of leaving unemployment has attracted more attention in the literature than any other question in this area. For some early work see, for example, Nickell (1979) and Lancaster (1979) for reduced-form models and Kiefer and Neuman (1979), Yoon (1981), Lancaster and Chesher (1983), Narendranathan and Nickell (1985), Flinn and Heckman (1982), and Heckman and Singer (1984) for structural models. Devine and Kiefer (1991) survey the empirical literature. See also Atkinson and Micklewright (1991) and the notes at the end of the policy chapter 9 for more discussion of the literature on unemployment compensation.

7 Labor Force Participation and Hours of Work

In this chapter we consider two of the more traditional issues in the theory of labor supply, labor force participation and hours of work. Variations in the participation rate are not important for unemployment in the steady state because of our assumption of constant returns to scale in the trade and production technologies. But the search externalities have some strong implications for the efficiency of the participation rate, which we will discuss in chapter 8 with the help of the model of this chapter. Also, because of the equilibrium nature of our model, we offer an equilibrium analysis of two traditionally partial effects, the added-worker and discouraged-worker effects.

In our discussion of hours of work we use a simple model without intertemporal substitution, a restriction that is not serious in the steady state. The search externalities do not have any implications for the choice of hours but the existence of a positive trading cost does. We argue that when there is a positive trading cost workers will always choose to work too few hours. This inefficiency is corrected when hours are determined jointly by the firm and the worker as part of the same Nash bargain that is used to determine wages.

7.1 Labor Force Participation

We analyze endogenous labor force participation by assuming that there are no stochastic job matchings and that the intensity of search is fixed. As in the preceding two chapters, job destruction is also exogenous. None of these restrictions makes an essential difference to the results that we derive. But we introduce a new assumption: When workers are out of the labor force, they enjoy leisure worth l_0, in real terms, which they lose when they enter the market. l_0 varies across individuals because of differences in preferences. In a model with endogenous determination of the value of leisure, l_0 will depend on the parameters of the utility function, and it will be an increasing function of the individual's wealth because leisure is a normal good. We discuss this issue again later in this chapter.

Leisure from nonparticipation is strictly greater than leisure during search, for two reasons. First, there may be direct search costs of various kinds, even for a fixed intensity of search. Second, and more important, there may be indivisibilities in the use of leisure time: Various nonmarket activities, like bringing up children, home improvements, and traveling, require a long time to complete. Persons who decide not to enter the labor force are able to participate in these activities and enjoy their full return. Persons who decide to enter the market and are looking for a job cannot take full advantage of them because they know that their free time is likely to be short and of uncertain duration. They are essentially standing in a queue waiting for a call and unable to commit themselves to long-term nonmarket activities.

Individuals of working age have the choice of staying out of the labor force and enjoy a stream of real return l_0, or they enter the labor force to look for a job, for a real present-discounted return U. We make the inessential assumption that U is the same for all individuals. We also assume zero net returns during search, $z = 0$, though relaxing this assumption is straightforward and gives rise to predictable results. The important new assumption of this section is that the return when out of the labor force, l_0, differs across individuals. Formally, we assume that it is a drawing from a distribution with cumulative density $H(l_0)$.

Once a person is in the labor force, his or her behavior is governed by the rules that we described in earlier chapters. Hence the present discounted value from entering the labor force is given by equation (1.12), with $z = 0$:

$$U = \frac{\theta q(\theta)w}{r[r + \lambda + \theta q(\theta)]}. \tag{7.1}$$

Outside the labor force, the present-discounted value of the person's return is

$$U_0 = \frac{l_0}{r}, \tag{7.2}$$

where l_0 varies across individuals according to the cdf $H(l_0)$. A person will participate whenever $U \geq U_0$, so the participation rule is

$$rU = \frac{\theta q(\theta)w}{r + \lambda + \theta q(\theta)} \geq l_0. \tag{7.3}$$

We argued in earlier chapters that rU can be given the interpretation of the reservation wage of those in the labor force. No one will be willing to work for less than rU. Condition (7.3) makes the maximum return that the individual is willing to give up to participate equal to the reservation wage. This is a desirable property of the model and an intuitive one. An unemployed worker can withdraw from the market at any time and enjoy return l_0. His reservation wage must exceed l_0: The lowest acceptable wage in the market is at least equal to the utility that has to be given up to participate. If the individual's utility outside the labor force is strictly less than rU, he enjoys some pure economic rent simply by participating. If he succeeds in finding a job that pays him strictly more than rU, he enjoys some more economic rent when he moves into employment.

The fraction of the population that participates is $H(rU)$. Thus in partial equilibrium more people participate when wages are higher, labor-market tightness is higher, and the rates of interest and job loss are lower. The dependence of the participation rate on labor-market tightness is the discouraged-worker effect: When the rate at which unemployed workers find jobs, $\theta q(\theta)$, falls, fewer workers participate. We return to a more detailed study of this effect in the next section.

We saw in the analysis of equilibrium in chapter 1 and elsewhere that the size of the labor force does not influence equilibrium. Thus, in converting the partial results to general equilibrium ones, we need not be concerned with the implications of variations in the labor force for equilibrium. We may simply use (7.3) to determine the size of the labor force as a fraction of the (exogenous) population of working age, but note that w and θ are jointly determined by (1.22) and (1.23). If we substitute w and $r + \lambda$ out of (7.3) by using (1.22) and (1.23), and impose also $z = 0$, we derive the equilibrium participation condition

$$\frac{\beta}{1-\beta} pc\theta \geq l_0, \tag{7.4}$$

with θ given by (1.24). The qualitative properties of the participation condition in equilibrium are the same as its partial properties because of (1.24). This feature of the model is similar to the one we derived for search intensity and job acceptance in equilibrium.

The size of the labor force is not a variable in the equations defining the equilibrium of the models that we have considered so far, so the same equilibrium conditions as before give the solutions for all the unknowns, except for the size of the labor force. When search intensity is fixed and there are no stochastic job matchings, equilibrium is given by the conditions derived in the simple model of chapter 1, (1.21) to (1.23). Then the condition

$$L = PH\left(\frac{\beta}{1-\beta}pc\theta\right),$$
(7.5)

where L is the size of the labor force and P, the size of the population of working age, closes the model by determining the participation rate, L/P. In equilibrium the participation rate depends on the share of labor in the wage bargain, labor-market tightness, and the cost of hiring. Because the cost of hiring depends on general productivity, the latter also influences the participation rate even if market tightness is independent of it.

7.2   The Discouraged- and Added-Worker Effects

The utility from nonparticipation, l_0, is not generally a constant, but it is likely to depend on the values taken by one or more of the variables determined in the labor market. If this were not the case, economic growth would have resulted in higher and higher participation rates. This is implausible and contradicted by the facts. A general specification for the value of leisure assigns a value to the subjective return from non-market activities that is proportional to the individual's wealth. Intuitively, richer individuals attach more value to leisure and require greater compensation to give it up.

In the case of leisure from nonparticipation, this argument becomes more relevant when we consider household wealth, and the participation decision of different members of the household. We show that the added- and discouraged-worker effects traditionally discussed in the participation literature can be given an immediate interpretation. Because of the equilibrium nature of the model, we are able to go further than the conventional partial analysis and show how the two effects interact in equilibrium to influence participation rates.

Consider a household which has nonhuman wealth A and no members in the labor force. We assume that the utility that a typical member of the household derives from nonparticipation is proportional to the permanent flow of income derived from household wealth,

$$l_0 = lrA,$$
(7.6)

where l is a positive constant. Different members of the household may have different factors of proportionality l, but for simplicity, we assume that they are equally productive once in the labor market. l is stochastically distributed among the population according to the cdf $H(l)$.

If a household has one employed member, its wealth consists of nonhuman wealth A and human wealth W, where W is the present-discounted value of income from employment, (1.13). The utility from nonparticipation derived by other household members is

$$l_0 = lr(A + W). \tag{7.7}$$

Finally, if a household has one unemployed participant and no employed members, its wealth is $A + U$, with U given by (1.12) or (7.1), so the utility of a nonparticipating member is

$$l_0 = lr(A + U). \tag{7.8}$$

We saw that participation takes place if $l_0 \leq rU$. We call the level of l at which $l_0 = rU$ the *reservation utility level* and denote it by l_r. An individual participates if $l \leq l_r$ and stays out of the labor force otherwise. For a household with no members in the labor force, l_r is simply equal to U/A. Wealthy households, those with a high nonhuman wealth A, may choose not to participate at all. When there is economic growth, the utility from participating, U, will grow along with the growth of wages, whereas nonhuman wealth will grow only to the extent that the household refrains from consumption and reinvests its wealth. If the growth in the two wealth variables is not the same, participation may change over time.

A member in a household with an employed participant will have reservation utility

$$l_r = \frac{U}{A + W}. \tag{7.9}$$

One in a household with an unemployed participant will have,

$$l_r = \frac{U}{A + U}. \tag{7.10}$$

Because $W \geq U$, it is always the case that given initial wealth, individuals in households with an employed member have lower reservation utility than similar individuals in households with an unemployed member. Hence the secondary worker in a household is more likely to participate when the primary worker is unemployed, than when he or she is employed: the added-worker effect of the empirical literature.

The discouraged-worker effect states that when unemployment is higher, the participation rate will fall, because of the reduced probability that a worker will get a job. In our model unemployment is higher when labor-market tightness, θ, is lower. The discouraged-worker effect is valid both in a partial and in a general equilibrium context and applies to both primary and secondary workers. In a partial context, we saw when discussing (7.3) that lower θ implies less expected return from participation. In the equation giving the equilibrium participation rate, (7.5), a lower θ implies again a lower participation rate. Finally, turning to the expressions for the participation of the secondary household member derived in this section, we find that when θ is lower, all three expressions we derived for l_r, U/A, $U/(A + W)$, and $U/(A + U)$ are also lower, both when wages are held constant and when they are allowed to vary according to the equilibrium wage equation (1.23).

Although labor-market tightness is an endogenous variable, as is the participation rate, the nature of the model (at least the one with exogenous job destruction rate) is such that we can study the interaction between the added and discouraged worker effects by treating θ as the control variable. The reason is that the model's solution is recursive and equilibrium unemployment depends only on one other unknown, θ. Thus the solution for θ obtained from, say, (1.24) is independent of both unemployment and the participation rate. Once θ is known, unemployment can be obtained from the Beveridge equation (1.21) and participation from (7.6) to (7.8).

Usually the added- and discouraged-worker effects are studied for their cyclical implications; that is, how participation responds to temporary changes in the economy. But since the effects of parameter changes on participation are transmitted through u and θ regardless of whether the change is permanent or temporary, the interaction of the added- and discouraged-worker effects when the change in θ is temporary should be similar to the steady-state interactions that we now study.

Suppose that the primary worker in a household always participates, and consider the participation of the secondary worker in the household. Suppose, to begin with, that nonhuman wealth is zero, $A = 0$. Then in equilibrium a fraction u of primary workers are unemployed, and for them $l_r = 1$. So the secondary worker in their household participates if $l \le l_r = 1$. With a large number of households, l over these workers is distributed according to $H(l)$, so the fraction of them that participates is $H(1)$. The remaining fraction $1 - u$ of households has an employed member, for whom when $A = 0$, $l_r = U/W$. So the secondary worker in their household participates if $l \le U/W$. In equilibrium

$$\frac{U}{W} = \frac{\theta q(\theta)}{r + \theta q(\theta)} < 1, \tag{7.11}$$

and θ satisfies (1.24). The fraction of secondary workers in households with employed primary member that participates is $H(U/W)$.

The difference between $H(1)$ and $H(U/E)$ consists of added workers. Secondary workers in households with unemployed primary member are not discouraged, because of our assumption that nonhuman wealth is zero. But the rest of the secondary workers are discouraged by higher unemployment, since U/W rises as θ falls.

The participation rate of secondary workers is

$$P_0 = uH(1) + (1-u)H\left(\frac{U}{W}\right). \tag{7.12}$$

In equilibrium u and θ are related by the steady-state condition (1.21). The participation effects of a change in θ are

$$\frac{\partial P_0}{\partial \theta} = \left[H(1) - H\left(\frac{U}{W}\right)\right]\frac{\partial u}{\partial \theta} + (1-u)H'\left(\frac{U}{W}\right)\frac{rq(\theta)(1-\eta)}{(r + \theta q(\theta))^2}, \tag{7.13}$$

where, as before, $-\eta$ is the elasticity of $q(\theta)$ with respect to θ and it is a number between zero and one. The first term on the right-hand side of (7.13) shows the added-worker effect of the change in θ, and it is negative because $\partial u/\partial \theta < 0$. The second term shows the discouraged-worker effect, and it is positive. However, it is not difficult to show that the overall effect on participation is likely to be positive.

We use the approximation

$$H(1) - H\left(\frac{U}{W}\right) = H'\left(\frac{U}{W}\right)\left(1 - \frac{U}{W}\right) \tag{7.14}$$

and note that

$$\frac{\partial u}{\partial \theta} = -\frac{\lambda q(\theta)(1-\eta)}{(\lambda+\theta q(\theta))^2} = -(1-u)\frac{\lambda(1-\eta)}{\theta(\lambda+\theta q(\theta))},$$ (7.15)

to get

$$\frac{\partial P_0}{\partial \theta} = (1-u)H'\left(\frac{U}{W}\right)\frac{r(1-\eta)}{\theta(r+\theta q(\theta))}\left[-\frac{\lambda}{\lambda+\theta q(\theta)}+\frac{\theta q(\theta)}{r+\theta q(\theta)}\right].$$ (7.16)

The term in the square brackets could be either positive or negative, which confirms that the resolution of the conflict between the added and discouraged-worker effects is empirical. It can easily be shown, however, that it is likely to be positive for plausible parameter values. The first term is, in the steady-state, the unemployment rate. The second term is, for $r = \lambda$, the employment rate. It will take implausibly high values of the real interest rate r for the expression on the right to fall down to the level of equilibrium unemployment. In most countries, λ, the inverse of the duration of a job, is about 0.20 to 0.25 on annual data, which are themselves implausibly high values for the rate of interest. Of course, r needs to be much higher than λ in (7.16) for the added-worker effect to dominate the discouraged-worker effect. This conforms with empirical analyses of added- and discouraged-worker effects over the cycle, where the latter is usually found to be dominant.

The results of the preceding paragraph, when applied to the business cycle, imply that participation rates should be pro-cyclical. There is, however, another, possibly stronger, reason for such pro-cyclicality in the model. This follows from the implications of taking into account non-labor wealth A. With positive nonhuman wealth, the reservation level of l which determines the equilibrium participation rate depends inversely on A for all households. If now the general level of productivities improves, through an increase in p, both forward-looking human wealth variables, U and W, increase by the same proportion because of the increase in wages. But nonhuman wealth does not increase, at least not for a while. Therefore the reservation utility level l_r increases for all household types. More household members participate regardless of the value of wealth. Intuitively, when market returns increase, the expected payoffs from participation increase, but the amount of nonhuman wealth, which increases the value of leisure, does not increase. Eventually, if the returns from participation remain high, nonhuman wealth also increases through higher savings. In that case the participation rate returns to its original value, but such a change takes place only asymptotically, as time tends to infinity.

7.3 Hours of Work

We analyze the choice of hours of work in the steady state by making use of a model that ignores intertemporal considerations, in contrast to the analysis of search intensity in chapter 5. This is not a serious restriction for our purposes, since the problems that we wish to highlight in the choice of hours of work do not depend on the differences between current income from work and permanent income. A dynamic analysis of the choice of hours of work along the lines of the analysis of the choice of hours of search in chapter 5 is, of course, possible. But in the steady state current income from work (the wage rate) is not very different from permanent income (rW in the notation of earlier chapters), so a model that ignores intertemporal considerations is likely to give similar results. In contrast, current income during search (unemployment income) is very different from permanent income (rU) even in the steady state, and the individual searches in order to make the transition from the current state to another, so ignoring intertemporal considerations in the choice of search intensity would eliminate the main results.

We assume that the worker's instantaneous utility depends on current income and current hours of work. We write instantaneous utility during employment as

$$w_E = wh\phi(1-h), \qquad \phi'(.) > 0, \ \phi''(.) \le 0, \ 0 \le h \le 1, \qquad (7.17)$$

where w now denotes the hourly wage rate, h denotes hours of work, and the length of the day is normalized to unity. The utility function is linear in income (wh) and nonlinear in hours of work. If income is higher, the marginal cost of hours of work is higher, indicating complementarity between consumption and leisure. These assumptions parallel the ones that we made in chapter 5 to analyze hours of search; see (5.31).

We assume for simplicity that the intensity of search is fixed and unemployed workers derive no direct utility from leisure and have no income. Hence the two equations giving the worker's present-discounted utility during unemployment and during employment in some job j are, respectively,

$$rU = \theta q(\theta)(W - U), \tag{7.18}$$

$$rW_j = w_j h_j \phi(1 - h_j) + \lambda(U - W_j). \tag{7.19}$$

The W without a subscript denotes utility in the representative job. The hourly wage rate is determined, as before, by the Nash solution to the bargaining problem. Hours of work may be determined either by the worker in such a way as to maximize his utility or by a bargain between the firm and the worker along the lines of the wage bargain. Since the search externalities do not influence the decision with regard to hours of work, nor does the chosen number of hours influence the number of jobs and number of workers that come into the market, the efficient number of hours of work is determined by a Nash bargain between the firm and the worker. We show that if workers choose their own hours of work, they will choose to work too few hours. The reason for this inefficiency is related to the existence of trading costs, though not to the search externalities.

If hours of work are chosen by workers, h_j maximizes W_j for given w_j and U. Hence optimum hours satisfy

$$\frac{\phi'(1 - h_j)}{\phi(1 - h_j)} h_j = 1. \tag{7.20}$$

The wage rate does not affect hours because the income and substitution effects offset each other, not an unreasonable property in the steady state. Labor-market tightness does not affect hours because the worker chooses his hours of work after he has found the job, and he knows he can revise his choice when he changes jobs.

If hours of work are chosen after a bargain between the firm and the worker, their determination is more complicated but still straightforward. Let p be the product per hour input. Then, the present-discounted value of profit from a vacant job and from a filled job j are, respectively,

$$rV = -pc + q(\theta)(J - V), \tag{7.21}$$

$$rJ_j = h_j p - h_j w_j - \lambda J_j. \tag{7.22}$$

Wages and hours of work in job j are chosen to maximize the product

$$(W_j - U)^\beta (J_j - V)^{1-\beta}, \qquad 0 < \beta < 1, \tag{7.23}$$

with W_j given by (7.19).

The wage rate that maximizes (7.23) satisfies the condition

$$\beta(J_j - V)\phi(1 - h_j) - (1 - \beta)(W_j - U) = 0. \tag{7.24}$$

Hours of work also maximize (7.23), and the condition they satisfy is

$$\beta(J_j - V)w_j\phi(1 - h_j)\left(1 - \frac{\phi'(.)}{\phi(.)}h_j\right) + (1 - \beta)(W_j - U)(p - w_j) = 0. \tag{7.25}$$

To derive a wage equation from (7.24), we make use of the property that in equilibrium wages and hours of work are the same in all jobs. Also in equilibrium $V = 0$, so from (7.21)

$$J = \frac{pc}{q(\theta)}. \tag{7.26}$$

Substituting into (7.22), we obtain

$$h(p - w) - \frac{r + \lambda}{q(\theta)}pc = 0. \tag{7.27}$$

Computing also $W - U$ from (7.18) and (7.19), we obtain

$$W - U = \frac{wh\phi(1 - h)}{r + \lambda + \theta q(\theta)}. \tag{7.28}$$

Hence, substituting $V = 0$, J from (7.26), $W - U$ from (7.28), and $r + \lambda$ from (7.27) into condition (7.24), we arrive at the wage equation

$$w = \beta p\left(1 + \frac{c}{h}\theta\right). \tag{7.29}$$

Wage equation (7.29) is of the same form as the one we had before, (1.23), except that now because w is an hourly wage rate, the cost of hiring is the hourly cost c/h and unemployment income z is zero. Equilibrium hours of work are determined from (7.25). Considering again (7.24) and (7.25) in equilibrium, when wages and hours are common to all jobs, we obtain, after substitution of $W - U$ from (7.24) into (7.25),

$$\frac{\phi'(1 - h)}{\phi(1 - h)}h = \frac{p}{w}. \tag{7.30}$$

The elasticity of the utility of leisure with respect to hours of work is equal to the ratio of the marginal product of labor to the wage rate. But in equilibrium the marginal product of labor must be strictly greater than the wage rate, as (7.27) implies, because firms must be compensated for their hiring costs. Hence (7.30) implies that when hours are set after a Nash bargain,

$$\frac{\phi'(1-h)}{\phi(1-h)}h > 1. \tag{7.31}$$

By the concavity of $\phi(1-h)$, the elasticity expression in (7.31) increases in h, so hours are now higher than implied by the worker's choice rule, (7.20). Now, if hours of work are determined by a bargain between the firm and the worker, they exceed the hours that maximize the worker's utility.

The discrepancy between utility-maximizing and Nash hours is not due to the search externalities; it is related to costly exchange. Workers choose the number of hours of work by comparing their marginal cost (loss of leisure) with the marginal benefit to themselves (the hourly wage rate). If the number of hours is determined by the Nash bargain, a similar marginal comparison is made but now the costs and benefits to the firm are also taken into account. The joint net marginal cost of one more hour to the firm and the worker is still the loss of leisure to the worker, but the joint gain is the product from one more hour. Thus the two methods of determining hours give the same result only when the wage rate is equal to the marginal product of labor. This cannot happen in equilibrium in this model because the firm's hiring costs drive a wedge between marginal product and wages.

In equilibrium (7.30) simplifies further by making use of (7.29). Substituting (7.29) into (7.30), we derive

$$\frac{\phi'(1-h)}{\phi(1-h)}h = \frac{1}{\beta(1+c\theta/h)}. \tag{7.32}$$

Labor-market tightness and the worker's share in the wage bargain influence optimal hours because they influence the wedge between the marginal product of labor and the equilibrium wage rate. Higher tightness or share of labor reduce the wedge, so they also reduce hours toward the level chosen by the utility-maximizing worker: The inefficiency that arises when workers choose their own hours is less in tight markets. (The inverse relation between tightness and hours of work is a feature of the steady state, and it does not necessarily hold over the cycle.)

Market equilibrium with variable hours of work is determined as before, except for small and obvious changes because of the reinterpretation of the wage rate and the product of labor in per-hour units. Thus in the steady state the Beveridge curve and the job creation curve, respectively, (1.21) and (1.24), are given by the same equations as before, and the hourly wage rate is also given by the same equation. Hours of work in the case where the worker chooses his own hours after he finds the job are given by the elasticity condition (7.20). In this case equilibrium hours depend only on the utility function, and they do not interact with the rest of the model. But in the efficient bargain case the hours condition changes to (7.32), so hours are influenced by all variables that influence equilibrium tightness. Any parameter that increases equilibrium tightness reduces equilibrium hours. Equation (7.32) is very much in the spirit of the other equilibrium relations that we have found in the labor market analysis of part II of the book, such as the intensity condition (5.29) and the participation condition (7.4). Equilibrium labor-market tightness (the ratio of vacancies to unemployment) is critical in all of them because it is the variable that transmits the effects of parameter changes to them.

7.4   Notes on the Literature

Labor force participation in the context of a job-matching model was considered by McKenna (1987). A partial treatment of added- and discouraged-worker effects in a model of search appeared in Pissarides (1976a, b). Other equilibrium matching models that considered changing labor force participation include Bowden (1980) and Blanchard and Diamond (1989).

The topics discussed in this chapter have received extensive treatment in the labor economics literature but not in the context of job-matching models. For example, partial models of added-worker and discouraged-worker effects were extensively discussed by Cain (1966) and Bowen and Finegan (1969). Generally, the early studies found that the discouraged-worker effect dominates the added-worker effect. More recently Lundberg (1985) has used a transitions approach to estimate a small but statistically significant added-worker effect for married women.

Issues in the supply of hours of work in dynamic models are discussed in several papers in the new classical macroeconomics, following the lead of Lucas and Rapping (1969). See, for example, Hall (1980) and Barro (1981). These papers tend to emphasize the short-run responses of employment to temporary shocks, and the contribution that the intertemporal substitution of leisure can make to an explanation of output fluctuations. For empirical evidence on the intertemporal substitution hypothesis, see Mankiw, Rotemberg, and Summers (1985) and Alogoskoufis (1987).

The contrast between utility-maximizing and bargaining solutions discussed in this chapter is closely related to the one discussed by McDonald and Solow (1981) in the context of employment determination under unions, though the inefficiency we derived here is not due to any of the reasons they discuss.

Our model of the choice of hours of work is deliberately simple to highlight the result of interest. Some general models of the allocation of time to work and search have appeared in the literature, but without important new results. See, for example, Whipple (1973), Siven (1974), Seater (1977), Barron and McCafferty (1977), and Burdett (1979).

III CONSTRAINED EFFICIENCY AND THE ROLE OF POLICY

8 Efficiency

The equilibrium that we described in the preceding chapters suffers from trading externalities. The chances that unemployed workers or vacant firms have of trading within a given period of time depend on the number of traders in the market and on what they do. In the context of the models that we described, the externalities are shown by the dependence of the transition probabilities of unemployed workers and vacant firms on the tightness of the market. We also saw that in equilibrium tightness depends on the wage rate. The critical question that we raise in this chapter is whether the Nash wage equation internalizes the search externalities; that is, whether in equilibrium social output is maximized despite the externalities.

The conditions under which wages are determined are not likely to lead to social efficiency. The externalities affect firms and workers still searching, yet wages are determined by the firm and the worker *after* they meet. The meeting firm and worker are not likely to take into account the effect of their choices on firms and workers still searching. We look at the implications of this for the efficiency of each of the decisions that we described in the preceding chapters, beginning with the efficiency of job creation in the simple model of chapter 1.

8.1 Job Creation

In the simple model of chapter 1, all jobs have the same productivity and search intensity is fixed. The critical variable that drives equilibrium is job creation, which is determined by profit-maximizing firms. The questions we investigate in this section are whether there is a wage rate that makes firms create the number of jobs that maximizes social output and whether the Nash bargaining solution gives rise to this wage rate in equilibrium.

We investigate these questions by ignoring capital, since it is obvious from the analysis of chapter 1 that under our assumptions about the structure of capital markets the choice of capital is optimal. See the discussion in section 1.6 and the condition for the choice of capital per job, (1.28). In other situations the search and bargaining environment may lead to inefficient capital choices associated with "hold-up" problems, a question that we do not investigate here (see the Notes on the Literature at the end of this chapter). Without capital, social output per job is simply p, and leisure enjoyed by each unemployed worker is z. Each vacancy costs society pc, and given the definition $\theta = v/u$, the social welfare function for an infinitely lived economy is

$$\Omega = \int_0^\infty e^{-rt}[p(1-u)+zu-pc\theta u]dt. \tag{8.1}$$

The social planner is subject to the same matching constraints as firms and workers. Therefore the evolution of unemployment that constrains social choices is the same as the one that constrains private choices,

$$\dot{u} = \lambda(1-u)-\theta q(\theta)u. \tag{8.2}$$

The social planner is not interested in wages, since wages determine only the distribution of output and distributional considerations are excluded from the social welfare function (by assumption). The approach that we will follow in the comparison of the social and private outcomes is to derive the social outcome by ignoring the private condition for job creation, (1.24), and then investigate whether there is a wage rate that makes the social and private conditions for job creation identical. If there is one, then clearly unemployment will be efficient for that wage, since both the private and social outcomes are constrained by the same steady-state condition, (8.2).

Let μ be a co-state variable. The optimal path of unemployment and market tightness satisfies (8.2) and the Euler conditions

$$-e^{-rt}(p-z+pc\theta)+[\lambda+\theta q(\theta)]\mu - \dot{\mu} = 0, \tag{8.3}$$

$$-e^{-rt}pcu+\mu u q(\theta)[1-\eta(\theta)] = 0. \tag{8.4}$$

$\eta(\theta)$ is the (negative of the) elasticity of $q(\theta)$, and it is a number between 0 and 1.

To derive the condition for the socially efficient number of jobs, we substitute μ from (8.4) into (8.3) and evaluate the outcome in the steady state to obtain

$$[1-\eta(\theta)](p-z)-\frac{\lambda+r+\eta(\theta)\theta q(\theta)}{q(\theta)}pc = 0. \tag{8.5}$$

Comparing now the social condition (8.5) with the private condition (1.24), reproduced here for easier reference,

$$(1-\beta)(p-z)-\frac{r+\lambda+\beta\theta q(\theta)}{q(\theta)}pc=0. \tag{8.6}$$

we find that the two are identical if, and only if,

$$\beta=\eta(\theta). \tag{8.7}$$

When (8.7) is satisfied, decentralized job creation is socially efficient.

The parameter β appears in (8.6) because of the wage equation and stands for labor's share of the surplus created by the job. So another way of stating the result that we have just derived is to say that if there is a wage equation of the same form as the one in the decentralized equilibrium, (1.23), but with β determined as in (8.7), then the search externalities that characterize the decentralized equilibrium are internalized. Now $\eta(\theta)$ is the elasticity of the expected duration of a vacancy (which in the steady state is equal to the inverse of $q(\theta)$).Because of the assumption of constant returns in the job-matching technology, $\eta(\theta)$ is also the elasticity of job matchings, $m(u, v)$, with respect to unemployment. Both β and $\eta(\theta)$ are numbers between 0 and 1, so condition (8.7) is feasible. But it is not likely to be satisfied when the wage equation is derived from the Nash solution to the wage bargain. In the Nash solution β is a constant, and normally it is assumed to equal $\frac{1}{2}$. $\eta(\theta)$ depends on the properties of the job-matching technology, and since $q(\theta)$ is a transition rate, $\eta(\theta)$ is not generally a constant. It is locally constant if the matching function can be approximated by a log-linear (Cobb-Douglas) function,

$$m=m_0 u^\eta v^{1-\eta}. \tag{8.8}$$

But even with Cobb-Douglas and a constant η, there is no reason why β should be equal to η, since β is determined in a different environment and without reference to the structural properties of the matching technology. Hence the Nash wage equation is not likely to internalize the search externalities.

However, since both firms and workers are causing congestion for each other, it is not possible to say whether equilibrium unemployment is in general above or below the socially efficient rate. One more hiring firm makes searching workers better off, but it makes other hiring firms worse off. The same is true of workers. One more searching worker makes hiring firms better off but other searching workers worse off. It follows easily from (1.24) and (8.2) that unemployment is higher when the share of labor in the wage bargain is higher. Hence equilibrium unemployment is above the socially efficient rate if $\beta > \eta(\theta)$, and it is below it if $\beta < \eta(\theta)$. Beyond that we cannot say much more about the efficiency of private outcomes in this model.

To provide some rationale for the efficiency condition (8.7), note that the elasticity of the expected duration of unemployment with respect to unemployment is $1 - \eta(\theta)$, and the elasticity of the expected duration of a job vacancy with respect to the number of job vacancies is $\eta(\theta)$. Hence, if $\eta(\theta)$ is high, it is an indication that at the margin firms are causing more congestion to other firms than the congestion that workers are causing to other workers. Firms are "taxed" by the social planner in this case by giving workers a higher share in the wage bargain. The same conclusions emerge if we consider the elasticity of the expected duration of unemployment with respect to vacancies, $-1 + \eta(\theta)$, and the elasticity of the expected duration of a job vacancy with respect to unemployment, $-\eta(\theta)$. We return to this question in the final section of this chapter.

Two other properties of the efficiency condition help to illustrate its nature. The first relates to the argument that we made in chapter 3, that the same market equilibrium as the one in chapter 1 can be derived from a model with large firms and costs of adjustment. The efficiency condition maximizes the present-discounted value of firms when account is taken of the dependence of the adjustment cost on the tightness of the market. The second property relates to the argument at the beginning of this chapter, that the private equilibrium outcome is likely to be inefficient because meeting firms and workers ignore the effects of their choices on those still searching. The efficiency condition maximizes the equilibrium returns of unemployed workers, who are the ones ignored in the wage bargain.

Consider first the model with large firms. Firm i chooses its capital stock and number of jobs to maximize the present-discounted value of profit

$$\Pi_i = \int_0^\infty e^{-rt}[F(K_i, N_i) - wN_i - pcV_i - \dot{K} - \delta K_i]dt \tag{8.9}$$

subject to the employment constraint

$$\dot{N}_i = q(\theta)V_i - \lambda N_i. \tag{8.10}$$

The firm takes the wage rate and labor-market tightness as given. The inefficiency in the supply of jobs arises from the fact that in market equilibrium labor-market tightness is influenced by the chosen supply of jobs, yet this is ignored by the firm. The socially optimum employment path maximizes an expression like (8.9) but replaces w by the social cost of employment (foregone leisure) and takes into account the link between θ and the chosen employment path. Comparison of (8.9) with the social welfare function (8.1) when K is ignored makes this obvious, and the argument need not be repeated.

A further property of the efficiency condition sheds more light on the reasons for the inefficiency of equilibrium wages. Unemployed workers enjoy expected return rU during search, given by equation (1.12). This return depends both on wages and on the number of available jobs. In equilibrium, if wages are higher, this does not necessarily mean that unemployed workers are better off, since the number of jobs may then be lower. This is the overall effect that the share of labor has on the expected returns of unemployed workers. A higher β raises expected wages but reduces the number of jobs, lengthening the expected duration of unemployment. In full equilibrium we can show that there is a unique β that maximizes the expected returns of unemployed workers, and this is the β that satisfies the efficiency condition (8.7).

To show this, we can go directly to the reduced-form equilibrium relation between the unemployed worker's net worth and market tightness, (1.19), reproduced below:

$$rU = z + \frac{\beta}{1-\beta} pc\theta. \tag{8.11}$$

Because this holds only in equilibrium, θ is constrained by (8.6). Maximization of (8.11) with respect to β, subject to (8.6), shows that rU attains a unique maximum at $\beta = \eta(\theta)$.

If firms and workers agree to share the surplus from employment in a way that maximizes the unemployed worker's expected returns, the search externalities will be internalized and social output maximized. This suggests another way of looking at the inefficiency of equilibrium, in terms of an insider-outsider dilemma: Unemployed workers are outsiders in the wage bargain, yet the chosen wage rate affects their welfare through the implications that it has for job creation. The insiders, employed workers and firms, are likely to ignore the welfare of the outsiders when setting the wage, so inefficiency is likely to result.

8.2 Job Destruction

Consider now the efficiency of equilibrium when there are idiosyncratic productivity shocks, as in the model analyzed in chapter 2. The two key equations of that model are (2.14) and (2.15), reproduced here for convenience:

$$(1-\beta)\frac{1-R}{r+\lambda} = \frac{c}{q(\theta)}, \tag{8.12}$$

$$R - \frac{z}{p} - \frac{\beta}{1-\beta}c\theta + \frac{\lambda}{r+\lambda}\int_R^1 (s-R)dG(s) = 0. \tag{8.13}$$

Jobs are created at maximum productivity p. After creation, shocks arrive at rate λ that moves productivity to px, where x is an idiosyncratic component constrained between 0 and 1. Jobs are destroyed when x drops below R, with R satisfying a zero-profit condition for occupied jobs. Equations (8.12) and (8.13) are solved for the equilibrium pair θ, R.

The decentralized equilibrium obtained from (8.12) and (8.13) depends on the sharing parameter β, so it is not likely to be efficient. We can show that efficiency again requires satisfaction of condition (8.7) and that although the decentralized value of market tightness may be either too high or too low, for the reasons explained in the preceding section, the decentralized value of the reservation productivity is always too low. That is, at given unemployment, there is always too little job destruction in equilibrium.

To demonstrate that the efficiency condition is still (8.7), we write the social welfare as

$$\Omega = \int_0^\infty e^{-rt}(y+uz-pc\theta u)dt, \tag{8.14}$$

where everything is as before except that now y denotes average output per person in the labor force. The evolution of unemployment that constrains social choices is given by

$$\dot{u} = \lambda G(R)(1-u) - \theta q(\theta)u, \tag{8.15}$$

since only jobs that get a productivity shock $x < R$ are destroyed. The evolution of y is given by

$$\dot{y} = p\theta q(\theta)u + \lambda(1-u)\int_R^1 psdG(s) - \lambda y. \tag{8.16}$$

The first term on the right-hand side of (8.16) shows new job creation, the output of each new job being p. The second term shows the fraction of existing jobs that are hit by a productivity shock. If the productivity shock s is between R and 1, the jobs continue in operation, producing ps each, but if the shock is below R, they close down and produce zero. The final term shows that the existing output from a typical worker is lost every time a shock arrives.

The socially efficient pair θ, R maximizes (8.14) subject to (8.15) and (8.16). In addition to (8.15) and (8.16), the optimal pair satisfies the Euler conditions (where μ_1 and μ_2 are co-state variables):

$$e^{-rt}(z - pc\theta) - [\lambda G(R) + \theta q(\theta)]\mu_1 + \dot{\mu}_1 + \mu_2\left[p\theta q(\theta) - \lambda\int_R^1 psdG(s)\right] = 0, \tag{8.17}$$

$$e^{-rt} - \mu_2\lambda + \dot{\mu}_2 = 0, \tag{8.18}$$

$$-e^{-rt}pcu - \mu_1(1 - \eta(\theta))q(\theta)u + \mu_2 p(1 - \eta(\theta))q(\theta)u = 0, \tag{8.19}$$

$$\lambda G'(R)(1-u)\mu_1 - (1-u)\lambda p R G'(R)\mu_2 = 0. \tag{8.20}$$

Evaluating the Euler conditions in the steady state and getting rid of the co-states μ_1 and μ_2, we arrive at two equations that are uniquely solved for the socially efficient θ and R:

$$[1 - \eta(\theta)]\frac{1-R}{r+\lambda} = \frac{c}{q(\theta)}, \tag{8.21}$$

$$R - \frac{z}{p} - \frac{\eta(\theta)}{1-\eta(\theta)}c\theta + \frac{\lambda}{r+\lambda}\int_R^1 (s-R)dG(s) = 0. \tag{8.22}$$

Comparison of (8.21) and (8.22) with the decentralized equilibrium (8.12) and (8.13) shows that social efficiency is again feasible and is obtained if the share of labor is $\eta(\theta)$, that is, if condition (8.7) is satisfied.

Efficiency in the model with idiosyncratic productivity shocks is not likely to be attained, for the same reasons that it fails in the model without shocks. Not surprisingly, idiosyncratic shocks do nothing to internalize the search externalities, and since the search externalities influence in the first instance job creation (those still searching), the extension of choice over the job destruction margin does not alter the internalizing rules. As before, there is a unique share of the surplus from job creation that makes firms create the efficient number of jobs. If the number of jobs created is efficient, then job destruction is also efficient, but if not, then job destruction will be inefficient too, since in equilibrium it depends on market tightness.

We saw in chapter 2 that market tightness is a decreasing function of the worker's share β. Therefore, as in the model with constant job destruction rate, at given unemployment job creation is above the efficient level if $\beta < \eta(\theta)$, and below it, if $\beta > \eta(\theta)$. We also saw in chapter 2 that R reaches a unique maximum at $\beta = \eta(\theta)$. Therefore, perhaps surprisingly, if job creation is not at the efficient level, job destruction is always too low.

To see the rationale for this result, we note from (8.13) and (8.11), that the reservation productivity satisfies

$$pR + \frac{\lambda p}{r+\lambda} \int_R^1 (s-R)dG(s) = rU. \tag{8.23}$$

The left-hand side of (8.23) is the expected profit from the marginal job: current product pR plus an option value from expected productivity shocks. The right-hand side is the reservation wage of the unemployed worker (or expected return from search). A job is destroyed when it fails to cover the worker's reservation wage because in equilibrium the expected return from a vacancy is zero. But we have already seen that the expected returns from search, rU, are maximized at the efficient point $\beta = \eta(\theta)$. Hence the reservation productivity is also maximized at $\beta = \eta(\theta)$. We return to a discussion of this issue in the concluding section of this chapter and in the next chapter, section 9.9.

8.3 Search Intensity and Job Advertising

The search externalities are likely to affect the decision with regard to the choice of search intensity. When the unemployed worker chooses how much to search, he ignores the effects that this is likely to have on other workers and firms—negative on the former and positive on the latter. Wages are not likely to internalize these externalities because, as before, the meeting firm and worker ignore the effects of their actions on firms and workers still engaged in trade. We now examine this proposition by using the techniques developed in chapter 5. We also examine the efficiency of job advertising which, as we saw, behaves like search intensity when the number of jobs is fixed but not when the number of jobs is variable. Job destruction in the analysis that follows is constant at the rate λ, as in the model of chapter 5, and all jobs produce output p.

Social output per head when workers search with intensity s and firms spend a on job advertising is given by

$$\Omega = \int_0^\infty e^{-rt}((1-u)p + u[z - \sigma(s, z)] - u\theta pc(a))dt. \tag{8.24}$$

As in chapter 5, $\sigma(s, z)$ is the cost of search, with $\sigma_s(.) > 0$ and $\sigma_z(.) \geq 0$, and $c(a)$ is the cost of advertising, with $c'(a) > 0$. The socially efficient solution maximizes (8.24) subject to the condition for the evolution of unemployment,

$$\dot{u} = \lambda(1-u) - \theta q(s, a, \theta)u, \tag{8.25}$$

with $q(.)$ given by

$$q = \frac{m(su, av)}{v}. \tag{8.26}$$

In choosing the search intensity and job advertising consistent with social efficiency, we take into account the fact that a variation in either influences the transition probability of the typical firm and worker. In deriving the private solutions in chapter 5, we ignored this influence, and this is where the private and social solutions differ.

The Euler conditions for the social maximization problem (8.24) to (8.26) are again equations (8.3) and (8.4), but now with $q(.)$ depending on a and s and z replaced by $z - \sigma(s, z)$ and two new equations for the two new control variables, a and s. Thus the condition that internalizes the externalities on job creation is again (8.7)—nothing has changed by the introduction of variable search intensity except that the elasticity η may now depend on other variables besides θ. The maximization conditions with respect to the two remaining control variables, s and a, satisfy

$$-e^{-rt}\sigma_s(s, z)u + \mu\theta q_s(s, a, \theta)u = 0, \tag{8.27}$$

$$-e^{-rt}u\theta p c'(a) + \mu\theta q_a(c, a, \theta)u = 0. \tag{8.28}$$

where μ is, again, the co-state variable associated with (8.25).

The question now is whether when (8.7) is satisfied, the private choices with respect to search intensity and job advertising are socially efficient. More generally, we ask whether there is a condition that makes (8.27) and (8.28) equivalent to the private equilibrium conditions derived in chapter 5. The pertinent conditions in chapter 5 are (5.29) and (5.30), which are reproduced here:

$$-s\sigma_s(s, z) + \frac{\beta}{1-\beta}pc(a)\theta = 0, \tag{8.29}$$

$$\frac{c'(a)a}{c(a)} = 1. \tag{8.30}$$

To answer this question, we note from (8.26) that

$$\frac{\partial q}{\partial s}\frac{s}{q} = \eta, \tag{8.31}$$

$$\frac{\partial q}{\partial a}\frac{a}{q} = 1 - \eta, \tag{8.32}$$

whereas (8.4) with $c(a)$ replacing c implies that

$$\mu = \frac{c(a)}{(1-\eta)q}. \tag{8.33}$$

Substitution of (8.31) and (8.33) into (8.27) gives the social condition for the optimal search intensity:

$$-s\sigma_s(s, z) + \frac{\eta}{1-\eta}pc(a)\theta = 0. \tag{8.34}$$

Comparison with the private condition (8.29) shows that given a, the condition that equalizes the social and private equilibrium is again (8.7).

To derive the social optimality of advertising, we substitute (8.32) and (8.33) into (8.28), to obtain

$$\frac{c'(a)a}{c(a)} = 1. \tag{8.35}$$

The choice of job advertising is always efficient, regardless of the relation between β and η. The social planner, like each individual firm, finds it beneficial to use the vacancy rate to attract workers to jobs and fixes the level of advertising for each vacancy according to the properties of the cost function.

As in the case of job destruction, we can derive a similar strong result for the inefficiency of search intensity. It is easy to calculate, by making use of the equilibrium conditions for s and θ, (5.28) and (5.29), that s reaches a unique maximum at the point $\beta = \eta$. In contrast, θ falls with β in the range $\beta \geq \eta$ but changes with ambiguous sign if $\beta < \eta$. Since $\beta = \eta$ is also the efficiency condition, we have that in equilibrium search intensity is never too high—it is too low unless it happens to be efficient by chance.

It is not difficult to see why s reaches its maximum at the efficiency point. We noted in the preceding sections that the expected return from search is maximized when the efficiency condition is satisfied. Equilibrium search intensity is a monotonically increasing function of the expected return from search, a result that can easily be derived from (8.29) and (8.11) when z in the latter is replaced by $z - \sigma(s, z)$. Thus intensity is also maximized when (8.7) is satisfied.

Consider now the efficiency of unemployment. At $\beta = \eta$ unemployment is efficient, and at $\beta > \eta$ it is too high, since both intensity and job creation are too low. If $\beta < \eta$, intensity is too low again but the number of jobs may be too high. We can say with certainty that the number of jobs is too high only when η is in a small neighborhood of β, since then intensity is arbitrarily close to a turning point. If η is not in a neighborhood of β, intensity becomes smaller and the number of jobs may actually fall as firms withdraw jobs in the face of declining efficiency units of search. Thus unemployment is too low if $\beta < \eta$ and close to it, but it may be either too high or too low if $\beta < \eta$ and not close to it.

It would appear from the analysis so far (and also from the subsequent analysis in this chapter) that the same condition internalizes the search externalities irrespective of whether the inefficiencies are due to decisions by firms or by workers. We should note, however, that the generality of the condition requires two other conditions, both of which are satisfied by our model. These conditions are the same as the ones that we met when discussing the uniqueness of equilibrium in chapter 5. First, the job-matching technology should have constant returns to scale, and second search intensity should enter the matching technology multiplicatively, like input-augmenting technical change.

We argued in chapter 5 that both restrictions are reasonable, though some authors prefer not to impose them. We have already seen the implications of increasing returns to scale for the uniqueness of equilibrium (chapter 5). With increasing returns there is no single internalizing rule for wages when both the number of jobs and search intensity are variable. We discuss here the implications of the second restriction satisfied by our matching technology, by referring to a result about efficiency due to Mortensen (1982b). This result requires a restriction on the matching technology that explicitly violates our restriction of input-augmenting search intensity.

The efficiency of search intensity was considered along similar lines by Mortensen (1982a) and Pissarides (1984b). Both authors ignored the negative externalities caused by higher intensity on other workers looking for jobs, so they concluded that intensity was unambiguously low (irrespective of what happens to the number of jobs in equilibrium). Mortensen (1982b) considered the condition needed for the optimality of intensity and concluded that if the matching technology is linear, assigning "property rights" to the job would give optimality. By property rights we mean that the side that initiates contact claims the entire surplus from the job. The other side is compensated only for its costs.

Thus Mortensen's rule requires knowledge of who initiates contact, and it gives $\beta = 1$ when the worker finds the job and $\beta = 0$ when the firm finds the worker. But, in practice, in most situations it is virtually impossible to attribute contact to one side or the other. For example, suppose that job contacts are realized through employment agencies, newspaper advertisements, or through mutual friends. In each of these cases both the firm and the worker need to make contact with the intermediary in order to establish a job match, so it would be impossible to assign exclusive property rights to the job to one side and not to the other.

With property rights, the job-matching technology would have to take an entirely different form from the one we have used in this book. The transition probability for each market participant would have to be written as the sum of two independent transition probabilities, one for the case where the participant initiates contact and one for the case where someone else does it. If property rights cannot be assigned to jobs, the case considered by Mortensen (1982a) and Pissarides (1984b) can never be efficient with a Nash wage equation, as the latter showed. The reason is that both models ignored the negative externalities from higher intensities, and considered only the effects of the positive externalities on participants on the other side of the market. We saw in this chapter that if both externalities are considered, an internalizing Nash wage equation exists, but interestingly, it confirms the earlier Mortensen-Pissarides result that search intensity is too low.

8.4 Stochastic Job Matchings

The introduction of stochastic job matchings does nothing to the block of equations that determines equilibrium labor-market tightness and search intensity, so the number of jobs and the intensity of search are efficient at the same condition as before, $\beta = \eta$. It is straightforward to show that the efficiency condition for the reservation productivity is also $\beta = \eta$. We will be brief here, because of the similarities between this model and the job destruction model of section 8.3. When there are stochastic job matchings, jobs and workers are ex ante identical, but the productivity of a match is a random variable $p\alpha$, with $p > 0$ constant and α distributed according to $G(\alpha)$. Once contact is made the value of α is discovered. The pair agree to form a match only if their idiosyncratic productivity α exceeds a reservation value α_r, which satisfies (6.33), reproduced here:

$$p\alpha_r = z + \frac{\beta}{1-\beta}pc\theta. \tag{8.36}$$

But by the Nash sharing rules, and as (8.11) shows, the right-hand side of (8.36) is the reservation wage of unemployed workers, rU, so the reservation productivity satisfies

$$p\alpha_r = rU. \tag{8.37}$$

The justification for (8.37) is the same as the justification for (8.23) in the job destruction model. Because once a worker arrives the firm's alternative to forming the job is a vacancy of zero value, the job is formed if the worker's expected return from search is covered.

Now we know from our previous analysis that social efficiency maximizes rU and that the maximization point satisfies $\beta = \eta$. Therefore the reservation productivity for the social problem always exceeds the decentralized value, and it is achieved at the unique point that satisfies (8.7). In decentralized equilibrium there is generally too much job acceptance, for the same reason that in the model with idiosyncratic productivity shocks there was too little job destruction.

It is not surprising that the condition for the efficiency of the reservation productivity is the same as the condition for general movements in and out of search. When a firm and a worker are considering whether to form a match or not, they look at their own costs and returns. If, say, they decide to form the job, they effectively remove one participant from each side of the market. The externalities from doing this are the same as the externalities that arise when a firm and a worker leave the market for any other reason. We saw that the condition $\beta = \eta$ internalizes the externalities when there is movement on both sides of the market, either through the exit and entry of jobs or through variations in workers' search intensities. Hence it also internalizes the externalities when the movement is due to job acceptance. As before, $\beta = \eta$ is the efficiency condition only when there are constant returns to scale in the matching technology. Without constant returns there cannot be simultaneous internalizing of the externalities when there is movement on both sides of the market as there always is when the decision margin is job acceptance.

Thus, as in the case of idiosyncratic productivity shocks when too many low-productivity jobs survive, workers are not likely to be allocated to jobs efficiently when the allocation is done by applying the reservation productivity rule (8.36). Too many jobs are likely to be accepted, so some workers will be underemployed. Unemployment will not necessarily be lower than the efficient level because the number of jobs may be below the efficient level and the intensity of search is also too low generally. These can offset the effects of underemployment on aggregate employment. But irrespective of the efficiency of unemployment, there is always inefficient underemployment in equilibrium.

8.5   Labor-Force Participation

The efficiency of the participation rate is straightforward to analyze, and technically the analysis is similar to the analysis of the efficiency of the reservation productivity when there are stochastic job matchings. We saw in chapter 7 that the participation rate depends on just one market variable, the expected return from search. All individuals whose utility from nonparticipation (leisure) is less than the expected return from search participate; others do not. We also saw that the determination of the expected return from search is independent of the participation rate. Hence the participation rate is efficient only when the expected return from search is efficiently determined. This is the same rule that determines the efficiency of job acceptance when there are stochastic job matchings.

The expected return from search is efficiently determined at the point $\beta = \eta$; otherwise, the private return from search is always less than the social return. Like unemployed workers, nonparticipants are outsiders in the wage bargain, so their costs and returns are ignored when wages are set. Thus the equilibrium participation rate is too low, except for the special case $\beta = \eta$, when it is efficient. The search externalities discourage some potential workers from coming into the market to look for work, even though from society's point of view they should participate. Conversely, changes in participation involve the movement of workers in and out of the market, so the externalities created are the same as the externalities created when workers move in and out of search because of changes in their search intensity or because of their decision to accept or reject a job. The same rule internalizes all externalities and in all cases worker search activity is too low.

8.6 Three Questions about Efficiency

The efficiency analysis of search equilibrium in this chapter has led to some common results in a variety of situations. The same condition ensures the efficiency of all decisions, and on the workers' side, if this condition is not satisfied, search activity is too low. On the firms' side results are different, because of the variable number of jobs and the zero-profit condition satisfied by the marginal job. Had the number of jobs been held fixed, the same too low activity result would have been derived for firms. Instead, the number of jobs may be either too high or too low. When firms have a nontrivial choice over job destruction, they destroy too few jobs, reducing labor turnover below the efficient level.

The similarity of results across the six decision margins leads to some questions that can conveniently be discussed here, at the risk of some repetition of the argument of the preceding sections. First, what is the reason for the similarity of results and what is the intuition behind the critical efficiency condition? Second, why is search activity always too low? And third, is equilibrium unemployment too high or too low?

The reason for the similarity of results is that the externalities affecting all decision margins are due to the number of efficiency units of inputs into trade (the generalized measure of the number of firms and workers searching). Recall that with search intensity s and job advertising a, the input of unemployed workers into trade is su and the input of firms with vacancies is av. Contacts are given by the matching technology $m(su, av)$, and the externalities arise because the rate at which each agent meets agents from the other side depends on the ratio av/su. The six decision margins create externalities to the extent that they affect this ratio: the supply of jobs through v, job advertising through a, search intensity through s, job destruction and job acceptance through u and v, and labor-force participation through u. Thus, if there is a rule that internalizes the search externalities caused by the ratio av/su, this rule will internalize simultaneously the externalities at all decision margins. This is what the rule $\beta = \eta$ does. Moreover, since the transition rates of both firms and workers depend on the single number av/su only when the matching technology has constant returns to scale and when intensities enter it multiplicatively, the latter two conditions are necessary for the existence of the single internalizing rule.

The critical efficiency condition relates a parameter of the resolution of bargaining conflict to a parameter of the technology of matchings. Thus we are not likely to find intuition for it, and existing results in the theory of externalities are not likely to help justify it. For example, the symmetric Nash solution implies that $\beta = \frac{1}{2}$; if the firm's rate of discount differs from the worker's, a more plausible resolution is one where β reflects this difference, being equal to the ratio of the firm's discount rate to the sum of the two rates. Other asymmetries in the firm's and worker's preferences in general imply other values for β. The elasticity η is the elasticity of the matching technology with respect to unemployment. If the matching technology is Cobb-Douglas, η is constant, otherwise it varies with the av/su ratio. Only in the case of a symmetric Cobb-Douglas technology, with firms and workers equally effective in making contacts, is η likely to be constant and equal to $\frac{1}{2}$.

Some rationale for the efficiency condition may be provided by using the fact that η is a measure of the relative effectiveness of the unemployed in making contacts, and consequently $1 - \eta$ is a measure of the relative effectiveness of firms in making contacts. We note also that in equilibrium the relative number of firms to workers searching (av/cu) is a decreasing function of β. So if the unemployed are more effective than firms in generating contacts (η is high), in equilibrium their number should be higher (β is high), and conversely. Of course, this argument may justify why η and β should be positively related in social equilibrium, not why they should be equal.

Turning now to the second question of why search activity is always too low, we have already seen that unemployed workers are excluded from the wage bargain. If unemployed workers were given the choice of setting the wage rule, their choice would coincide with the social planner's. They would choose the wage that balanced out the positive externalities from the entry of more jobs with the negative externalities from the increased search activity of other unemployed workers. Employed workers are not interested in this kind of consideration, since they have already established contact with a firm. The inefficiencies arise because the allocative role of the wage rate in this market environment affects unemployed workers and firms with vacancies, yet it is chosen by employed workers and firms with filled jobs. The insiders in the wage bargain ignore the interests of the outsiders, yet the wage decisions affect mainly the allocation decisions of the outsiders.

Since the interests of unemployed workers and the social planner coincide, the social rule maximizes unemployed workers' expected returns from search. Workers choose too low search activity because the returns from it are not, in general, as high as they should be. Thus too few workers come into the market to search, they search with too low intensity, and they give up search too readily.

Firms would suffer from a similar problem if there was no unlimited supply of jobs at given positive marginal profit (in contrast to this, worker entry is restricted by the valuation of leisure from nonparticipation). With limited job entry, the expected return from one more vacancy would be too low. But with unlimited entry the movement of jobs in and out of the market dominates the effects of the externalities. Unlimited entry, as we saw in chapter 3, corresponds to the existence of a downward-sloping labor-demand curve with costs of adjustment, and in equilibrium it implies an inverse monotonic relation between the ratio av/cu and the parameter β. Thus labor-market tightness v/u may be either too high or too low, depending on the relation between β and η, in contrast to decisions on the worker's side.

Of all the questions that can be asked about the efficiency of search equilibrium, the one that is most frequently asked is whether unemployment is too high or too low. The reason for the interest in this question is that if the answer is that unemployment is too high, it will justify governmental intervention to reduce it. Our model, however, does not give grounds for such a simplistic approach to policy. Although the question of whether unemployment is too high or too low can be answered, what is more important for social efficiency is the allocation of resources to different economic activities and whether this is efficient in the private equilibrium. Unemployment is one of the outcomes of this allocation mechanism, not a cause of misallocations.

The important allocation question is whether firms and workers devote enough resources to search. We have seen that firms may devote either too much or too little, in the form of new jobs, depending on the relation between β and η, but workers devote always too few resources to search. The problem is with translating this into whether the final unemployment outcome is above or below the efficient one, since sometimes too little search by workers implies too high unemployment and sometimes it implies too low unemployment. Whether unemployment turns out to be too high or too low depends partly on whether there are enough jobs and partly on which margin dominates workers' decisions, search intensity, or job acceptance: Too little search intensity lengthens search durations; too low reservation wages reduce search durations. Another factor to note in the case where reservation wages play a role in job allocations is that in equilibrium there is underemployment, since too many low-productivity jobs are accepted. Employment in jobs that would be socially efficient to accept is unambiguously too low when $\beta \neq \eta$, regardless of whether search intensity dominates reservation wages, and vice versa.

A similar ambiguity arises in the determination of unemployment when there are idiosyncratic productivity shocks and endogenous job destruction. Recall that unemployment in the steady state in that model is given by

$$u = \frac{\lambda G(R)}{\lambda G(R) + \theta q(\theta)}. \tag{8.38}$$

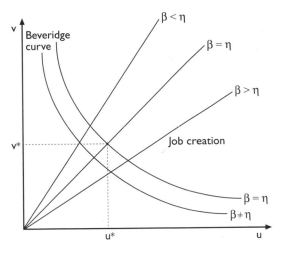

Figure 8.1
Efficient unemployment (u^*) and vacancies (v^*) with endogenous job creation and job destruction

If we treat β as a parameter that varies between zero and one, R reaches a maximum at $\beta = \eta$ and θ decreases monotonically as β increases. Hence, in vacancy-unemployment space, the Beveridge curve in (8.38) lies too close to the origin if $\beta \neq \eta$, but the job creation line through the origin may be to the left or to the right of the efficient line (see figure 8.1).

It is clear from figure 8.1 that because β shifts both curves, it is not possible, in general, to determine the effects of the inefficiencies on both vacancies and unemployment. For the case drawn, unemployment is too low when $\beta < \eta$ and job vacancies are too low when $\beta > \eta$, with ambiguity in vacancies in the former case and in unemployment in the latter case. But in both cases there is a misallocation of resources because too many low-productivity jobs survive.

8.7   Notes on the Literature

Questions about the efficiency of search equilibrium were first raised by Phelps (1972) and Tobin (1972) and argued against by Prescott (1975). The first formal models of efficiency analysis with congestion were due to Diamond (1981, 1982b), following on from the related work by

Mortensen (1978), Baily (1978), and Diamond and Maskin (1979). In Diamond (1981) the inefficiency is due to a positive externality which we did not consider here: At higher unemployment rates the quality of the average job match improves, because, say, more suitable workers are likely to be conveniently placed to search a given vacancy. In Diamond (1982b) the externalities are more generally related to the movement of workers, though the overall number of workers and jobs was assumed fixed. In contrast to these models and to later work on the efficiency of search equilibrium, the first formal model of search equilibrium, by Lucas and Prescott (1974), was not characterized by a matching technology, and it was free of other search externalities. Therefore equilibrium in it was efficient.

The efficiency of search intensity and job advertising was discussed in closely related models by Mortensen (1982a) and Pissarides (1984b). Mortensen considered the implications of property rights to jobs, whereas Pissarides considered the implications of endogenous number of jobs. Mortensen (1982b) is a generalization of Mortensen (1982a) to other related situations. Both works considered only the positive externalities affecting the other side of the market, so they concluded that inputs into search are always too low. In a related model of two-sided search with both positive and negative externalities but with increasing returns to scale in the matching technology, Howitt and McAfee (1987) concluded that there is no feasible wage that can internalize the search externalities.

The efficiency analysis with stochastic job matchings is an extension of the one in Pissarides (1984a), which addressed the efficiency questions for a fixed number of jobs and for matching technologies with nonconstant returns to scale. For an analysis of the efficiency implications of transferable skills (i.e., productivity differences that are not match-specific), see Lockwood (1986). In a model related to the one in this chapter, Deree (1987) considered the efficiency of job-to-job movements when jobs differ in their productivities and concluded that reservation wages are likely to be too low (and so turnover is likely to be too high). McKenna (1987) considered the efficiency of participation decisions and derived the same efficiency condition as in this chapter.

The efficiency of search equilibrium when there is also a competitive sector was considered by Davidson, Martin and Matusz (1987), who concluded that the search sector is likely to be too small.

The generality of the efficiency condition (8.7) in models with two-sided search and other related models was demonstrated by Hosios (1990). More recently some authors have considered different wage determination mechanisms to examine whether the efficiency condition is satisfied or not. Moen (1997) has demonstrated that it holds in models where firms set wages subject to the constraint that higher wages imply shorter waiting times. Similar wage-setting assumptions are used by Acemoglu and Shimer (1997) who argue that wage dispersion for homogeneous workers is efficient under these circumstances, since it gives incentives to workers to collect information and erodes firms' monopoly power in wage setting.

Related efficiency questions in markets with frictions are raised by Grout (1984), Caballero and Hammour (1996), MacLeod and Malcomson (1993), and Acemoglu and Shimer (1997b)—see also Malcomson (1997) for a review—who discuss the hold-up problem, when a firm commits itself to irreversible capital investments before wage negotiations. In our framework this problem is avoided by the assumptions of the existence of a perfect second-hand market in capital goods.

There is a large literature on the efficiency of other kinds of matching problems that goes back at least to Koopmans and Beckmann (1957) and Becker (1973). See, for example, Sattinger (1991), Montgomery (1991), McLaughlin (1994), Smith (1997), and Coles and Burdett (1997).

Questions about the divergencies of the interests of the insiders and outsiders in the wage bargain and their implications for wage determination and unemployment are discussed by Solow (1985) and Lindbeck and Snower (1988). See also the next chapter for a discussion of this issue.

9 The Role of Policy

In the analysis of the preceding chapters we saw that equilibrium unemployment depends on several parameters and that, in general, it is inefficient. We now turn our attention to the analysis of policy. We first introduce some policy instruments and study their effects on the equilibrium of the model. We then ask whether there are optimal policy rules that remove the inefficiencies caused by the search externalities. We consider only microeconomic policy and study its role in the model of the labor market without capital and with exogenous rate of interest.

The policy rules that we will study are linear and derived from wage taxes and employment or unemployment subsidies. The approach we follow is first to consider some general principles underlying wage determination in the presence of policy and then to study subsequently the effects of linear policy rules on job creation, job destruction, the intensity of search, and the reservation rules that govern the decision of whether or not to form a match.

9.1 Policy Instruments

We consider five policy instruments, wage taxes paid by the worker; employment subsidies, hiring subsidies, and firing taxes received or paid by the firm; and unemployment compensation. If there are also wage taxes paid by the firm, such as employer contributions to social security, their analysis is similar to that of wage taxes paid by workers because of the equilibrium nature of the model. In general, tax incidence is independent of who pays the tax.

Wage taxes are linear and smooth functions of income. The smoothness assumption is made for analytical tractability, without loss of essential generality. We introduce the possibility of progressive or regressive taxation by assuming that if the gross wage at a job j is w_j, the net wage received by the worker is $(1 - t)(w_j + \tau)$. It is convenient to think of workers as receiving a tax subsidy τ, and subsequently taxed on their total labor earnings, including the subsidy, at the proportional rate t. With this tax the net transfer from the worker to the tax authorities is

$$T(w_j) = tw_j - (1 - t)\tau. \tag{9.1}$$

The marginal tax rate t is in the range $0 \le t < 1$, and in general, we will be interested in situations where there are some net tax payments, that is, the tax instruments are such that at the equilibrium wage w, $T(w) \geq 0$. The tax subsidy τ may be either positive or negative. If $\tau > 0$, taxation is progressive, since the average tax rate rises with the wage; if $\tau < 0$, taxation is regressive, and if $\tau = 0$, it is proportional. Our assumptions regarding the structure of the tax system imply that t plays the role of a proportional tax rate, irrespective of the sign or value of τ. Changes in t do not affect the wage subsidization that is implicit in a progressive or regressive tax system.

Employment is subsidized at the rate a per job. Although, in general, we will refer to a as if it were a positive number, it can have any sign. The employment subsidy is paid to firms throughout the duration of the job. It is assumed to be independent of the skill of the occupant of the job or the wage rate, though it is straightforward to see the implications of making it proportional to p in the formulas that follow.

Firms in addition receive a hiring subsidy when a worker is hired and pay a firing tax when a separation takes place. In contrast to employment subsidies, we assume that the hiring and firing taxes depend on the worker's skill; for example, they may be tied to the wage rate. We will follow a simple approach to the modeling of hiring and firing taxes by assuming that the firm that hires a worker whose initial (general) productivity is p receives a hiring subsidy of pH, and when the separation takes place, it has to pay a tax pT. The tax paid on separation is not a compensation given to the worker but a cost borne by the firm, which might be a shadow tax reflecting firing restrictions imposed by the government. Any transfer given by the firm on separation has no influence on the model because it is absorbed by the negotiated wage. Firing taxes are assumed to depend on skill because it is plausible to assume that in markets where there are firing restrictions, it is more difficult to get rid of a skilled worker than of an unskilled one.

Unemployed workers receive some compensation, which is policy-determined. We assume that the policy parameter is the after-tax replacement rate, that is, the ratio of net unemployment benefit to average net income from work. We define the net unemployment benefit b by

$$b = \rho[w - T(w)], \tag{9.2}$$

where ρ is the policy parameter and $w - T(w)$ is the average net wage rate. We assume that $0 \leq \rho < 1$. Of course b is not taxed because it is already defined in after-tax terms.

In some applications, working with (9.2) creates complications because the equilibrium is characterized by a conditional wage distribution and not a unique wage rate. In those cases a convenient shortcut that does not sacrifice important generality is to define benefits in terms of the general productivity parameter p, which is unique and exogenous. In those cases we define net unemployment benefit by

$$b = \rho[p - T(p)]. \tag{9.3}$$

The policy instruments are the tax subsidy τ, the marginal tax rate t, the replacement rate ρ, the employment subsidy a, the hiring subsidy pH, and the firing tax pF. If there are financing constraints on policy makers, the policy instruments are not independent of each other. We will discuss the implications of financing constraints later in this chapter, but first we treat the policy instruments as independent parameters.

9.2 Wage Determination

The question whether policy influences wages in equilibrium is critical for our analysis. We begin by considering some general principles underlying their interaction, by making use of the simple model of wage determination introduced in chapter 1.

Thus suppose that there are no idiosyncratic productivity shocks, no stochastic job matchings, fixed intensity of search, and net imputed income during unemployment (excluding unemployment compensation) which is also fixed at some level z. The net marginal product of labor is p, and the firm's cost of hiring is pc. The supply of jobs is variable and determined by profit maximization. In the absence of policy, the equilibrium number of jobs (or labor-market tightness) and equilibrium wages are given by the equations of chapter 1, (1.22) and (1.23), reproduced here for easier reference:

$$p - w - \frac{(r + \lambda)pc}{q(\theta)} = 0, \tag{9.4}$$

$$w = (1 - \beta)z + \beta(1 + c\theta)p. \tag{9.5}$$

Job destruction takes place at the constant rate λ. To derive the equations with policy, we first have to compute the worker's and firm's present discounted values with policy. The unemployed worker's net worth with policy is given by

$$rU = z + b + \theta q(\theta)(W - U), \tag{9.6}$$

where W is the average net worth of employed workers. The employed worker's net worth in a job that pays w_j is given by

$$rW_j = w_j - T(w_j) + \lambda(U - W_j). \tag{9.7}$$

The firm's net worth from a vacancy and from a job paying w_j are given by

$$rV = -pc + q(\theta)(J + pH - V), \tag{9.8}$$

$$rJ_j = p + a - w_j - \lambda(J_j + pF). \tag{9.9}$$

In (9.8) the firm receives a hiring subsidy pH when the worker arrives and the job is created. When the job is occupied, the subsidy is a flow a that is added to revenue and when the job is destroyed the firm pays a firing tax pF in addition to losing the surplus from the job.

Wages are chosen, as before, to maximize the Nash product, and they can be renegotiated any time. In the model without policy, the application of this rule was straightforward, and it gave rise to the simple wage equation in (9.5). In the present context, however, the application of the Nash rule is more problematic, because of the existence of the hiring subsidy and firing tax.

To see this, consider the choices facing the firm and the worker when they first meet. If they sign a contract, the payoff to the firm is $J_j + pH$, since the firm will receive the subsidy pH upon completion of the signing. Therefore the initial wage is chosen to maximize the product

$$B_0 = (W_j - U)^{\beta}(J_j + pH - V)^{1-\beta}. \tag{9.10}$$

But after the worker is taken on, the benefit to the firm from continuation of the contract is only J_j, since no further hiring subsidies are received. In contrast, now the firing tax becomes operational, and if the firm fails to agree to a continuation wage, its loss will be $J_j + pF$. Therefore, if the worker can force a renegotiation of the wage after he is hired, the new wage will maximize the product

$$B = (W_j - U)^{\beta}(J_j + pF - V)^{1-\beta}. \tag{9.11}$$

Clearly, the wage outcome in the two cases is different. The key question then is whether the worker can force a renegotiation of the wage after he is hired. We will assume that he can, so we will compute two wages, one denoted by w_{0j} and negotiated initially so as to maximize (9.10) and one denoted w_j and negotiated subsequently so as to maximize (9.11). This assumption is the natural generalization of the assumptions about wage determination that we have followed throughout this book. Following the terminology introduced in the literature by Lindbeck and Snower (1988), we refer to w_{0j} as the "outside" wage and to w_j as the "inside" wage: w_{0j} is negotiated by those still outside the firm, before the firm gets locked in by turnover taxes, and w_j is negotiated by those inside the firm, who benefit from the firing restrictions imposed on the firm.

Some authors reject the plausibility of the two-tier wage structure, either on empirical grounds (Lindbeck and Snower 1988) or on the grounds that the worker cannot force a renegotiation because he has no credible threat if the firm refuses to renegotiate (McCleod and Malcomson 1993). An examination of the implications of these alternative mechanisms would take us beyond the scope of our analysis, though we may note that they give the same job destruction outcomes, even when job destruction is endogenous. But the job creation outcomes are generally different, since job creation depends on the firm's expected profits which are in turn influenced by the wage outcomes.

Given our assumptions, the outside (initial) wage solves

$$\beta \frac{\partial W_j}{\partial w_{0j}}(J_j + pH - V) + (1 - \beta)\frac{\partial J_j}{\partial w_{0j}}(W_j - U) = 0, \tag{9.12}$$

and the inside (continuation) wage solves

$$\beta \frac{\partial W_j}{\partial w_j}(J_j + pF - V) + (1 - \beta)\frac{\partial J_j}{\partial w_j}(W_j - U) = 0. \tag{9.13}$$

In the presence of taxes,

$$\frac{\partial W_j}{\partial w_{0j}} = \frac{\partial W_j}{\partial w_j} = \frac{1 - T'(w_j)}{r + \lambda},$$

$$\frac{\partial J_j}{\partial w_{0j}} = \frac{\partial J_j}{\partial w_j} = -\frac{1}{r + \lambda},$$

so labor's share of the total surplus now is $\beta[1 - T'(w_j)]/[1 - \beta T'(w_j)]$, instead of the constant β as in the model without taxes. The marginal tax rate influences labor's share, whereas the total tax paid and subsidies received influence the surplus that is shared, not the relative shares. If the marginal tax rate is positive, labor's share falls; whether wages fall or rise depends also on what happens to the surplus from the job and to labor's alternative return.

This result is general: Marginal tax rates influence the division of the surplus from a job, whereas average tax rates and subsidies influence the outcome of the bargain only through their effect on the surplus shared. It is obvious from the previous analysis that if there was a marginal element in unemployment compensation, that is, if the benefit paid depended on the worker's previous wage, this would also influence the division of the surplus. Also, if the firm had to pay a wage tax, or if the other subsidies and taxes were related to the wage rate, the firm's net marginal tax rate would also influence the division of the surplus. We will not consider any of these extensions because they do not have interesting implications for the behavior of equilibrium unemployment, over and above those due to the worker's marginal tax rate.

The worker's marginal tax rate reduces labor's share of the surplus, because a unit rise in wages conceded by the firm yields benefit to the worker of one unit less the marginal tax rate. Thus the marginal tax rate imposes a joint loss to the firm and worker that can be reduced by keeping wages low. In contrast, subsidies and other parameters of the tax system impose the same loss to the firm and the worker irrespective of the level of wages, so the firm and the worker share the loss from them as they share the rest of the surplus from the job. (Clearly, with earnings-related unemployment benefits labor's share would rise, since a unit concession by the firm yields benefit to the worker of one unit when employed and of some additional compensation in the event of unemployment.)

With taxes and unemployment benefits given by (9.1) and (9.2), the outside and inside wage equations derived in equilibrium from (9.12) and (9.13), respectively—that is, imposing $V = 0$ and $w_j = w$ for all j—are

$$w_0 = \frac{1-\beta}{1-\rho(1-\beta)}\left[\frac{z}{1-t} - (1-\rho)\tau\right]$$

$$+ \frac{\beta}{1-\rho(1-\beta)}[(1 + c\theta - \lambda F + (r + \lambda)H)p + a],$$

(9.14)

$$w = \frac{1-\beta}{1-\rho(1-\beta)}\left[\frac{z}{1-t} - (1-\rho)\tau\right] + \frac{\beta}{1-\rho(1-\beta)}[(1+c\theta+rF)p+a]. \quad (9.15)$$

The two wage schedules differ to the extent that there are hiring subsidies and job-separation taxes. The outside wage increases by a fraction of the hiring subsidy because the payment of the subsidy is conditional on the worker's agreement to accept the job offer. But it decreases by a fraction of the firing tax, since if the worker agrees to sign the contract, the firm becomes liable to the firing tax. In contrast, the inside wage is independent of the hiring subsidy, since it has already been received, but now increases in the firing tax, since the firm has to pay the tax if the worker does not agree to continue the job match.

In the absence of hiring subsidies, wages are low at first and increase after renegotiation; to reflect the fact that once the job has started, the firm is locked into it by the firing tax. But hiring subsidies increase the initial wage. The outside wage is lower than the inside wage if $F > H$, that is, if the firing tax exceeds the hiring subsidy.

Apart from this difference in the two wage schedules, they share common properties. The replacement rate raises wages because it raises income from unemployment and so improves the worker's threat point in the Nash bargain. The employment subsidy also raises wages, but now because the total return from the job is higher: Workers get a fraction of the subsidy paid to firms. Similarly the firm and worker share the tax subsidy τ, which is implicitly paid to workers. The net subsidy received when a job is formed is $(1 - \rho)\tau$: Employed workers receive the full subsidy τ, and unemployed workers receive a fraction ρ of it as part of their unemployment benefit.

The marginal tax rate influences equilibrium wages because the imputed value of leisure (or home production) is not taxed, so taxation makes leisure more attractive relative to work. Had taxation been proportional, this would have been the only effect of the tax system on wages. However, we argued in chapter 3 that in the steady state it is not reasonable to hold the imputed return from leisure constant. If the imputed return from leisure is generalized in the way we argued in chapter 3 (e.g., if it depends on wealth), the tax system still has an effect on wages but only because of the implicit tax subsidy. The marginal tax rate in the case where the imputed value of leisure is proportional to productivity is absorbed entirely by workers.

The formal demonstration of these propositions is straightforward and so omitted. Intuitively the way that we defined taxation in equation (9.1) implies that the marginal tax rate works as if taxation were proportional. With proportional taxation $\tau = 0$, so the tax system does not introduce any distortion in the workers' relative rewards from taking a job. Proportional taxation plays the same role as labor-augmenting productivity change. Labor-augmenting productivity change multiplies the labor input by a constant; proportional taxes multiply the wage rate by a constant. If the two are proportional because the imputed value of leisure is proportional to wealth (or wages or productivity), the effect is the same.

In contrast, income during unemployment, progressive or regressive taxation, and employment subsidies change wages, since they introduce distortions in the relative rewards from taking a job. The wage equations imply that (for given θ) the replacement rate raises wages, so it increases the cost of labor to the firm. The employment subsidy also raises wages but reduces the net cost of labor, since the firm and worker share it. The tax subsidy reduces the cost of labor to the firm, by reducing the negotiated wage, and raises net wages, again because it is shared by the firm and worker.

9.3 Equilibrium with Policy

We now close the model with the wage equations (9.14) and (9.15) by considering the supply of jobs. We still assume no idiosyncratic shocks, so the interesting decision margin is job creation. This is easily derived from (9.8) and (9.9) by imposing the equilibrium condition $V = 0$, giving

$$p - w + a + p\left[(r + \lambda)H - \lambda F - \frac{r + \lambda}{q(\theta)}c\right] = 0. \tag{9.16}$$

This condition generalizes (9.4) as substitution of $a = H = F = 0$ makes clear. The question that arises here, however, is if H or F are positive, which is the relevant wage equation that should be used to solve (9.16), the inside wage (9.15) or the outside wage (9.14)? Our previous discussion suggests the use of the outside wage, since the firm calculates the expected returns from a new vacancy, (9.8), on the basis of the expected profit from a new job. This assumes that if $F > H$, the outside wage is feasible, for example, that it is positive and does not violate any minimum wage restrictions. Substitution of wages from (9.14) into (9.16) gives the job creation condition

$$p + a + \tau - \lambda pF + (r + \lambda)pH$$

$$= \frac{z}{(1-\rho)(1-t)} + \frac{pc}{(1-\rho)(1-\beta)}\left(\beta\theta + [1 - (1-\beta)\rho]\frac{r+\lambda}{q(\theta)}\right). \tag{9.17}$$

Equilibrium unemployment is derived, as before, from the Beveridge curve, given the solution for tightness in (9.17):

$$u = \frac{\lambda}{\lambda + \theta q(\theta)}. \tag{9.18}$$

With fixed rate of job destruction and search intensity and no stochastic job matchings, policy does not influence the rate of job matchings, for given θ, or the rate of job separations. The system (9.17) and (9.18) can be represented diagrammatically as before, with (9.18) showing the downward-sloping Beveridge curve and (9.17) a line through the origin that represents job creation. Policy in this model influences job creation and so rotates the line through the origin, clockwise when the effect on job creation is negative and counterclockwise when the effect is positive. Given our discussion of wage determination, it is predictable which policies have positive job creation effects and which negative: employment subsidies, hiring subsidies, and the implicit tax subsidy τ (or progressive taxation) all increase job creation and reduce unemployment; firing taxes, unemployment compensation, and wage taxes reduce job creation.

9.4 Job Destruction

Consider now the implications of policy for job destruction, when there are idiosyncratic productivity shocks and jobs with idiosyncratic productivity below a reservation R are destroyed. The model was described in some detail in chapter 2, so we restate here the key equation when there are idiosyncratic shocks for the asset value of a job:

$$rJ(x) = px - w(x) + \lambda \int_R^1 J(s)dG(s) - \lambda J(x). \tag{9.19}$$

The firm opens a job at the maximum value of the idiosyncratic productivity parameter, $x = 1$. Idiosyncratic shocks arrive at the rate $\lambda > 0$ and are drawn from the distribution $G(s)$. Each time an idiosyncratic shock arrives wages are renegotiated. The Nash wage equation is a natural extension of the equation without shocks:

$$w(x) = (1 - \beta)z + \beta(x + c\theta)p. \tag{9.20}$$

Jobs are destroyed when their idiosyncratic productivity drops below R, defined by $J(R) = 0$.

With policy, equations (9.19) and (9.20) change in ways that are the natural generalizations of (9.9) and (9.14)–(9.15). As before, the initial (outside) wage is different from the continuation (inside) wage, for the reasons earlier explained. Since productivities now differ, there is no unique inside wage but a distribution of wages across jobs. This introduces some complexities in the definition of unemployment compensation. A natural way to define unemployment compensation, which generalizes (9.2) given the definition of taxes in (9.1), is to write

$$b = p(1 - t)[E(w(x) \,|\, x \geq R) + \tau], \tag{9.21}$$

where $w(x)$ is the wage rate at a job with idiosyncratic productivity x. Then, $E(w(x) \,|\, x \geq R)$ is the average wage in the market, at least for the insiders.

Making use of (9.21), however, introduces far too many complexities into the model. Similar results can be obtained about the role of unemployment compensation if we assume that benefits are fixed according to starting productivity, p, as defined in (9.3). That is, instead of (9.21) we use

$$b = p(1 - t)(p + \tau). \tag{9.22}$$

We will use (9.22) in what follows. When there is a distribution of wages, the simplicity gained in the modeling is worth the sacrifice of some generality.

Since initial idiosyncratic productivity is $x = 1$, the outside wage with endogenous job destruction is identical to the one earlier derived for exogenous job destruction, (9.14), except for the use of (9.22) in place of the earlier $p(1 - t)(w + \tau)$. The equation is

$$w_0 = (1 - \beta)\left[\frac{z}{1-t} - (1-\rho)\tau + \rho p\right] + \beta[1 + c\theta - \lambda F + (r + \lambda)H]p + \beta a. \quad (9.23)$$

The inside wage is a natural generalization of (9.15), with x replacing 1 as the idiosyncratic component of productivity:

$$w(x) = (1 - \beta)\left[\frac{z}{1-t} - (1-\rho)\tau + \rho p\right] + \beta[x + c\theta + rF]p + \beta a. \quad (9.24)$$

Thus, although the derivation of these wage equations is now more complicated, as in chapter 2, the principles governing wage determination in the presence of policy intervention are the same as the ones discussed earlier in this chapter.

To derive the job destruction rule, we note that (9.19) with policy becomes

$$rJ(x) = px + a - w(x) + \lambda \int_R^1 J(s)dG(s) - \lambda G(R)pF - \lambda J(x), \quad (9.25)$$

whereas the returns from a vacancy satisfy

$$rV = -pc + q(\theta)(J^0 + pH - V). \quad (9.26)$$

Here J^0 is the asset value in (9.25) for $x = 1$, but with the wage rate satisfying the outside wage equation, (9.23); this is in contrast to the $J(1)$ in the integral expression, which is derived from (9.25) for the inside wage (9.24).

When a job is destroyed, the firm gives up $J(x)$ and pays a termination tax pF. So a job with idiosyncratic productivity x will be destroyed if $J(x) < -pF$, giving the reservation productivity equation

$$J(R) + pF = 0. \quad (9.27)$$

Substitution of $J(R)$ from (9.25) into (9.27) gives

$$pR + a - w(R) + \lambda \int_R^1 J(s)dG(s) + [r + \lambda(1 - G(R))]pF = 0, \quad (9.28)$$

with $w(R)$ satisfying (9.24) for $R = x$.

Now, since

$$w(x) - w(R) = \beta p(x - R),$$

(9.25) and (9.27) imply that

$$(r + \lambda)[J(x) - J(R)] = (1 - \beta)p(x - R),$$

so

$$J(x) = (1 - \beta)\frac{p(x - R)}{r + \lambda} - pF. \tag{9.29}$$

Hence substitution of $w(R)$ from (9.24) into (9.28) and of $J(s)$ from (9.29) into (9.28) gives the job destruction rule,

$$R + \frac{a + (1 - \rho)\tau}{p} - \rho + rF - \frac{z}{p(1 - t)} - \frac{\beta c}{1 - \beta}\theta + \frac{\lambda}{r + \lambda}\int_R^1 (s - R)dG(s) = 0. \tag{9.30}$$

The job destruction rule (9.30) generalizes the rule without policy derived in chapter 2, (2.15), in an obvious way. The employment subsidy and income tax subsidy, a and τ, respectively, both reduce the reservation productivity for given θ, since they increase the returns from a job. The firing tax also reduces the reservation productivity, since it is now more expensive to destroy jobs. The tax rate t increases the reservation productivity because leisure is untaxed, and the replacement rate also increases it because it reduces the cost of unemployment.

To close the model, we need to derive the equation for market tightness (job creation), which is derived from (9.26) for $V = 0$. Noting from (9.23) and (9.24) that

$$w_0 - w(R) = \beta[1 - R + (r + \lambda)(H - F)]p,$$

we obtain from (9.25),

$$(r + \lambda)[J^0 - J(R)] = (1 - \beta)(1 - R)p - \beta(r + \lambda)(H - F)p. \tag{9.31}$$

Therefore, from (9.26), which for $V = 0$ implies that

$$J^0 = \frac{pc}{q(\theta)} - pH, \tag{9.32}$$

and from (9.27), we get the job creation condition

$$(1 - \beta)\left(\frac{1 - R}{r + \lambda} - F + H\right) = \frac{c}{q(\theta)}. \tag{9.33}$$

Condition (9.33) generalizes the job creation condition in the absence of policy, (2.14). As before, it gives a negative relation between the reservation productivity and tightness, since at higher reservaticn productivity jobs have smaller expected lifetimes and so fewer are created. The net subsidy to hiring and firing, $H - F$, increases θ. Here it is the net subsidy that matters because before job creation the firm expects to receive H and pay F with probability 1. This contrasts with the job destruction rule, where only the firing tax mattered because the hiring subsidy was bygone.

To derive the effects of the policy parameters on job creation and job destruction, we make use of the diagram that we used in chapter 2 for other parameter changes. In a space with R on the vertical axis and θ on the horizontal, equation (9.30) is shown as an upward-sloping curve labeled JD and equation (9.33) as a downward-sloping curve labeled JC. Equilibrium R and θ are at the intersection of the two curves (figure 9.1). We discuss the policy effects by holding unemployment constant, that is, any policy change that increases R increases job destruction at given unemployment and any policy change that increases θ increases job creation at given unemployment. Wc rcturn to a discussion of unemployment later.

It turns out that for given unemployment, all policy parameters have well-defined effects on job creation and job destruction flows. The

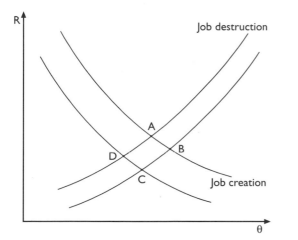

Figure 9.1
Policy effects on job creation and job destruction: (a) Employment subsidies, tax subsidies, A to B; (b) proportional tax rate, unemployment compensation, B to A; (c) hiring subsidy, D to A; (d) firing taxes, A to C.

employment subsidy a and tax subsidy τ both shift the job destruction curve down and so reduce job destruction and increase job creation at given unemployment. The tax rate t shifts the job destruction curve up, so it has opposite effects. The hiring subsidy H shifts the job creation curve to the right and so increases both job creation and job destruction. The reason for the increase in job creation is obvious: The hiring subsidy increases the rewards from matching. Job destruction increases because of the increase in market tightness, which improves the worker's options in the labor market. In contrast to employment subsidies, which are given to continuing jobs as well, hiring subsidies are paid only at job creation time. Therefore, when negative shocks hit, they are not present to offset the effects of higher tightness.

Firing taxes shift the JC curve left and the JD curve down, so job destruction decreases. The effect on job creation is ambiguous in the diagram, but differentiation of (9.30) and (9.33) with respect to F easily establishes that job creation falls as well. Job creation falls because, once created, the job will pay the firing tax with probability 1, so the overall expected return from the job declines. The effect is ambiguous in the diagram because the increased duration of jobs restores some of the lost expected profit, but clearly not enough.

Finally unemployment compensation shifts the JD curve up, decreasing job creation and increasing job destruction. The reason is that with higher unemployment income, wages are higher at given productivity, reducing expected profits from both new jobs and continuing ones.

Equilibrium unemployment is obtained from the Beveridge equation

$$u = \frac{\lambda G(R)}{\lambda G(R) + \theta q(\theta)},$$
(9.34)

which is downward-sloping and convex to the origin in vacancy-unemployment space (figure 9.2). Then, from our previous analysis, higher subsidies a or τ shift the Beveridge curve in and rotate the job creation line counterclockwise, reducing unemployment. The tax rate has the opposite effect, increasing unemployment. Since a linear tax system with both t and τ positive corresponds to a progressive tax, the effects of a progressive tax on unemployment could be either positive or negative. We discuss this point further below.

The hiring subsidy H shifts the Beveridge curve out and rotates the job creation line counterclockwise, having ambiguous effects on unem-

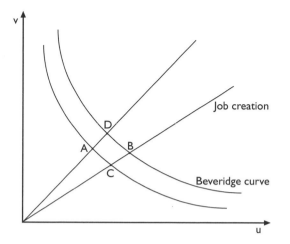

Figure 9.2
Policy effects on unemployment and vacancies: (a) Employment subsidies, tax subsidies, *B* to *A*; (b) proportional tax rate, unemployment compensation, *A* to *B*; (c) hiring subsidy, *C* to *D*; (d) firing taxes, *D* to *C*.

ployment. The firing tax causes shifts in the opposite direction, so the effect on unemployment is also ambiguous. Note, however, from (9.33) and (9.30) that if the same hiring subsidy and firing tax are imposed $(F = H)$, then the net effect is a shift of the JD curve in figure 9.1 down. This decreases job destruction and increases job creation at given unemployment and so shifts the Beveridge curve in and rotates the job creation line counterclockwise in figure 9.2. Unemployment unambiguously falls.

Finally the replacement rate shifts the Beveridge curve out and rotates the job creation line clockwise, unambiguously increasing unemployment.

9.5 Search Intensity

The preceding section has demonstrated that the introduction of policy parameters in the model of job creation and job destruction enriches the model with plausible results. But labor supply still plays only an indirect role in the determination of the policy effects, through its effects on wage determination. In this section and the next we consider the implications of the richer labor-supply models of chapters 5 and 6 for policy. In this section we allow search intensity to vary. As in the model of chapter 5, we assume that if worker i supplies s_i efficiency units during search, the rate at which jobs arrive becomes

$$q_i^w = \frac{s_i}{su} m(su, v). \tag{9.35}$$

Here s is the equilibrium search intensity supplied by the representative worker. We do not consider variable advertising intensity because of the results of chapter 5, that with endogenous vacancies optimal advertising depends only on the properties of the cost-of-advertising function. Also we assume that there are no idiosyncratic productivity shocks, so job destruction takes place at the constant rate λ.

The worker's cost of s_i units of search is

$$\sigma_i = \sigma(s_i, z), \tag{9.36}$$

so net income during unemployment is $z + b - \sigma_i$. Here z is imputed income during unemployment and b is actual income. The cost function satisfies the usual concavity properties listed in (5.9). The unemployed worker maximizes his expected returns during search, U_i, by choosing his efficiency units s_i. In equilibrium all workers choose the same s_i. The procedure for deriving the equation for the equilibrium s was described in chapter 5. Nothing fundamental is changed by the introduction of taxes and unemployment income.

The equilibrium equation with policy is similar to the one without policy, (5.26),

$$s\sigma_s(s, z) = \frac{\beta(1-t)}{1-\beta} pc\theta. \tag{9.37}$$

We suggested in (5.31) that a reasonable approximation to the cost of search function is

$$\sigma(s, z) = zh(s), \tag{9.38}$$

where $h(s)$ is the number of hours devoted to search and satisfies $h'(s) > 0$, $h''(s) \geq 0$. Then (9.37) becomes

$$szh'(s) = \frac{\beta(1-t)}{1-\beta} pc\theta. \tag{9.39}$$

Thus, under (9.38), intensity depends on the marginal tax rate. In equilibrium it may also depend on the other policy instruments, because of the dependence of θ on them, but it is interesting that when we control for θ, neither the progressivity of taxation nor the replacement rate influence intensity.

It is clear from the derivation of (9.39) that two features of the model contribute to this property. First, the marginal tax rate influences intensity because it influences the worker's share of the surplus from a job. Since the marginal tax rate reduces the worker's share, intensity falls. Other policy instruments that affect the surplus from the job, but not the relative shares, have their effect on intensity through the equilibrium value of market tightness. Second, unemployment compensation does not influence intensity.

This is because of the assumption of risk neutrality and the assumption that the cost of time is independent of actual income, as stated in (9.38). We discussed the merits of this assumption in chapter 5, and we will not repeat the arguments here. We have also argued that under risk aversion the replacement rate can reduce intensity at given θ.

Now, with variable intensity, the equilibrium condition for unemployment is

$$u = \frac{\lambda}{\lambda + \theta q(s, \theta)}.$$
(9.40)

Substitution of s from (9.39) into (9.40) gives the equilibrium relation between vacancies and unemployment (the Beveridge curve) consistent with maximization. The marginal tax rate is a shift variable in this relation, but other tax instruments and the replacement rate are not. A rise in the marginal tax rate shifts the Beveridge curve to the right, implying more unemployment at each level of vacancies.

Labor-market tightness is determined, as before, by an equation like (9.17) which is generalized to include variable search intensity. The introduction of variable intensity does not have important new implications for the equation determining tightness, and repeating the argument here is unnecessary. The conclusion that we draw from the introduction of variable search intensity in the policy model is that the model previously described for fixed intensity remains largely unaltered, and the only new policy channel introduced is that higher taxes shift the Beveridge curve out. A more general specification of income during unemployment also has the implication that higher unemployment compensation shifts the Beveridge curve out, because of disincentive effects on intensity. But the model that follows in the next section is a better way of obtaining the disincentive effects of unemployment compensation on search decisions.

9.6   Stochastic Job Matchings

We consider next the implications of policy for job rejection and job acceptance. As in the model of chapter 6, we assume that there are match-specific differences in productivities distributed according to $G(\alpha)$. (Of course, this is a different $G(.)$ from the one used to denote the distribution of idiosyncratic productivity shocks in section 9.4.) The Nash rule for sharing the surplus from a job implies that the meeting firm and worker agree to form all matches with productivity at least as high as some reservation α_r. In the model without policy, the reservation productivity is given by (6.33). To simplify the analysis, we assume that there are no idiosyncratic productivity shocks and no hiring subsidies or firing taxes. There are only employment subsidies, taxes on wage income, and unemployment benefits.

The effect of policy on the reservation productivity is easy to analyze, given the results of chapter 6 and the wage equation derived earlier in this chapter. We saw in chapter 6 that all workers who cover the cost of their employment are accepted. With an employment subsidy a this implies that the reservation productivity satisfies

$$p\alpha_r + a - w(\alpha_r) = 0, \tag{9.41}$$

where $w(\alpha_r)$ is the wage rate paid by the firm. The net wage rate received by the worker from this job is $(1 - t)\,[w(\alpha_r) + \tau]$, and in equilibrium this must be equal to the worker's reservation wage, rU. This equality follows from the Nash sharing rule: The firm and the worker always agree which is the marginal job. From (9.6) and the Nash sharing rule, we derive the equilibrium relation:

$$rU = z + b + \frac{\beta(1-t)}{1-\beta}\,pc\theta. \tag{9.42}$$

The reservation wage therefore satisfies

$$(1-t)[w(\alpha_r)+\tau] = z+b+\frac{\beta(1-t)}{1-\beta}pc\theta. \tag{9.43}$$

By substituting $w(\alpha_r)$ from (9.41) into (9.43), we obtain the equation for the reservation productivity that generalizes (6.33):

$$p\alpha_r = \frac{z+b}{1-t}-\tau-a+\frac{\beta}{1-\beta}pc\theta. \tag{9.44}$$

The reservation productivity falls with the tax subsidy τ and the employment subsidy a. The subsidies are payable either to firms or workers when they form a match, so both are more willing to form matches. Since an increase in τ for given marginal rate implies a more progressive income tax, progressive taxation reduces the reservation productivity. The rationale behind this result is that progressive taxation reduces the rewards from holding out for a higher-productivity job, since these jobs are taxed more heavily.

The marginal tax rate and unemployment compensation raise the reservation productivity. They both reduce the relative rewards from holding a job. The marginal tax rate has the effect regardless of the progressivity of the tax. But this result depends on a fixed z and b, that is, on untaxed leisure.

Suppose now that unemployment compensation is defined as in (9.22), which is again a useful simplification because of the existence of a wage distribution. Substituting into (9.44) and collecting terms, we obtain the following condition satisfied by the reservation productivity:

$$\alpha_r = \frac{z}{p(1-t)}-\frac{a+(1-\rho)\tau}{p}+\rho+\frac{\beta}{1-\beta}c\theta \tag{9.45}$$

Condition (9.45) generalizes condition (6.33). By straightforward differentiation we then find that the replacement rate raises the reservation productivity and the tax subsidy reduces it. Employment subsidies reduce the reservation productivity. The marginal tax rate increases the reservation productivity because leisure is untaxed.

The implications of stochastic job matchings for equilibrium unemployment are somewhat different from the implications of variable search intensity and much richer. The equation for labor-market tightness generalizes (6.34) in an obvious way, given our earlier results on the influence of policy:

$$(1-\beta)\left(\alpha^e + \frac{a+(1-\rho)\tau}{p} - \rho - \frac{z}{p(1-t)}\right) - \beta c\theta - \frac{(r+\lambda)c}{q(\theta)[1-G(\alpha_r)]} = 0. \quad (9.46)$$

The equation for the Beveridge curve is now

$$u = \frac{\lambda}{\lambda + \theta q(\theta)[1-G(\alpha_r)]}. \quad (9.47)$$

Hence the Beveridge curve shifts out when the replacement rate or tax rate rise, and it shifts in when the tax subsidy or the employment subsidy rise. These effects are shown in figure 9.3. The replacement rate unambiguously raises unemployment, by moving the economy from a point such as A to another point B. But unlike the search-intensity case, now the tax subsidy shifts the Beveridge curve toward the origin by making workers and firms more willing to accept jobs. Hence the effects of the tax subsidy are now exactly opposite to those of unemployment compensation. Unemployment unambiguously falls, and vacancies may either rise or fall in response to wage subsidies. In addition employment

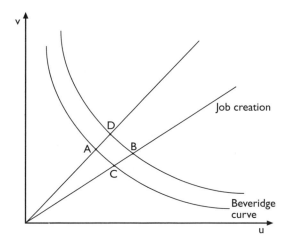

Figure 9.3
Effects of policies with stochastic job matchings: (a) Replacement rate, A to B; (b) progressivity of taxation, B to A; (c) employment subsidies, B to A; (d) proportional tax rate, A to B.

subsidies now have a double effect on unemployment equilibrium by shifting the Beveridge curve inward and rotating the job creation line counterclockwise. Unemployment falls. The marginal tax rate reduces job creation and shifts the Beveridge curve out, having opposite effects to those of the tax subsidy τ.

9.7 Compensating Policy Changes

We now turn our attention to the normative aspects of policy. First, we ask, in this section, whether it is possible to design policy in such a way as to have no effect on equilibrium. This may be possible because of the flexibility that a policy maker has when there are several policy instruments. Second, we ask, in the next section, whether policy can be designed in such a way as to offset the effects of the search externalities identified in chapter 8.

The reason for the interest in compensating policy changes is the following: Often governments have objectives that are outside the market environment that we have been analyzing. For example, they may have equity objectives, such as income support for the unemployed and wage subsidies for the low-paid, which stem from considerations not present in our models.. Or they may have revenue-raising objectives, again for reasons unrelated to the structure of our models. In such cases the most efficient way to choose policy is to do it in a way that does not distort the equilibrium of the labor market that we have derived.

This contrasts with the analysis of policy in the next two sections, where the reason for policy intervention is an externality generated within the model. The optimal policy in the latter case is not compensating but influences the equilibrium in the desired direction.

We will analyze policy for the job creation-job destruction model of section 9.4, leaving the modifications necessary for the other cases to interested readers. The simple model with no idiosyncratic productivity shocks is a special case of the model that we analyze, for a degenerate distribution of productivities. The model with stochastic job matchings is close to the one with idiosyncratic productivity shocks, whereas the model with variable search intensity is simple to analyze with predictable results, given the results of section 9.5.

Now the two key equations of the model with idiosyncratic productivity shocks are (9.30) and (9.33). A compensating policy combination then has to satisfy the following two equations, respectively, derived from (9.33) and (9.30):

$$F = H, \tag{9.48}$$

$$a + (1 - \rho)\tau - p\rho + rpF - \frac{z}{1-t} = -z. \tag{9.49}$$

When (9.48) and (9.49) are satisfied, the equilibrium R, θ pair, and therefore job creation, job destruction, and unemployment are the same as they are in a policy-free environment. Of course there may still be effects on wages, unemployment income and tax revenue, a point to which we now turn.

Condition (9.48) states that if there are firing taxes or job security regulations, there should be corresponding hiring subsidies to offset their effects. Otherwise, job creation would be adversely affected. Suppose then that there are firing taxes F compensated as in (9.48). We re-write (9.49) as follows:

$$a + \tau = -rpF + \frac{t}{1-t}z + \rho(p + \tau). \tag{9.50}$$

Equation (9.50) then states that marginal wage taxes and unemployment benefits have to be compensated by employment subsidies or implicit income tax subsidies but firing taxes (and hiring subsidies) reduce the need for employment subsidies. Since when both τ and t are positive we have in effect a progressive income tax, (9.50) also justifies the implementation of either progressive income taxes or firing taxes and hiring subsidies to compensate for unemployment benefits.

Given the large number of instruments, we restrict the policy choices further to discuss some salient features of the compensating structure. The implications of firing taxes have already been discussed, so we set from now on $F = 0$. Suppose also that for the moment $z = 0$, that is, the unemployed do not enjoy untaxed income or leisure during search, and $a = 0$. Then, in the absence of untaxed leisure, (9.50) implies that the marginal tax rate can be used to raise tax revenue without causing distortions anywhere. Workers pay the entire tax. Suppose now that some of this revenue is used to finance unemployment benefits. The formula for benefits is given by (9.22), so, if the objective of policy is to finance a given level of net benefit per worker b, without causing distortions in job creation and job destruction decisions, the compensation rule in (9.50) implies that a tax subsidy τ should be chosen that satisfies

$$\tau = \frac{b}{1-t}. \qquad (9.51)$$

If, on the other hand, the objective of policy is to provide a given replacement rate ρ, the compensation rule should be $\tau = \rho (p + \tau)$, namely

$$\tau = \frac{\rho}{1-\rho} p. \qquad (9.52)$$

In both cases unemployment benefits need to be compensated by tax subsidies, or put differently, the taxation that finances them needs to be progressive.

When the unemployed worker enjoys untaxed leisure during unemployment, the condition for the efficient compensation changes but not fundamentally. With $z > 0$, (9.50) implies that the policy distortions on job creation and job destruction are avoided when

$$\tau = \frac{t}{1-t} z + \rho(p + \tau). \qquad (9.53)$$

If the net level of benefit is the policy objective, a rearrangement of (9.53) gives

$$\tau = \frac{tz + b}{1-t}. \qquad (9.54)$$

With positive leisure during unemployment, the income tax needs to be more progressive to compensate a given replacement rate. Progressivity needs to be bigger the higher the tax. A similar result is obtained when the replacement rate is the objective of policy.

Progressive taxation eliminates the distortions introduced by unemployment compensation and taxes because one of its components, τ, is equivalent to an employment subsidy given to workers. With the sharing rules that we have used, a similar objective could be achieved if the subsidy was given to firms instead of workers, that is, if we set $\tau = 0$ but subsidized employment according to the compensating rule in (9.50).

The compensation rule in (9.50) allows the government to raise revenue with no influence on equilibrium unemployment. Given that the average pre-tax wage is the conditional expectation w^e, earned by a fraction $1 - u$ of the workers, and the remaining fraction u of workers receive net benefits b, the net revenue raised by the government is, from (9.1),

$$T = [tw^e - (1 - t)\tau](1 - u) - ub. \tag{9.55}$$

Assuming that the tax subsidy is chosen to compensate for the effects of the policy on equilibrium, according to formula (9.54), the tax revenue in (9.55) becomes, after a rearrangement of terms,

$$T = t(w^e - z)(1 - u) - b. \tag{9.56}$$

Clearly, given that $w^e > z$, an appropriate choice of t can always give positive tax revenue for any value of unemployment compensation b.

The compensatory policy rules, however, will generally influence the distribution of the surplus between firms and workers. To see this, we note from the wage equations (9.23) and (9.24) that the inside and outside wage schedules are the same when $F = H$. From (9.24) then we note that the pre-tax wage rate for given x is also

$$w(x) = (1 - \beta)\left(\frac{z + b}{1 - t} - \tau\right) + \beta(x + c\theta + rF) + \beta a. \tag{9.57}$$

Let again, for simplicity, $F = a = 0$, and substitute τ from the compensation rule (9.54) into (9.57):

$$w(x) = (1 - \beta)z + \beta(x + c\theta). \tag{9.58}$$

Under the compensation rules pre-tax (gross) wages are the same as in the policy-free equilibrium. Hence, if there is a positive tax revenue, workers pay the entire tax.

The reason that under the compensation rules workers bear all taxes is not difficult to see. Job creation and job destruction are determined by zero-profit conditions, respectively, for new vacancies and existing job matches. If these rules are to remain unaffected by policy, firms have to continue making zero profits at the two margins at the same reservation productivity and market tightness. Therefore the firm's profit flow at given R and θ has to be unaffected by policy, which can only be achieved if workers bear all taxes. The compensating rules that we derived ensure that the Nash bargaining solution for wages is such that wage costs to the firm are unaffected by policy.

9.8 Search Externalities and Policy

The second normative policy question that we investigate concerns the role of policy in internalizing the search externalities. We saw in chapter 8 that the existence of the search externalities makes equilibrium inefficient. There is an efficient equilibrium, but the determination of wages by the meeting firm and worker is not likely to attain it. We ask here whether policy can be designed in such a way as to ensure that the private equilibrium is the efficient one.

The efficiency condition that we derived in chapter 8 is that the share of labor in the wage bargain, β, should be equal to the absolute value of the elasticity of the firm's transition rate, η. In practical terms, β is unobservable. In the symmetric Nash case it is equal to $\frac{1}{2}$, but more generally, it depends on the relative discount rates of firms and workers. In other market situations it may also depend on labor-market tightness. However, in the market environment that we have adopted throughout this book, the value $\frac{1}{2}$ is a reasonable benchmark.

The absolute elasticity of $q(\theta)$, $\eta(\theta)$, can more easily be tied down, since it can be estimated empirically. It is either the absolute elasticity of the mean duration of vacancies with respect to the v/u ratio, or alternatively one minus the elasticity of the mean duration of unemployment with respect to v/u.

The policy problem that we analyze is the following. Suppose: we know the elasticity $\eta(\theta)$ and we take the benchmark value of $\frac{1}{2}$ for β. Is there a policy package that can ensure that the private equilibrium can be described by a set of equations where the effective share of labor is not $\frac{1}{2}$ but $\eta(\theta)$? (Of course, if empirically $\eta(\theta) = \frac{1}{2}$, the problem does not arise.)

As in the preceding section, we concentrate on the case of idiosyncratic productivity shocks and the job creation and job destruction rules that they imply. Then for efficiency, (9.30) and (9.33), respectively, require that

$$\frac{a+(1-\rho)\tau}{p} - \rho + rF - \frac{z}{p(1-t)} - \frac{\beta}{1-\beta}c\theta = -\frac{z}{p} - \frac{\eta}{1-\eta}c\theta, \qquad (9.59)$$

$$-F + H - \frac{c}{(1-\beta)q(\theta)} = -\frac{c}{(1-\eta)q(\theta)}. \qquad (9.60)$$

From (9.60) we find that the optimal hiring subsidy now is

$$H = F + \left(\frac{1}{1-\beta} - \frac{1}{1-\eta}\right)\frac{c}{q(\theta)}. \tag{9.61}$$

Thus the subsidy needs to be bigger when $\beta > \eta$ and smaller otherwise. Intuitively, if $\beta > \eta$, the cost of labor is higher than in the efficient equilibrium, and therefore not enough jobs come into the market. A higher hiring subsidy can correct this inefficiency.

Suppose now that F has been fixed exogenously and that H has been chosen to correct the distortion in the job creation condition for given R. Then (9.59) implies that the other instruments should satisfy

$$a + \tau = \rho(p + \tau) + \frac{t}{1-t}z - rpF + \left(\frac{\beta}{1-\beta} - \frac{\eta}{1-\eta}\right)cp\theta. \tag{9.62}$$

Comparing with (9.50), we find that if $\beta > \eta$, the required employment subsidies, a or τ, are higher. The reasons are the same as before: $\beta > \eta$ implies inefficiently low job creation, which influences job destruction decisions, so employment subsidies are needed to correct it. Although more precise policy rules can be derived for some special cases, no additional insights stem from this analysis.

9.9   An Alternative Approach to the Design of Policy

The efficiency analysis of job destruction rules (and also, if we allowed it, of search intensity and job acceptance) in the preceding section was conducted under the assumption that labor-market tightness is always made efficient, by choosing the tax instruments in such a way as to satisfy $\beta = \eta$.

An alternative approach to the problem of designing an optimal policy is to argue that since in general the search externalities have an ambiguous effect on tightness and β is unobservable, in practice, policy may not succeed in improving this aspect of resource allocation. But the effects of the externalities on job destruction, search intensity, and the reservation productivity are clear-cut: All are too low in equilibrium, irrespective of the relation between β and η. So a welfare-improving policy may simply aim to raise intensity and reservation productivities, and either not interfere with market tightness or aim to compensate the effect of the policy on it.

We have argued that search intensity is not likely to be very responsive to policy instruments. A more effective way of improving the intensity of search, which so far we did not discuss, might rely on structural measures. A central agent sets up employment agencies or subsidizes the information networks in labor markets that bring together firms and workers. Since the role of intensity in our model is to bring agents together, rather than make them form jobs, a structural policy is an effective way of achieving this. In terms of the formal model, a structural policy increases the rate of job matchings for given vacancies and unemployment. For example, it may be shown by a neutral productivity improvement in the job-matching function,

$$m = \mu m(su, v), \tag{9.63}$$

where $\mu > 0$ and an increase in μ indicates improved structural measures. Then μ enters as a multiplicative parameter in the rate $q(s, \theta)$, and so it shifts the Beveridge curve inward, just as an exogenous rise in intensity does.

Our efficiency analysis has also shown that the search externalities imply that the reservation productivity is too low in both the job destruction model and when there are stochastic job matchings and the acceptance decision is governed by reservation rules. Improved contacts through direct policy intervention corrects the inefficiently low search intensity but not necessarily the inefficiently low reservation productivities. Some other policy is needed to induce firms and workers to be more choosey about the jobs they form and retain. An obvious policy that can have this effect is unemployment compensation. Paying the unemployed a subsidy will unambiguously increase the reservation productivities applied to both the job acceptance and job destruction decisions.

The combination of structural policies to improve contacts between firms and workers and unemployment compensation to increase their reservation standards is one response to the search externalities when the efficient number of jobs that should be created is not known. Unemployment compensation, however, is likely to decrease equilibrium labor-market tightness through its wage effects and may lead to too low job creation. More formally, are there policies that can increase the reservation productivity chosen by firms and workers but have no influence on labor-market tightness? We consider this question within the job creation–job destruction model given by equations (9.30) and (9.33).

From (9.30) it follows that the reservation productivity R with policy intervention is higher than in the policy-free environment if

$$a + (1 - \rho)\tau - p\rho + rpF - \frac{z}{1-t} < -z.$$

As in the analysis of compensating policy changes, it is more convenient to write this condition as

$$a + \tau < \frac{tz + b}{1 - t} - rpF, \qquad (9.64)$$

where b is the level of unemployment compensation.

Suppose that a policy combination is adopted that satisfies (9.64) and that this leads to an increase in the reservation productivity of $dR > 0$. Then, from (9.33), the effect on job creation is neutralized if hiring subsidies and firing taxes are chosen such that

$$-\frac{dR}{r + \lambda} - F + H = 0. \qquad (9.65)$$

Let $F = 0$, to simplify matters. Then (9.65) says that a policy that induces firms to destroy more jobs should be compensated by hiring subsidies, not by employment subsidies, if the objective of policy is to increase job destruction but not influence job creation. The introduction of firing taxes makes no difference to this conclusion, since generally $F > 0$, except to the extent that firing taxes reduce job destruction and so call for more interventionist policy to increase job destruction and offset the negative effects on job creation.

Returning now to (9.64) and letting $F = 0$, we find that the policy needed to achieve the objective of raising job destruction can be one of the following: more unemployment compensation, more taxes on employment, or less subsidization of employment. For as long as these policies are compensated by hiring subsidies to correct the distortionary effects on job creation, any one of these policies improves welfare in the presence of search externalities, even if we do not know the direction of these externalities.

9.10   Notes on the Literature

Of all the policy effects considered in this chapter, the question of the effects of unemployment compensation on reservation wages and the duration of unemployment has occupied most space in the theoretical and empirical literature on job search. More recently, however, questions of employment and hiring subsidies and firing taxes are also attracting some attention, as is taxation.

On unemployment insurance see, for example, the papers in the Phelps (1970) volume which address the positive aspects of the question of unemployment compensation and search, as do numerous papers on partial models of search; see, for example, Mortensen (1977) and the other papers collected in the same issue of the journal. For empirical work on the effect of unemployment compensation on search activity, see the survey by Devine and Kiefer (1991), the book by Layard, Nickell and Jackman (1991), and the critical evaluations by Atkinson and Micklewright (1985, 1991).

The efficient design of unemployment compensation was discussed (in essentially partial models) by Baily (1978), Flemming (1978), Sampson (1978), and Shavell and Weiss (1979). Generally, the early literature has considered normative questions within a narrow framework, in particular, how unemployment insurance can be designed to reduce its disincentive effects. An early exception is the paper by Diamond (1981), which considered unemployment compensation as a policy to correct the inefficiencies introduced by the externalities in the model. More recently there has been a resurgence of interest in the optimal design of unemployment insurance within equilibrium models; see, for example, Hopenhayn and Nicolini (1997), Wang and Williamson (1996), Andolfatto and Gomme (1996), Costain (1995), Valdivia (1995), Fredriksson and Holmlund (1998), and Acemoglu and Shimer (1999a).

Questions of financing and compensating policy changes were studied in a partial framework in Pissarides (1983), with results similar to the ones derived here. A similar question was addressed in an equilibrium model by Ljungqvist and Sargent (1995b), where it is shown that progressive taxation can offset the disincentive effects of unemployment insurance but at the cost of less efficient labor allocation. The equilibrium effects of policy were considered in Pissarides (1985b), in a model that is a precursor to some of the analysis in this chapter. Some policy questions in related models are surveyed and analyzed by Johnson and Layard (1986). Other questions of financing, related to experience rating and falling outside the scope of our model, were analyzed by Feldstein (1976) and surveyed by Topel and Welch (1980).

The role of policy in the model with endogenous job destruction was considered in a number of papers. See, for example, Millard and Mortensen (1996) and Mortensen and Pissarides (1999a) for calibrations. For other approaches see Ljungqvist and Sargent (1995a, 1998), Bertola and Rogerson (1997), Jackman, Pissarides and Savouri (1990), Burdett (1990), and Boeri and Burda (1996).

The role of firing restrictions in search models were analyzed by Burda (1992), Millard (1995), Garibaldi (1998), Ljungqvist (1997), and Mortensen and Pissarides (1999c). The latter considered the claim made by Krugman (1994) and others that the increase in wage inequality in the United States and in unemployment in Europe are the result of more generous welfare benefits in Europe, with favorable results.

For an empirical study of the effects of unemployment insurance on search intensity that finds that the unemployed who receive benefits search more intensely because of better integration into the labor market, see Wadsworth (1989).

For an analysis of tax effects within the search framework, see, in addition to most of the papers above, Pissarides (1998).

The elasticity of the matching function with respect to unemployment was estimated by Pissarides (1986) and Layard, Nickell, and Jackman (1991) with British data to be about 0.7 and by Blanchard and Diamond (1989) with U.S. data to be about 0.4. Both papers find that a Cobb-Douglas search technology, with implied constant elasticity, is a reasonable empirical assumption. Later estimates, cited in the Notes on the Literature in chapter 1, largely confirmed these findings. In calibration exercises the elasticity is often fixed at 0.5, as is the share of labor, ensuring an efficient equilibrium. Calibrations show that the results are not very sensitive to small variations in the elasticity estimate, for example, in the range 0.4–0.6.

Bibliography

Abbring, J. H. 1997. *Essays in Labour Economics*. Amsterdam: Free University.

Abraham, K. G., and L. F. Katz. 1986. Cyclical unemployment: Sectoral shifts or aggregate disturbances? *Journal of Political Economy* 94: 507–22.

Acemoglu, D. 1997. Matching, heterogeneity, and the evolution of income distribution. *Journal of Economic Growth* 2: 61–92.

Acemoglu, D., and R. Shimer. 1997. Efficient wage dispersion. Unpublished paper MIT.

Acemoglu, D., and R. Shimer. 1999a. Efficient unemployment insurance. *Journal of Political Economy* 107: 893–928.

Acemoglu, D., and R. Shimer. 1999b. Holdups and efficiency with search frictions. *International Economic Review*, forthcoming.

Aghion, P., and P. Howitt. 1994. Growth and unemployment. *Review of Economic Studies* 61: 477–94.

Aghion, P., and P. Howitt. 1998. *Endogenous Growth Theory*. Cambridge: MIT Press.

Akerlof, G. A., A. K. Rose, and J. L. Yellen. 1988. Job switching and job satisfaction in the U.S. labor market. *Brookings Papers on Economic Activity* 2: 495–594.

Albaek, K., and B. E. Sorensen. 1998. Worker flows and job flows in Danish manufacturing, 1980–91. *Economic Journal* 108: 1750–71.

Albrecht, J. W., and B. Axell. 1984. An equilibrium model of search unemployment. *Journal of Political Economy* 92: 824–40.

Alchian, A. A. 1969. Information costs, pricing and resource unemployment. *Western Economic Journal* 7: 109–28.

Alogoskoufis, G. 1987. On intertemporal substitution and aggregate labor supply. *Journal of Political Economy* 95: 938–60.

Anderson, P. M., and S. M. Burgess. 1995. Empirical matching functions: Estimation and interpretation using disaggregate data. Working Paper 5001. National Bureau of Economic Research.

Andolfatto, D. 1996. Business cycles and labor market search. *American Economic Review* 86: 112–32.

Andolfatto, D., and P. Gomme. 1996. Unemployment insurance and labor-market activity in Canada. *Carnegie-Rochester Conference Series on Public Policy* 44: 47–82.

Arellano, M., and C. Meghir. 1992. Female labour supply and on-the-job search: An empirical model estimated using complementary data sets. *Review of Economic Studies* 59: 537–57.

Arrow, K. J. 1965. The theory of risk aversion. In *Aspects of the Theory of Risk-Bearing*, ed. K. J. Arrow. Helsinki: Yrjo Jahnssonin Saatio.

Atkinson, A. B., and J. Micklewright. 1985. *Unemployment Benefits and Unemployment Duration*. London: STICERD, London School of Economics.

Atkinson, A. B., and J. Micklewright. 1991. Unemployment compensation and labor market transitions: A critical review. *Journal of Economic Literature* 29: 1679–727.

Bailey, M. N. 1978. Some aspects of optimal unemployment insurance. *Journal of Political Economy* 10: 379–402.

Barlevy, G. 1998. The sullying effect of recessions. Unpublished paper. Northwestern University.

Barro, R. J. 1981. Intertemporal substituion and the business cycle. *Carnegie-Rochester Conference Series on Public Policy* 14: 237–68.

Barron, J., and S. McCafferty. 1977. Job search, labor supply and the quit decision: Theory and evidence. *American Economic Review* 67: 683–91.

Barron, J. M. 1975. Search in the labor market and the duration of unemployment: Some empirical evidence. *American Economic Review* 65: 934–42.

Bean, C., and C. A. Pissarides. 1993. Unemployment, consumption and growth. *European Economic Review* 37: 837–54.

Becker, G. 1973. A theory of marriage, part I. *Journal of Political Economy* 81: 813–46.

Belzil, C. 1994. Relative efficiencies and comparative advantages in job search. Unpublished manuscript. Concordia University.

Benhabib, J., and C. Bull. 1983. Job search: The choice of intensity. *Journal of Political Economy* 91: 747–64.

Berman, E. 1997. Help wanted, job needed: Estimates of a matching function from employment service data. *Journal of Labor Economics* 15: S251–93.

Bertola, G., and R. J. Caballero. 1994. Cross-sectional efficiency and labour hoarding in a matching model of unemployment. *Review of Economic Studies* 61: 435–56.

Bertola, G., and R. Rogerson. 1997. Institutions and labor reallocation. *European Economic Review* 41: 1147–71.

Beveridge, W. H. 1944. *Full Employment in a Free Society.* London: George Allen and Unwin.

Bilsen, V., and J. Konings. 1998. Job creation, job destruction, and growth of newly established, privatized, and state-owned enterprises in transition economies: Survey evidence from Bulgaria, Hungary, and Romania. *Journal of Comparative Economics* 26: 429–445.

Binmore, K. G., A. Rubinstein, and A. Wolinsky. 1986. The Nash bargaining solution in economic modelling. *Rand Journal of Economics* 17: 176–88.

Black, M. 1981. An empirical test of the theory of on-the-job search. *Journal of Human Resources* 16: 129–40.

Blanchard, O. J., and P. A. Diamond. 1989. The Beveridge Curve. *Brookings Papers on Economic Activity* 1: 1–60.

Blanchard, O. J., and P. A. Diamond. 1990. The cyclical behavior of the gross flows of U.S. workers. *Brookings Papers on Economic Activity* 2: 85–155.

Blanchard, O. J., and P. A. Diamond. 1994. Ranking, unemployment duration and wages. *Review of Economic Studies* 61: 417–34.

Blanchflower, D. G., and S. M. Burgess. 1996. Job creation and job destruction in Great Britain in the 1980s. *Industrial and Labor Relations Review* 50: 17–38.

Blanchflower, D. G., and A. J. Oswald. 1994. *The Wage Curve.* Cambridge: MIT Press.

Boeri, T. 1996. Is job turnover countercyclical? *Journal of Labor Economics* 14: 603–25.

Boeri, T., and M. C. Burda 1996. Active labour market policies, job matching and the Czech miracle. *European Economic Review* 40: 805–17.

Boeri, T., and U. Cramer. 1992. Employment growth, incumbents and entrants: Evidence from Germany. *International Journal of Industrial Organization* 10: 545–65.

Bowden, R. J. 1980. On the existence and secular stability of the u-v loci. *Economica* 47: 35–50.

Bowen, W. G., and T. A. Finegan. 1969. *The Economics of Labor Force Participation.* Princeton: Princeton University Press.

Broersma, L., and F. A. G. den Butter. 1994. A consistent set of time series data on labour market flows for the Netherlands. Research Memorandum 1994–43. Free University, Amsterdam.

Broersma, L., and J. C. van Ours. 1998. Job searchers, job matches and the elasticity of matching. unpublished paper. University of Tilburg.

Burda, M., and C. Wyplosz. 1994. Gross worker and job flows in Europe. *European Economic Review* 38: 1287–315.

Burda, M. C. 1992. A note on firing costs and severance benefits in equilibrium unemployment. *Scandinavian Journal of Economics* 39: 479–89.

Burda, M. C., and S. Profit. 1996. Matching across space: Evidence on mobility in the Czech republic. *Labour Economics* 3: 255–78.

Burdett, K. 1978. A theory of employee job search and quit rates. *American Economic Review* 68: 212–20.

Burdett, K. 1979. Search, leisure, and individual labor supply. In *Studies in the Economics of Search*, eds. S. A. Lippmann, and J. J. McCall. Amsterdam: North-Holland.

Burdett, K. 1981. A useful restriction on the offer distribution in job search models. In *Proceedings of a Symposium at the Industrial Institute for Economic and Social Research*. Stockholm.

Burdett, K. 1990. A new framework for labor market policy. In *Panel Data and Labor Market Studies*, eds. J. Hartog, G. Ridder, and J. Theeuwes. Amsterdam: North Holland.

Burdett, K., and D. T. Mortensen. 1998. Wage differentials, employer size, and unemployment. *International Economic Review* 39: 257–73.

Burgess, S. M. 1993. A model of competition between unemployed and employed job seekers: An application to the unemployment outflow rate in Britain. *Economic Journal* 103: 1190–204.

Burgess, S. M., J. Lane, and D. Stevens. 1994. Job flows, worker flows and churning. Unpublished paper. University of Bristol.

Burgess, S. M., and S. Profit. 1998. Externalities in the matching of workers and firms in Britain. Discussion Paper 1857. Centre for Economic Policy Research.

Butters, G. R. 1977. Equilibrium distributions of sales and advertising prices. *Review of Economic Studies* 44: 465–91.

Caballero, R. J., and M. L. Hammour. 1994. The cleansing effect of recessions. *American Economic Review* 84: 1350–68.

Caballero, R. J., and M. L. Hammour. 1996. On the timing and efficiency of creative destruction. *Quarterly Journal of Economics* 111: 805–52.

Cain, G. G. 1966. *Married Women in the Labor Force: An Economic Analysis.* Chicago: University of Chicago Press.

Campbell, J. R., and J. D. M. Fisher. 1998. Aggregate employment fluctuations with microeconomic asymmetries. Unpublished manuscript. University of Rochester.

Cohen, D., and G. Saint-Paul. 1994. Uneven technical progress and job destructions. Working Paper 9412. CEPREMAP.

Cole, H. L., and R. Rogerson. 1996. Can the Mortensen-Pissarides matching model match the business cycle facts? Staff Report 224. Federal Reserve Bank of Minneapolis, Research Department.

Coles, M. G., and K. Burdett. 1997. Marriage and class. *Quarterly Journal of Economics* 112: 141–68.

Coles, M. G., and E. Smith. 1996. Cross-section estimation of the matching function: Evidence from England and Wales. *Economica* 63: 589–98.

Coles, M. G., and E. Smith. 1998. Market places and matching. *International Economic Review* 39: 239–354.

Contini, B., L. Pacelli, M. Filippi, G. Lioni, and R. Revelli. 1995. *A Study of Job Creation and Job Destruction in Europe.* Brussels: Commission of the European Communities.

Contini, B., and R. Revellli. 1997. Gross flows vs. net flows in the labor market: What is there to be learned? *Labour Economics* 4: 245–63.

Cooley, T. F., and V. Quadrini. 1998. A neoclassical model of the Phillips curve relation. Unpublished manuscript. University of Rochester.

Costain, J. S. 1995. Unemployment insurance in a general equilibrium model of job search and precautionary savings. Working Paper. University of Chicago.

Davidson, C., L. Martin, and S. Matusz. 1987. Search unemployment and the production of jobs. *Economic Journal* 97: 857–76.

Davis, S. J. 1987. Fluctuations in the pace of labor reallocation. *Carnegie-Rochester Conference Series on Public Policy* 27: 335–402.

Davis, S. J., and J. C. Haltiwanger. 1990. Gross job creation and destruction: Microeconomic evidence and macroeconomic implications. *NBER Macroeconomics Annual* 5: 123–68.

Davis, S. J., and J. C. Haltiwanger. 1992. Gross job creation, gross job destruction, and employment reallocation. *Quarterly Journal of Economics* 107: 819–63.

Davis, S. J., J. C. Haltiwanger, and S. Schuh. 1996. *Job Creation and Destruction.* Cambridge: MIT Press.

Deree, D. R. 1987. Labor turnover, job-specific skills, and efficiency in a search model. *Quarterly Journal of Economics* 102: 815–33.

Devine, T. J., and N. M. Kiefer. 1991. *Empirical Labor Economics: The Search Approach.* Oxford: Oxford University Press.

Diamond, P. A. 1981. Mobility costs, frictional unemployment, and efficiency. *Journal of Political Economy* 89: 789–812.

Diamond, P. A. 1982a. Aggregate demand management in search equilibrium. *Journal of Political Economy* 90: 881–94.

Diamond, P. A. 1982b. Wage determination and efficiency in search equilibrium. *Review of Economic Studies* 49: 217–27.

Diamond, P. A. 1984a. Money in search equilibrium. *Econometrica* 52: 1–20.

Diamond, P. A. 1984b. *A Search-Equilibrium Approach to the Micro Foundations of Macroeconomics.* Cambridge: MIT Press.

Diamond, P. A., and E. Maskin. 1979. An equilibrium analysis of search and breach of contract. *Bell Journal of Economics* 10: 282–316.

Dicks-Mireaux, L. A., and J. C. R. Dow. 1959. The determinants of wage inflation: United Kingdom, 1946–56. *Journal of the Royal Statistical Society* A 122: 145–174.

Dow, J. C. R., and L. A. Dicks-Mireaux. 1958. The excess demand for labour: A study of conditions in Great Britain, 1946–56. *Oxford Economic Papers* 10: 1–33.

Dunne, T., M. J. Roberts, and L. Samuelson. 1989. Plant turnover and gross employment flows in the manufacturing sector. *Journal of Labor Economics* 7: 48–71.

Entorf, H. 1998. *Mismatch Explanations of European Unemployment: A Critical Evaluation.* Berlin: Springer.

Eriksson, C. 1997. Is there a trade-off between employment and growth? *Oxford Economic Papers* 49: 77–88.

Falkinger, J., and J., Zweimuller. 1998. Learning for employment, innovating for growth. Discussion Paper 1856. Centre for Economic Policy Research.

Farber, H. S. 1994. The analysis of inter-firm worker mobility. *Journal of Labor Economics* 12: 554–93.

Feinberg, R. M. 1977. Search in the labor market and the duration of unemployment: A note. *American Economic Review* 67: 1011–13.

Feldstein, M. S. 1977. Temporary layoffs in the theory of unemployment. *Journal of Political Economy* 84: 937–57.

Feve, P., and F. Langot. 1996. Unemployment and the business cycle in a small open economy: G.M.M. estimation and testing with French data. *Journal of Economic Dynamics and Control* 20: 1609–39.

Flemming, J. S. 1978. Aspects of optimal unemployment insurance: Search, leisure, savings and capital market imperfections. *Journal of Public Economics* 10: 403–25.

Flinn, C. J., and J. J. Heckman. 1982. New models for analyzing structural models of labor force dynamics. *Journal of Econometrics* 18: 115–68.

Foote, C. L. 1998. Trend Employment Growth and the Bunching of Job Creation and Destruction. *Quarterly Journal of Economics* 113: 809–34.

Fredriksson, P., and H. Bertil. 1998. Optimal unemployment insurance in search equilibrium. Working Paper 1998:2. Uppsala University.

Friedman, M. 1968. The role of monetary policy. *American Economic Review* 58: 1–17.

Fuentes, A. 1998. On-the-job search and the Beveridge curve. Unpublished paper. Wolfson College, Oxford.

Garibaldi, P. 1998. Job flow dynamics and firing restrictions. *European Economic Review* 42: 245–75.

Gautier, P. 1997. *The Flow Approach to the Labor Market.* Amsterdam: Free University.

Gautier, P., and L. Broersma. 1994. The timing of labor reallocation and the business cycle. Unpublished paper. Tinbergen Institute.

Gomes, J., J. Greenwood, and S. Rebelo. 1997. Equilibrium unemployment. Unpublished paper. University of Rochester.

Gorter, C., and J. C. van Ours. 1994. Matching unemployment and vacancies in regional labour markets: An empirical analysis for the Netherlands. *Papers in Regional Science* 73: 153–67.

Greenwood, J., G. M. MacDonald, and G.-J. Zhang. 1996. The cyclical behavior of job creation and job destruction: A sectoral model. *Economic Theory* 7: 95–112.

Gregg, P., and B. Petrongolo. 1997. Non-random matching and the performance of the Beveridge curve. Discussion Paper 347, Centre for Economic Performance, London School of Economics.

Gronau, R. 1971. Information and frictional unemployment. *American Economic Review* 61: 290–301.

Gross, D. M. 1997. Aggregate job matching and returns to scale in Germany. *Economics Letters* 56: 243–8.

Grout, P. 1984. Investment and wages in the absence of binding contracts: A Nash Bargaining approach. *Econometrica* 52: 449–60.

Gujarati, D. 1972. The behaviour of unemployment and unfilled vacancies. *Economic Journal* 82: 195–204.

Haan den, W. J., G. Ramey, and J. Watson. 1997. Job destruction and propagation of shocks. Discussion Paper 97–23. University of California, San Diego.

Hall, R. E. 1979. A theory of the natural unemployment rate and the duration of employment. *Journal of Monetary Economics* 5: 153–69.

Hall, R. E. 1980. Labor supply and aggregate fluctuations. *Carnegie-Rochester Conference Series on Public Policy* 12: 7–33.

Hansen, B. 1970. Excess demand, unemployment, vacancies and wages. *Quarterly Journal of Economics* 84: 1–23.

Hansen, G. D. 1995. Indivisible labor and the business cycle. *Journal of Monetary Economics* 16: 309–27.

Heckman, J. J., and B. Singer. 1984. A method for minimizing the impact of distributional assumptions in econometric models for duration data. *Econometrica* 52: 271–320.

Holt, C. C. 1970. Job search, Phillip's wage relation, and union influence. In *The Microeconomic Foundations of Employment and Inflation Theory*, eds. E. S. Phelps et al. New York: Norton.

Holt, C. C., and M. H. David. 1966. The concept of job vacancies in a dynamic theory of the labor market. In *The Measurement and Interpretation of Job Vacancies*. New York: Columbia University Press.

Holzer, H. 1987. Job search by employed and unemployed youth. *Industrial and Labor Relations Review* 40: 601–11.

Hopenhayn, H., and R. Rogerson. 1993. Job turnover and policy evaluation: A general equilibrium analysis. *Journal of Political Economy* 101: 915–38.

Hopenhayn, H. A., and J. P. Nicolini. 1997. Optimal unemployment insurance. *Journal of Political Economy* 105: 412–38.

Hosios, A. J. 1990. On the efficiency of matching and related models of search and unemployment. *Review of Economic Studies* 57: 279–98.

Howitt, P. 1988. Business cycles with costly search and recruiting. *Quarterly Journal of Economics* 103: 147–65.

Howitt, P., and R. P. McAfee. 1987. Costly search and recruiting. *International Economic Review* 28: 89–107.

Hughes, G., and B. McCormick. 1985. An empirical analysis of on-the-job search and job mobility. *Machester School* 53: 76–95.

Ioannides, Y. M. 1997. Evolution of trading structures. In *The Economy as an Evolving Complex System II*, eds. W. B. Arthur, S. N. Durlauf, and D. A. Lane. Reading, MA: Addison-Wesley.

Jackman, R., C. A. Pissarides, and S. Savouri. 1990. Labour market policies and unemployment in the OECD. *Economic Policy* 11: 449–90.

Jackman, R. J., R. Layard, and C. A. Pissarides. 1989. On vacancies. *Oxford Bulletin of Economics and Statistics* 51: 377–94.

Johnson, G. E., and R. Layard. 1986. The natural rate of unemployment: Explanation and policy. In *Handbook of Labor Economics*, eds O. Ashenfelter and R. Layard. Amsterdam: North-Holland.

Jones, R., and G. Newman. 1995. Adaptive capital, information depreciation and Schumpeterian growth. *Economic Journal* 105: 897–915.

Jovanovic, B. 1979. Job matching and the theory of turnover. *Journal of Political Economy* 87: 972–90.

Jovanovic, B. 1984. Matching, turnover and unemployment. *Journal of Political Economy* 92: 108–22.

Julien, B., J. Kennes, and I. King. 1998. Bidding for labor. Unpublished paper. Concordia University.

Kahn, L., and S. Low. 1984. An empirical model of employed search, unemployed search and nonsearch. *Journal of Human Resources* 19: 104–17.

Kennes, J. 1994. Underemployment, on-the-Job search, and the Beveridge curve. Unpublished paper. University of Western Ontario.

Kiefer, N. M., and G. R. Neumann. 1979. An empirical job search model, with a test of the constant reservation-wage hypothesis. *Journal of Political Economy* 87: 89–107.

King, I., and L. Welling. 1995. Search, unemployment, and growth. *Journal of Monetary Economics* 35: 499–507.

Konings, J. 1995. Job creation and job destruction in the UK manufacturing sector. *Oxford Bulletin of Economics and Statistics* 57: 5–24.

Konings, J., H. Lehmann, and M. E. Schaffer. 1996. Job creation and job destruction in a transition economy: Ownership, firm size, and gross job flows in Polish manufacturing 1988–91. *Labour Economics* 3: 299–317.

Koopmans, T., and M. Beckman. 1957. Assignment problems and the location of economic activities. *Econometrica* 25: 53–76.

Krugman, P. 1994. Past and prospective causes of high unemployment. In *Reducing Unemployment: Current Issues and Policy Options*. Kansas City: Federal Reserve Bank of Kansas City.

Lagarde, S., E. Maurin, and C. Torelli. 1994. Job reallocation between and within plants: Some evidence from French micro data on the period 1984–1992. INSEE. Paper originally published in French in *Economie et Provision* 1(1994-4): 113–114.

Lagos, R. 1997. An alternative approach to market frictions: An application to the market for taxicab rides. Unpublished paper. London School of Economics.

Lagos, R., and G. L. Violante. 1998. What shifts the Beveridge curve? A microfoundation for the aggregate matching function. Unpublished paper. London School of Economics.

Laing, D., T. Palivos, and P. Wang. 1995. Learning, matching and growth. *Review of Economic Studies* 62: 115–29.

Lancaster, T. 1979. Econometric models for the duration of unemployment. *Econometrica* 47: 939–56.

Lancaster, T., and A. Chesher. 1983. An econometric analysis of reservation wages. *Econometrica* 51: 1661–76.

Layard, R., S. Nickell, and R. Jackman. 1991. *Unemployment: Macroeconomic Performance of the Labour Market*. Oxford: Oxford University Press.

Leonard, J. S. 1987. In the wrong place at the wrong time: The extent of frictional and structural unemployment. In *Unemployment and the Structure of Labor Markets,* eds. K. Lang and J. S. Leonard. New York: Basil Blackwell.

Lilien, D. 1982. Sectoral shifts and sectoral unemployment. *Journal of Political Economy* 90: 777–93.

Lindbeck, A., and D. J. Snower. 1988. *The Insider-Outsider Theory of Employment and Unemployment*. Cambridge, MA: MIT Press.

Lindeboom, M., J. C. van Ours, and G. Renes. 1994. Matching employers and workers: An empirical analysis on the effectiveness of search. *Oxford Economic Papers* 46: 45–67.

Lipsey, R. G. 1960. The relation between unemployment and the rate of change of money wage rates in the United Kingdom, 1862–1957. *Economica* 27: 62–70.

Lipsey, R. G. 1974. The micro theory of the Phillips curve reconsidered: A reply to Holmes and Smyth. *Economica* 41: 62–70.

Ljungqvist, L. 1997. How do layoff costs affect employment? Unpublished paper. Stockholm School of Economics.

Ljungqvist, L., and T. J. Sargent. 1995a. The Swedish unemployment experience. *European Economic Review* 39: 1043–70.

Ljungqvist, L., and T. J. Sargent. 1995b. Welfare states and unemployment. *Economic Theory* 6: 143–60.

Ljungqvist, L., and T. J. Sargent. 1998. The European unemployment dilemma. *Journal of Political Economy* 106: 514–50.

Lokwood, B. 1986. Transferable skills, job matching and the inefficiency of the "natural" rate of unemployment. *Economic Journal* 96: 961–74.

Lucas, R. E., and E. C. Prescott. 1974. Equilibrium search and unemployment. *Journal of Economic Theory* 7: 188–209.

Lucas, R. E., and L. A. Rapping. 1969. Real wages, employment and inflation. *Journal of Political Economy* 77: 721–54.

Lundberg, S. 1985. The added worker effect. *Journal of Labor Economics* 3: 11–37.

MacLeod, B. W., and J. M. Malcomson. 1993. Investments, holdup, and the form of market contracts. *American Economic Review* 83: 811–37.

Malcomson, J. M. 1997. Contracts, hold-up and labor markets. Discussion Paper 9703. University of Southampton.

Mankiw, N. G., J. J. Rotemberg, and L. H. Summers. 1985. Intertemporal substitution in macroeconomics. *Quarterly Journal of Economics* 100: 225–51.

McCall, J. J. 1970. Economics of information and job search. *Quarterly Journal of Economics* 84: 113–26.

McDonald, I. M., and R. M. Solow. 1981. Wage bargaining and employment. *American Economic Review* 71: 896–908.

McKenna, C. J. 1987. Labour market participation in matching equilibrium. *Economica* 57: 325–33.

McLaughlin, K. J. 1994. Rent sharing in an equilibrium model of matching and turnover. *Journal of Labor Economics* 12: 499–523.

Merz, M. 1995. Search in the labor market and the real business cycle. *Journal of Monetary Economics* 36: 269–300.

Millard, S. P. 1995. The effect of employment protection legislation on labour market activity: A search approach. Unpublished paper. Bank of England.

Millard, S. P., and D. T. Mortensen. 1996. The unemployment and welfare effects of labour market policy: A comparison of the U.S. and U.K. In *Unemployment Policy: How Should Governments Respond to Unemployment?* eds. D. Snower and G. de la Dehesa. Oxford: Oxford University Press.

Moen, E. R. 1997. Competitive search equilibrium. *Journal of Political Economy* 105: 385–411.

Montgomery, J. 1991. Equilibrium wage dispersion and interindustry wage differentials. *Quarterly Journal of Economics* 106: 163–79.

Mortensen, D. T. 1970. A theory of wage and employment dynamics. In *The Microeconomic Foundations of Employment and Inflation Theory,* eds. E. S. Phelps et al. New York: Norton.

Mortensen, D. T. 1977. Unemployment insurance and job search decisions. *Industrial and Labor Relations Review* 30: 505–17.

Mortensen, D. T. 1978. Specific capital and labor turnover. *Bell Journal of Economics* 9: 572–86.

Mortensen, D. T. 1982a. The matching process as a non-cooperative/bargaining game. In *The Economics of Information and Uncertainty,* ed. J. J. McCall. Chicago: University of Chicago Press.

Mortensen, D. T. 1982b. Property rights and efficiency in mating, racing, and related games. *American Economic Review* 72: 968–79.

Mortensen, D. T. 1986. Job search and labor market analysis. In *Handbook of Labor Economics,* eds. O. C. Ashenfelter and R. Layard. Amsterdam: North-Holland.

Mortensen, D. T. 1990. Equilibrium wage distributions: A synthesis. In *Panel Data and Labor Market Studies*, eds. J. Hartog, G. Ridder, and J. Theeuwes. Amsterdam: North-Holland.

Mortensen, D. T. 1994. The cyclical behavior of job and worker flows. *Journal of Economic Dynamics and Control* 18: 1121–42.

Mortensen, D. T., and C. A. Pissarides. 1993. The cyclical behavior of job creation and job destruction. In *Labour Demand and Equilibrium Wage Formation*, eds. J. C. van Ours, G. A. Pfann, and G. Ridder. Amsterdam: North-Holland.

Mortensen, D. T., and C. A. Pissarides. 1994. Job creation and job destruction in the theory of unemployment. *Review of Economic Studies* 61: 397–415.

Mortensen, D. T., and C. A. Pissarides. 1998. Technological progress, job creation and job destruction. *Review of Economic Dynamics* 1: 733–53.

Mortensen, D. T., and C. A. Pissarides. 1999a. New developments in models of search in the labor market. In *Handbook of Labor Economics*, eds. O. Ashenfelter and D. Card. Amsterdam: North-Holland.

Mortensen, D. T., and C. A. Pissarides. 1999b. Taxes, subsidies and equilibrium Labor Market Outcomes. In, ed. E. S. Phelps. New York: Russell Sage Foundation. Paper presented at the conference on Low-Wage Employment Subsidies, Russell Sage Foundation, New York, December 8, 1997.

Mortensen, D. T., and C. A. Pissarides. 1999c. Unemployment responses to "skill-biased" shocks: The role of labour market policy. *Economic Journal*, 109: 242–65.

Narandanathan, W., and S. Nickell. 1985. Modelling the process of job search. *Journal of Econometrics* 28: 29–49.

Nickell, S. J. 1979. Estimating the probability of leaving unemployment. *Econometrica* 47: 1249–66.

OECD 1996. *Job Creation and Loss: Analysis, Policy, and Data Development.* Paris: OECD.

Ours van, J. C. 1991. The efficiency of the Dutch labour market in matching unemployment and vacancies. *De Economist* 139: 358–78.

Ours van, J. C., and G. Ridder. 1991. Cyclical variation in vacancy durations and vacancy flows: An empirical analysis. *European Economic Review* 35: 1143–55.

Ours van, J. C., and G. Ridder. 1992. Vacancies and recruitment of new employees. *Journal of Labor Economics* 10: 138–55.

Parsons, D. O. 1973. Quit rates over time: A search and information approach. *American Economic Review* 63: 390–401.

Parsons, D. O. 1991. The job search behavior of employed youth. *Review of Economics and Statistics* 73: 597–604.

Phelps, E. S. 1967. Phillips curves, expectations of inflation and optimal unemployment. *Economica* 34: 254–81.

Phelps, E. S. 1968. Money–wage dynamics and labor-market equilibrium. *Journal of Political Economy* 76: 678–711.

Phelps, E. S. 1972. *Inflation Policy and Unemployment Theory: The Cost-Benefit Approach to Monetary Planning.* New York: Norton.

Phelps, E. S. 1994. *Structural Slumps.* Cambridge, MA: Harvard University Press.

Phelps, E. S., and H. T. Hoon. 1999. Low-wage employment subsidies in a Labor-turnover model of the "natural rate." In, ed. E. S. Phelps. New York: Russell Sage Foundation. Paper presented at the conference on Low-Wage Employment Subsidies, Russell Sage Foundation, New York, December 8, 1997.

Phelps, E. S., et al. 1970. *Microeconomic Foundations of Employment and Inflation Theory.* New York: Norton.

Pissarides, C. A. 1976a. Job Search and Participation. *Economica* 43: 333–49.

Pissarides, C. A. 1976b. *Labour Market Adjustment: Microeconomic Foundations of Short-Run Neoclassical and Keynesian Dynamics.* Cambridge: Cambridge University Press.

Pissarides, C. A. 1979. Job matchings with state employment agencies and random search. *Economic Journal* 89: 818–33.

Pissarides, C. A. 1983. Efficiency aspects of the financing of unemployment insurance and other government expenditures. *Review of Economic Studies* 50: 57–69.

Pissarides, C. A. 1984a. Efficient job rejection. *Economic Journal* 94: 97–108.

Pissarides, C. A. 1984b. Search intensity, job advertising and efficiency. *Journal of Labor Economics* 2: 128–43.

Pissarides, C. A. 1985a. Short-run equilibrium dynamics of unemployment, vacancies, and real wages. *American Economic Review* 75: 676–90.

Pissarides, C. A. 1985b. Taxes, subsidies and equilibrium unemployment. *Review of Economic Studies* 52: 121–34.

Pissarides, C. A. 1986. Unemployment and vacancies in Britain. *Economic Policy* 3: 499–559.

Pissarides, C. A. 1987. Search, wage bargains and cycles. *Review of Economic Studies* 54: 473–84.

Pissarides, C. A. 1988. The search equilibrium approach to fluctuations in employment. *American Economic Review* 78: 363–69.

Pissarides, C. A. 1994. Search unemployment with on-the-job search. *Review of Economic Studies* 61: 457–75.

Pissarides, C. A. 1998. The impact of employment tax cuts on unemployment and wages: The role of unemployment benefits and tax structure. *European Economic Review* 42: 155–83.

Pissarides, C. A., and J. Wadsworth. 1994. On-the-job search: Some empirical evidence from Britain. *European Economic Review* 38: 385–401.

Prescott, E. C. 1975. Efficiency of the natural rate. *Journal of Political Economy* 83: 1229–36.

Ramey, G., and J. Watson. 1997. Contractual fragility, job destruction, and business cycles. *Quarterly Journal of Economics* 112: 873–912.

Rogerson, R. D. 1998. Indivisible labor, lotteries, and equilibrium. *Journal of Monetary Economics* 21: 3–16.

Rothschild, M. 1973. Models of market organization with imperfect information: A survey. *Journal of Political Economy* 81: 1283–1308.

Salop, S. C. 1973. Wage differentials in a dynamic theory of the firm. *Journal of Economic Theory* 6: 321–44.

Sampson, A. A. 1978. Optimal redundancy compensation. *Review of Economic Studies* 45: 447–52.

Satinger, M. 1991. Consistent wage distributions. *Quarterly Journal of Economics* 106: 277–88.

Schager, N. H. 1987. *Unemployment, Vacancy Durations and Wage Increases: Applications of Markov Processes to Labour Market Dynamics.* Research Report. 29. Stockholm: Industrial Institute for Economic and Social Research.

Seater, J. J. 1977. A unified model of consumption, labor supply and job search. *Journal of Economic Theory* 14: 349–72.

Seater, J. J. 1979. Job search and vacancy contacts. *American Economic Review* 69: 411–19.

Shavell, S., and L. Weiss. 1979. The optimal payment of unemployment insurance payments over time. *Journal of Political Economy* 87: 1347–62.

Shi, S., and Q. Wen. 1997. Labor market search and capital accumulation: Some analytical results. *Journal of Economic Dynamics and Control* 21: 1747–76.

Siven, C.-H. 1974. Consumption, supply of labour and search activity in an intertemporal perspective. *Swedish Journal of Economics* 76: 44–61.

Smith, L. 1997. The marriage model with search frictions. Unpublished paper. MIT.

Solow, R. 1985. Insiders and outsiders in wage determination. *Scandinavian Journal of Economics* 87: 411–28.

Stiglitz, J. E. 1985. Equilibrium wage distributions. *Economic Journal* 95: 595–618.

Tobin, J. 1972. Inflation and unemployment. *American Economic Review* 62: 1–18.

Topel, R., and F. Welch. 1980. Unemployment insurance: Survey and extensions. *Economica* 47: 351–79.

Valdivia, V. 1995. Evaluating the welfare benefits of unemployment insurance. Working Paper. Northwestern University.

Wadsworth, J. 1989. Unemployment benefits and search effort in the UK labour market. *Economica* 43: 13–27.

Wang, C., and S. Williamson. 1996. Unemployment insurance with moral hazard in a dynamic economy. *Carnegie-Rochester Conference Series on Public Policy* 44: 1–41.

Warren, R. S. 1996. Returns to scale in a matching model of the labor market. *Economics Letters* 50: 135–42.

Wasmer, E. 1996. Competition for jobs in a growing economy and the emergence of dualism. Working Paper 9715. CREST, INSEE.

Whipple, D. 1973. A generalized theory of job search. *Journal of Political Economy* 81: 1170–88.

Wilde, L. L. 1979. An information-thoeretic approach to job quits. In *Studies in the Economics of Search,* eds. S. A. Lippman and J. J. McCall. Amsterdam: North-Holland.

Wilson, B. A. 1995. Unemployment and underlying productivity shocks: Were the Luddites right? Unpublished manuscript. Board of Governors of the Federal Reserve.

Wright, R. 1986. Job search and cyclical unemployment. *Journal of Political Economy* 94: 38–55.

Yashiv, E. 1997a. Aggregate labor market fluctuations: The interaction of search and frictions. Unpublished manuscript. Tel Aviv University.

Yashiv, E. 1997b. The determinants of equilibrium unemployment. Working Paper CR 600/1997. HEC School of Management, Paris.

Yoon, B. J. 1981. A model of unemployment duration with variable search intensity. *Review of Economics and Statistics* 63: 599–609.

Index